JAMES KOUZES | BARRY POSNER

THE STUDENT LEADERSHIP CHALLENGE

FIVE PRACTICES FOR BECOMING AN
EXEMPLARY LEADER

FOURTH EDITION

THE LEADERSHIP CHALLENGE®
A Wiley Brand

Published by John Wiley & Sons, Inc., Hoboken, New Jersey.
Published simultaneously in Canada.

For general information on our other products and services or for technical support, please contact our Customer Care Department within the United States at (800) 762-2974, outside the United States at (317) 572-3993 or fax (317) 572-4002.

Wiley also publishes its books in a variety of electronic formats. Some content that appears in print may not be available in electronic formats. For more information about Wiley products, visit our web site at www.wiley.com.

Library of Congress Cataloging-in-Publication Data
Names: Kouzes, James M., 1945- author. | Posner, Barry Z., author.
Title: The student leadership challenge : five practices for becoming an
   exemplary leader / James M. Kouzes and Barry Z. Posner.
Description: Fourth edition. | [San Francisco] : Jossey-Bass, [2024] |
   Includes index.
Identifiers: LCCN 2024001122 (print) | LCCN 2024001123 (ebook) | ISBN
   9781394206087 (paperback) | ISBN 9781394206094 (adobe pdf) | ISBN
   9781394206100 (epub)
Subjects: LCSH: College student government. | Leadership.
Classification: LCC LB2346 .K68 2024 (print) | LCC LB2346 (ebook) | DDC
   378.1/01—dc23/eng/20240214
LC record available at https://lccn.loc.gov/2024001122
LC ebook record available at https://lccn.loc.gov/2024001123

Cover Design: Wiley
Author Photos: Courtesy of the Author
Printed and bound by CPI Group (UK) Ltd, Croydon, CR0 4YY

C9781394206087_120324

We dedicate this edition to our grandchildren, Leo Lopez and Rosie and Julian Collins, who will be part of the next generation of young people who will lead us into a better future.

Important Information About the Student Leadership Practices Inventory® Self Online

If you purchased a *new* copy of this book, you are eligible to receive one single-use access code for the Student Leadership Practices Inventory Self Online assessment. Follow these instructions to retrieve your code:

- Go to www.studentlpi.com/ebook
- Fill out the required information to verify your purchase.
- Your code will be automatically e-mailed to you.
- Go to: slpiself.studentleadershipchallenge.com and enter your code to take the inventory.
- If you are using a free-sample, used, rented, or borrowed copy of this e-book, you are not eligible to receive a free code, but may purchase one at www.studentlpi.com/assess

The *Student Leadership Practices Inventory* (Student LPI®) is the cornerstone of The Five Practices of Exemplary Leadership® model. Created by leadership educators James M. Kouzes and Barry Z. Posner, this powerful leadership development model approaches leadership as a measurable, learnable, and teachable set of behaviors, because everyone can be a leader—whether in a designated leadership role or not. The Student LPI offers you a method for accurately assessing your leadership skills based on The Five Practices of Exemplary Leadership, by measuring the frequency with which you engage in 30 behaviors that research shows lead to the best leadership outcomes.

Contents

Five Practices for Becoming an Exemplary Leader

The Student Leadership Challenge is about how students—people just like you—mobilize others to make extraordinary things happen, from the classroom, stadium, residence hall, Greek chapters, clubs, and student government to the campus, neighboring community, and nation. It's about student leaders' daily leadership practices to get people moving toward a better future. They use these practices to transform values into actions, visions into realities, obstacles into innovations, separateness into solidarity, and risks into rewards. Leadership is what creates the opportunity to turn challenging situations into remarkable successes.

This fourth edition of *The Student Leadership Challenge* comes out six years after the previous edition's publication. Since then, we have continued to research, consult, teach, and write about what student leaders do and how anyone, regardless of age, can learn to be a better leader. We're honored by the reception in the education marketplace and by hearing that students, educators, and practitioners continue to find *The Student Leadership Challenge* conceptually and practically useful.

The Student Leadership Challenge has stood the test of time, and we continue to ask the same question we asked when we started our inquiry into exemplary leadership: *What did you do when you were at your personal best as a leader?*

When reflecting on this question, one of the most common yet profound realizations students have is that leadership is an identifiable set of skills and abilities available to anyone, regardless of age or position. As one student explained: "Growing up, I assumed leaders had certain traits and qualities that I didn't seem to have. I thought there were 'natural' leaders who were born to lead. I thought leadership was the description of what these people did. When you asked me to describe my personal-best leadership experience, I found, to my surprise, that I had those leadership abilities myself." Another student said that they learned "that anybody can be a leader. I had never considered myself a leader, but when I needed to step up and deal with a difficult situation, I was able to find the leader within me and do so."

We've talked to thousands of young people, and their stories and the behaviors and actions they've described—combined with examples from thousands of other leaders around the world—reveal The Five Practices of Exemplary Leadership® framework. When students do their best as leaders, they Model the Way, Inspire a Shared Vision, Challenge the Process, Enable Others to Act, and Encourage the Heart. We describe each of these practices in detail in this book and discuss how to use them to become a more effective leader.

The Student Leadership Challenge is evidence-based. We derived The Five Practices from research, and we illustrate them with examples from real student leaders doing real things. In this fourth edition, we report new stories, examples, and illustrations of exactly what students like you do when they are at their leadership best. We make concepts easy to understand so you can focus on applying what works. Also, in this new edition, you have the opportunity to complete the *Student*

Leadership Practices Inventory, enabling you to get an evidence-based assessment of how you see yourself as a leader. With this information, you can make decisions about practical ways you can act to improve your leadership capacity and make a difference in the lives of those you lead. We've left space throughout the book for you to reflect on and discover new ways to be the best leader you can be.

The more we research and write about leadership, the more confident we become that leadership is within the grasp of everyone and that leadership opportunities are everywhere. No matter what your experience is, and whether you've had few opportunities to exercise leadership or many, we know that you have the capacity to lead if you choose to. Leadership is not about a position or title, as too many people presume. It is about the choices you make throughout your life.

In reading this book, we want you to realize that there are no shortages of leadership opportunities and that the "future" requires your leadership. As you take advantage of them, others will begin to take note and look to you to help them figure out how they can develop themselves as leaders. You don't just owe it to yourself to become the best leader you can be. You have a responsibility to others as well. You may not yet know it, but people around you need you to do your best and be your best.

A GUIDE FOR STUDENTS AND YOUNG LEADERS

How do you get other people to want to follow you? How do you get people to move forward together for a common purpose? How do you energize people to work hard and accomplish something that everyone can feel proud of? These are only some of the important questions that are answered in *The Student Leadership Challenge*. Think of this book as a guide to take along on any leadership journey. You can consult it when you want advice and guidance on how to get extraordinary things done. Think of it as a place to go when you need help figuring out what to do as a leader.

We recommend that you first read the Prologue, but after that, there is no prescribed order to proceed through the rest of this book. Go wherever your interests are. We wrote *The Student Leadership Challenge* to support you in your leadership development. Just remember that each practice is essential. Although you might skip around in the book, you can't skip understanding and doing any of these fundamentals of leadership.

In the Prologue, we introduce our leadership framework by sharing a Personal-Best Leadership Experience—a case study about how one leader acted on her values and pursued a path of commitment and action to make a difference in gender equality education in her country and others. An overview of The Five Practices of Exemplary Leadership summarizes the findings about what student leaders do when they are at their best and shows how these actions make a difference. A major benefit of learning and adopting this leadership operating system is that it isn't difficult to understand, doesn't cost any money, nor require anybody's permission to use it. What is required is an initial commitment from you and ongoing practice to make these leadership behaviors habits in your life.

The ten chapters that follow describe the *Ten Commitments of Leadership*—the essential behaviors—that student leaders use to get extraordinary things done. We explain the fundamental principles supporting each of The Five Practices, provide numerous examples, and offer data and research evidence. At the end of every chapter, use the interactive worksheets to identify opportunities for improvement and to strengthen your leadership capabilities. Reflect on what you learned from reading the chapter and decide how you will put this into action.

Continuing to develop your leadership capabilities is the theme of the concluding chapter. The Five Practices gives you a framework for liberating the leader within you, and we remind you that your leadership makes a difference. Leadership is a skill that can be learned and honed, and we explore various avenues for doing so while being mindful that there are no guarantees in life. Leadership happens *in the moment,* and there is no time like the present for thinking about what kind of leader you aspire to be.

This book will contribute to your success working with others, the creation of new ideas and enterprises, the renewal of healthy schools and prosperous communities, and greater respect and understanding worldwide. Exercising leadership will enrich your life.

Meeting the leadership challenge is a personal—and a daily— challenge for everyone. We know *you* can meet it if you have the will and the way to lead. You must supply the will. We'll do our best to keep supplying the way.

James M. Kouzes
Orinda, California

Barry Z. Posner
*Berkeley, California*Preface

Leadership is the art of mobilizing others to want to struggle for shared aspirations.

—*Leadership* as defined by Jim Kouzes and Barry Posner

Prologue

When Leaders Are at Their Personal Best

Madeline Price grew up on a beef cattle farm in rural Queensland, Australia. After high school graduation, she joined fifteen other recent graduates on a trip to see the world and do volunteer work in Cambodia and Thailand. While visiting a school in Cambodia, Madeline noticed that all twenty-three students in the first-grade classroom were male. When she asked the teacher where the girls were, she was shocked by his answer: "Boys are more valuable to educate," he told Madeline.[1]

As soon as she returned to Australia, it clicked that the teacher's answer represented a problem that occurred everywhere. "I just hadn't perceived it yet," Madeline said. "But those simple words, 'Boys are more valuable,' opened my eyes to the gender disparities faced abroad and in Australia." Madeline's growing sensitivity to the gender inequality she saw back home in Australia clarified for her the need to speak out about it. However, she didn't find a receptive audience among her friend groups—at least, not at first.

"I talked about it with my friends, and very few people felt what I was feeling," she told us. "My friends all truly believed that women

1

were as equal as we could get. It wasn't that my friends didn't care; it was just that they didn't know." To Madeline, however, it was evident that just because not everyone agreed with her, gender inequality was still a global issue. She couldn't get it out of her mind and didn't stop trying to speak to others about it.

A few years later, Madeline enrolled in a community development and leadership seminar while at university. "Going into the class, I knew I had to do something related to gender inequality," Madeline said. She proposed conducting educational seminars for high school students and community organizations to open their eyes to how gender inequality still played a role in their lives and how they might combat it.

"I couldn't stop talking and thinking about it, even when other people I knew didn't seem to think it was as big a problem in Australia as I did," Madeline said. She created the One Woman Project (OWP) and recruited volunteers to help her develop and lead the seminars. "The name comes from the idea that if we educated just one woman to empower herself, the world is already a better place," Madeline said.

OWP works with schools and community organizations through invitation. Schools call OWP to conduct an educational seminar when an incident of gender bias has occurred on campus or just because they believe in the importance of gender inequality education. In addition, before the pandemic, OWP hosted the largest feminist festival in Queensland for three years running before transitioning to an online program. They also publish two feminist periodicals and host both in-person and online events.

Framing the information in ways students could identify with was an early challenge for OWP. "It's not enough to say, 'Gender inequality is a problem,' especially for the girls in the high schools. They think it's a 'me thing, not a culture thing.'" One of the best ways of engaging students, Madeline found, was to enable them to find their voices. She explained:

> They're students, and they're not given many platforms to say, "This is what I think about sexuality or gender." Student voices aren't often listened to regarding curriculum or educational issues. We want to hear their answer regarding those questions, and I think it's essential to let them know you want to listen to them. That makes a huge difference in getting them to share their opinions and feelings.

OWP also works to show that gender inequality is not an issue that affects women alone. The curriculum covers how a patriarchal culture reinforces beliefs and behaviors that harm men and women. For example, in cultures where masculinity is measured by "toughness" and the expectation that men do not show emotion, men have higher rates of suicide and accidental death and an increased chance of mental health concerns during their lifetime. In addition, Madeline recruited male volunteers to OWP, which helps give male students a visual connection to the idea that gender inequality is not an issue that affects only women. "I wanted to find ways to make sure that students see that both men and women are affected by these issues. Making certain that we have men going into schools to give these seminars along with our female volunteers is extremely helpful in that respect," Madeline told us.

Starting the first gender inequality education program in the country was not without its challenges. "There was no one else in Australia running an educational program like this," Madeline said. "That meant there was both a huge vacancy in the space and no template for us to work from." As a young woman in the midst of her collegiate career tackling a sensitive issue head-on in local schools and communities,

Madeline enabled others in her community to believe that their ideas for making the world a better place could be achieved. Within OWP, Madeline supports that principle by cultivating an atmosphere of sharing ideas and developing leadership skills with her volunteers. She has even worked to convert the organization's structure to be in line more closely with the principles of OWP: where work is based upon autonomy and peer relationships rather than top-down management strategies. "Rather than having singular leadership in the organization, we've become leader full," Madeline said. The move from hierarchies mirrored the organization's values: "We didn't want to continue to perpetuate the dynamics that we are fighting against in the outside world. We needed to change ourselves in order to change the world."

Today, the One Woman Project works in an average of 200 schools yearly and has reached more than 25,000 young people through in-school educational programs and workshops. OWP has also gone on the road, conducting rural road trip visits to schools with less access to organizations like theirs—including the school Madeline attended. Outposts in China, Tanzania, and India have grown organically from volunteers who were so engaged in Australia that they wanted to stay connected and spread the message in their home countries. OWP also created a wealth redistribution fund for volunteers to dip in as needed—whether that means covering rent for the month or for professional development training a volunteer wants to undertake, even if it doesn't directly benefit OWP. "We have put together these practices and structures that can enable people to get from the organization what they need, so they can put into the organization what they want," Madeline said.

Madeline's story speaks to a fundamental question: When does leadership begin? The answer is: whenever anyone seizes the moment to make something extraordinary happen. Anyone can do it! Madeline put it to us this way:

> There is no set formula for creating change and making it happen. You just decide to do something, to make a

difference, and then do it. If you want to make the pledge to achieve gender equality, all you really need is passion and the drive to take the first step.

Madeline saw an opportunity and took it, first when she returned from Cambodia and started talking with her friends about gender issues, and then at university, where she hatched her plan to launch the One Woman Project. Those relatively small opportunities transformed into something much more significant. Madeline didn't wait for someone to appoint her as "the" leader. She recognized an issue, had a passion for it, found others with a similar vision, and just got started. Then she kept going. Leadership, like any other skill in life, can be learned and strengthened through coaching and practice, and you don't have to wait until that support and preparation are lined up before you start to lead. No amount of coaching or practice can make much of a difference if you don't care deeply about making something better than it currently is.

Everyone can lead, whether or not they are in a formal position of authority or even part of an organized group.[2] That's what we mean when we say *leadership is everyone's business*. It is not about being a student government officer; team, chapter, or club captain; program director; editor; supervisor; president; CEO; military officer; or government official. Nor is leadership about fame, wealth, or even age. It's not about your family status, the neighborhood you come from, or your gender, sexual orientation ethnic, or racial background. It's about knowing your values and those of the people around you and taking the steps, however small, to make what you do every day demonstrate that you live by those values.

Also, as Madeline's experience illustrates, leadership is about transforming values and goals into action. When members of her community and students at her university heard of OWP, enthusiastic volunteers showed up looking to become a part of her project because they shared the vision of eradicating gender inequality through education. "People wanted to get on board almost immediately because it was a cause they believed in," Madeline said. "Like me, they'd experienced friends telling them things they knew were false: that misogyny was no longer an issue, that things were okay as they were. The One Woman Project gave them a place to say, 'That's not true; let's change things.'"

From that outpouring of volunteer support, Madeline learned a valuable lesson in leadership. "I'm here," said Madeline, "to facilitate the passion of other people as well as my own, and from that, OWP has grown into monthly events, conferences, and International Women's Day events—all because of the passion of the people I work with." Within the OWP, Madeline has cultivated an atmosphere encouraging people to share their ideas and aspirations. During weekly meetings, for example, volunteers pitch ideas for potential projects for the OWP to implement. In one case, a volunteer proposed the idea of a monthly calendar, with art from local artists, to be sold to help fund some of the OWP initiatives, and it turned out to be a huge success.

Madeline made it a point to encourage everybody involved because she realized how much it helped everyone keep going as they worked toward making their hopes and dreams come true. What's more, she told us how much she appreciates that there isn't a single leader in their organization; instead, everyone takes the lead in different ways, making leadership development of its volunteers an integral part of OWP's growth plan. "These are exactly the kind of team members I want, people willing to take an idea and grow it and find new opportunities for us," Madeline said. "I want them to take an idea or existing endeavor and ask, 'How can I make this better?'"

Because OWP's success depends on the support of volunteers, Madeline worked hard to ensure an atmosphere of fun for everyone involved. She emphasized the importance of mental health and taking care of yourself. To that end, she arranged seminars for the volunteers to learn to recognize the symptoms of burnout in themselves and other team members. After all, she explained, "Everyone who works with us comes to us in their spare time."

> Most of them are students, but some have full-time jobs. In other words, it's easy to get burned out just from the sheer volume of work. We have a no-fault policy where anyone can back away from their work at any time, no questions asked—maybe it's the middle of finals, maybe it's a problem at home, maybe someone needs a break. The only way to keep passion and commitment high is to let people know they need to take care of themselves first, and I try very hard to encourage that.

For example, Madeline made sure that every volunteer team member attending a meeting completed a self-care survey on which they ranked their well-being on a scale from 1 to 10. Anyone who self-reported being under heavy stress received ideas from Madeline and other team members on how to relieve it. "Self-care has to be a priority," Madeline said.

Madeline also hosted social events for her community of volunteers, such as dinners or events in the town, where the focus is on having fun and promoting teamwork. These celebrations fostered a sense of community and friendship and helped keep the passion high among the OWP team. Madeline explained that she had "a lot of people saying, 'I've never had feminist friends before, and now I get to go out and do fun projects with them.' Everyone is so excited to see and work with each other."

Madeline knows that it's essential to acknowledge the contributions of everyone on the team because her volunteers are taking on responsibility outside of their daily student lives. At their social events, she takes the time to recognize volunteers who have put together proposals outside of their usual work or who have done an exceptional job in recent projects. By attending these dinners and social gatherings herself, Madeline reinforces the idea that she's still one of them and just as much a part of the team as the volunteers.

Madeline is no longer with the One Woman Project as director, although she remains on OWP's board to help support and coach her teammates in the new evolutions of the organization. "I went on leave for a month and a half, and when I came back, the organization was running like clockwork. The whole organization just felt embodied in the values we hold. There wasn't a single decision made while I was gone I didn't agree with," Madeline said, which turned out to be a light bulb moment: the values she had worked to instill in OWP had taken on a life of their own, and it was time for her to move on. "I felt like there wasn't anything I could give OWP that they couldn't do without me—that if I held on longer, I would have been more of a burden to the organization than a benefit."

Reflecting on her work at OWP, Madeline said:

> I'm most proud to see that other people are invested in the same vision I had and that we've achieved incredible things. But when I think of OWP, I don't think of any particular thing we've done. I think of the people that I got to spend the most time with, the conversations I had with them, and the lifelong friendships that I've built. What I'm most proud of is having found a community that shares my collective vision for a better society. That's what fills my heart.

Madeline's experience shows something we have seen over and over: leadership begins when you find something you care about and grabs hold of you. It doesn't necessarily require an organization, a budget, a hierarchy, a position, or a title. It requires the willingness to step up to a challenge, the passion for a worthy purpose, the determination to persist in the face of adversity, and the desire to engage others in making something extraordinary happen.

THE FIVE PRACTICES OF EXEMPLARY LEADERSHIP

In undertaking her leadership challenge, Madeline seized on an opportunity to make a difference. And although her story is unique, it is not unlike countless others. We've been conducting original global research for more than forty years, and when we ask young leaders to tell us about their personal-best leadership experiences—experiences that they believe are their individual standards of excellence—there are countless stories just like Madeline's.[3] We've found them everywhere, and it proves that leadership knows no ethnic, cultural, or geographical borders; no racial or religious bounds; no differences between young and old. Leaders reside in every city and every country, in every function and every organization. We find exemplary leadership everywhere we look.

After analyzing these leadership experiences, we discovered, and continue to find, that individuals who guide others along pioneering journeys follow surprisingly similar paths regardless of the times or settings. Although each experience was distinctive in its expression, there were clearly identifiable behaviors and actions that made a difference. When getting extraordinary things done with others, leaders engage in what we call The Five Practices of Exemplary Leadership®:

- Model the Way
- Inspire a Shared Vision
- Challenge the Process
- Enable Others to Act
- Encourage the Heart

These practices are not restricted to the people we studied. Nor do they belong to a few select shining stars. Leadership is not about personality, power, or privilege; it's about behavior. The Five Practices are available to anyone who accepts the leadership challenge—the challenge of taking people and organizations to places they have never been before. It is the challenge of moving beyond the ordinary to the extraordinary.

The Five Practices framework is not an accident of a particular historical moment. It has passed the test of time. Although the *context* of leadership has changed dramatically over the years, the *content* of leadership has not changed much at all. The fundamental behaviors and actions of leaders have remained essentially the same, and they are as relevant today as they were when we began our study of exemplary leadership. We predict the same for the foreseeable future. The truth of each personal-best leadership experience multiplied thousands of times and substantiated empirically by hundreds of thousands of students and scores of scholars establishes The Five Practices of Exemplary Leadership as an "operating system" for leaders everywhere. Here's a brief overview of The Five Practices of Exemplary Leadership and how they result in the *Ten Commitments of Exemplary Leadership*.

Model the Way

Titles are granted, but it's your behavior that earns you respect. Exemplary leaders know that if they want to gain commitment and achieve the highest standards, they must be models of the behavior they expect of others. To effectively Model the Way, you must be clear about your guiding principles. You must *clarify values by finding your voice*. When you understand your values and who you are, you can authentically give voice to those values.

But *your* values aren't the only values that matter. Finding your voice encourages others to do the same, paving the way for mutual understanding. In every team, organization, and community, others also feel strongly about matters of principle. As a leader, you also must help identify and *affirm the group's shared values*. Leaders' actions are far more important than their words when others want to determine how serious leaders are about what they say. Words and actions must be consistent. Exemplary leaders *set the example by aligning actions with shared values*. Their daily actions demonstrate their deep commitment to their beliefs and the groups they are part of. One of the best ways to prove something is important is when you "walk the talk" yourself.

Inspire a Shared Vision

Students described their personal-best leadership experiences as times when they imagined an exciting, highly attractive future for themselves and others. They had visions and dreams of what *could* be. They had absolute and total personal faith in those dreams and were confident in their abilities to make those extraordinary things happen. Every organization, every social movement, and every significant event begins with a vision. It is the force that propels the creation of the future.

Leaders *envision the future by imagining exciting and ennobling possibilities*. Before starting any project, you must appreciate the past and envision what the results should look like, much as an architect draws a blueprint or an engineer builds a model. But you can't command commitment to a new future; you have to inspire it. You must *enlist others in a common vision by appealing to shared aspirations*. You do this by talking to others and, even more important, listening to them to understand what motivates them. You enlist others by helping them feel they are part of something that matters and something everyone believes is vital to accomplish together. When you express your enthusiasm and excitement for the vision, you ignite a similar passion in others.

Challenge the Process

Challenge is the crucible for greatness. Every single personal-best leadership case involved a change from the status quo. Not one student achieved a personal best by keeping things the same. The challenge might have been launching an innovative new event, tackling a problem differently, rethinking a service their group provides, creating a successful campaign to get students to join an environmental program, starting up a new student group or team, achieving a revolutionary turnaround of a school or university policy, or getting a new event underway with the intent that it become a new institutional tradition. It could also be dealing with daily obstacles and challenges, such as finding ways to resolve a group conflict or designing and delivering an important class or school project. Regardless of the specifics, all the personal-best experiences involved overcoming adversity and embracing opportunities to grow, innovate, and improve.

Leaders are pioneers willing to step out into the unknown. However, leaders aren't the only creators or originators of new ideas, projects, services, or processes. Innovation comes more from listening than telling and from continuously looking outside yourself and your group for new and innovative ways to do things. You need to *search for opportunities by seizing the initiative and by looking outward for innovative ways to improve.*

Because innovation and change involve *experimenting and taking risks*, one way of dealing with experimentation's potential risks and failures is *by consistently generating small wins and learning from experience.* There's a strong correlation between the process of learning and the approach leaders take to make extraordinary things happen: the best leaders are simply the best learners.[4] Leaders are always learning from their errors and failures. Life is the leader's laboratory, and exemplary leaders use it to conduct as many experiments as possible.

School is a great incubator environment for learning how to become the best leader you can be.

Enable Others to Act

Grand dreams don't become meaningful realities through the actions of a single student. Achieving greatness requires a team effort. It requires solid trust and enduring relationships. It requires group collaboration and individual accountability.[5] No leader ever got anything extraordinary done by working solo. All leadership requires a team effort.

Leaders *foster collaboration by building trust and facilitating relationships*. You must engage all those who make the project work—and involve in some way all who must live with the results. Leaders appreciate that people don't perform at their best or stick around for long if they feel weak, dependent, or alienated. When you *strengthen others by increasing self-determination and developing competence*, they are likelier to give it their all and exceed expectations. Focusing on serving the needs of others rather than one's self-interest builds trust in a leader. The more people trust their leaders and each other, the more they take risks, improve, and move forward. When students are trusted, have choices in how they do their work, feel in control, and have ample information, they are more likely to use their energies to produce extraordinary results. Through trusting relationships, leaders turn others into leaders themselves.

Encourage the Heart

The climb to the top is arduous and steep. People can become exhausted, frustrated, and disenchanted, and are often tempted to give up. Genuine acts of caring keep people in the game and draw them forward.

Leaders *recognize contributions by showing appreciation for individual excellence.* Appreciation can be expressed one to one or with many people. It can come from dramatic gestures or simple actions. Being a leader requires showing appreciation for people's contributions and creating a culture of *celebrating the values and victories by creating a spirit of community.* Recognitions and celebrations need to be personal and personalized. They aren't necessarily about fun and games, though there is much fun, and there are a lot of games when students acknowledge people's accomplishments. Neither are they necessarily about formal awards. Ceremonies designed to create "official" recognition can be effective, but only if participants perceive them as sincere. Encouragement is valuable and important because it connects what people have done with the successes the group gathers to celebrate. Leaders make sure that people appreciate how their actions connect with their and the group's values. Celebrations and rituals, when done sincerely and from the heart, give a group a strong sense of identity and team spirit that can carry them through tough times.

THE TEN COMMITMENTS OF EXEMPLARY LEADERSHIP

The Five Practices of Exemplary Leadership are the core leadership competencies that emerged from analyzing thousands of personal-best leadership cases. When student leaders do their best, they Model the Way, Inspire a Shared Vision, Challenge the Process, Enable Others to Act, and Encourage the Heart.

Embedded in The Five Practices are behaviors that can serve as the basis for your learning to lead. We call these the Ten Commitments of Exemplary Leadership. They focus on actions you need to both apply to yourself and that you need to take with others. Think of them with a mindset of "Thou Shalt."

The Five Practices and Ten Commitments of Exemplary Leadership

MODEL THE WAY

1. Clarify values by finding your voice and affirming shared values.
2. Set the example by aligning actions with shared values.

INSPIRE A SHARED VISION

3. Envision the future by imagining exciting and ennobling possibilities.
4. Enlist others in a common vision by appealing to shared aspirations.

CHALLENGE THE PROCESS

5. Search for opportunities by seizing the initiative and by looking outward for innovative ways to improve.
6. Experiment and take risks by consistently generating small wins and learning from experience.

ENABLE OTHERS TO ACT

7. Foster collaboration by building trust and facilitating relationships.
8. Strengthen others by increasing self-determination and developing competence.

ENCOURAGE THE HEART

9. Recognize contributions by showing appreciation for individual excellence.
10. Celebrate the values and victories by creating a spirit of community.

The Ten Commitments serve as a guide for explaining, understanding, appreciating, and learning how leaders get extraordinary things done with others. Each is discussed in depth in the following chapters, through real-life examples, research studies, empirical evidence, and practical applications.

Before doing so, take a few minutes to complete *the Student Leadership Practices Inventory* and use the Appendix ("How You Behave Matters") to reflect on how you currently behave and engage in various leadership behaviors. (You will find information on how to access and complete The *Student Leadership Practices Inventory* in the Appendix on page 311 of this book.) Armed with this information, you can consider those leadership practices that you find most comfortable doing. Particularly note those behaviors that you may not fully appreciate, have missed opportunities to use, and want to pay particular attention to developing.

In the Appendix, we also look at the evidence that these practices, commitments, and behaviors matter. To your question "Do they truly make a difference in how students want to struggle to achieve shared aspirations?" the research and empirical evidence make the case that they do.[6]

In the following chapters, you have more opportunities to reflect on your leadership behaviors and review the empirical evidence that leadership, and how you behave, makes a difference. You'll discover in-depth discussions of each practice and commitment and review many examples from the real-life experiences of students like Madeline, who accepted the leadership challenge and mobilized their teams and organizations to achieve the extraordinary. The Five Practices and Ten Commitments serve as the organizing structure for learning this operating system and becoming the best leader you can be.

MODEL
THE WAY

The first step you must take along the path to becoming an exemplary student leader is inward. It's a step toward discovering who you are and what you believe in. Leaders stand up for their beliefs. They practice what they preach. They also ensure that others stand by the values that they agree on. It is consistency between words and actions that builds credibility.

In the next two chapters, we take a look at how you as a student leader must:

➤ **Clarify Values** by finding your voice and affirming shared values.
➤ **Set the Example** by aligning actions with shared values.

MODEL THE WAY

Reflections from the *Student Leadership Practices Inventory*

1. My overall score from the *Student Leadership Practices Inventory* for Model the Way was:

   _____

2. Of the six leadership behaviors that are part of Model the Way, the statement that I indicated engaging in most frequently was:

   _____

   _____

3. The leadership behavior statement that I engaged in the least often was:

   _____

   _____

   Based on your self-assessment with the leadership practice of Model the Way, complete the following two statements. As you read and review the following two chapters, keep in mind these reflections and observations.

4. Of the leadership behaviors associated with Model the Way, the one(s) I feel most comfortable engaging in is/are:

   _____

   _____

   _____

5. The leadership behaviors that I feel I could engage in more often and be more comfortable with doing are:

   _____

   _____

   _____

1

Commitment #1:
Clarify Values

"Who are you?" You need to know the answer to this question. It is foremost on the mind of anyone willing to follow you. Leadership is fundamentally a relationship, and for someone to join you on a journey, they first want to know something about you, who you are, and what you stand for. Your leadership journey begins when you set out to discover "this is who I am" and are able and willing to express it.

John Banghoff, for example, knew that he wanted to be in the university marching band since he was nine years old when he attended his first college football game with his father. Making the band his first year felt like a dream come true. "I was on cloud nine," John said. "It was the coolest experience to hear my name called." However, shortly after that, the band's student leaders took John and his new bandmates under the bleachers, where they passed around a flask; afterward, they were escorted to a party and introduced to a band tradition of hazing first-year student recruits. "This turned out to be the worst night of my life," John said. "Seeing all of these people that I looked up to drinking and harassing me and the other new band members left me seriously questioning whether I wanted to be part of this organization."

John's struggle about staying in the band or leaving pushed him to think deeply about what mattered to him. Did his personal values align with the band's culture? Being part of a team, having an opportunity to put his passion for music into practice, and expressing his gratitude for being involved in the marching band were important values he discovered in the process of asking himself, "Who am I, and what do I care about?" John told us.

> I realized that the marching band was something that I still wanted to be a part of because it gave me the opportunity to play the trumpet and that I should work on my own feelings of gratitude for the experience rather than focusing on parts that weren't what I wanted.

With this clarity, John soon found other band members who shared his beliefs and concerns. "Once I talked about values, I realized that there were other people who felt the way that I did. Together, we could focus on what was right about marching band and figure out what we might do about the negative aspects," John said. However, before they could do much, the band's hazing tradition became public news and eventually resulted in the college firing the band director.

It was a time of intense challenge for everyone in the band, as John explained: "It felt like we had no direction and were being punished for the mistakes of a few. We weren't sure who we could trust, and the leaders we'd come to know and respect within the band were just trying to keep the ship afloat." The band felt directionless and unmoored, not at all like the prestigious group that John had once yearned to join.

Amid this crisis, John and a few of his peers were selected as squad leaders for the following season of the marching band. Under the leadership of the newly appointed band director, John and the other squad leaders helped design a cultural blueprint for the band, which articulated new values to help guide it: a tradition of excellence, extraordinary respect, and an attitude of gratitude. "These values gave us signposts to move to when we noticed things that didn't align with them," John said. The group's ability to relate to each other and feel gratitude even through difficult times helped sustain the marching band's excellence and return it to national prominence.

In implementing the new values and practices, John helped facilitate workshops on the new cultural blueprint, including exercises to show how the band's values could be lived in real life. John recalls, "Although the process of redefining the band's culture was not an easy one, it was extremely rewarding to see everyone rally around the new set of cultural values." At the end of the season, at the annual concert where the band plays for the community and presents awards to its members, John received the Most Inspirational Bandperson Award for helping bring the band back together after its crisis. "That night, as I drove home, I was in tears," John said. "I was in tears the first night of my band experience and my last night, but in two very different circumstances and for very different reasons. It was the journey between point A and point B that made me the leader I am."

The personal-best leadership cases we've collected are, at their core, the stories of people like John who were clear about their values and used this clarity as a bedrock to give them the courage to make tough choices and navigate difficult terrain. Leaders are expected to be clear about their values and comfortable speaking out on matters of principle and conscience. But to speak out, you have to know what to speak about. To stand up for your beliefs, you have to know the beliefs you stand for. To walk the talk, you have to have a talk to walk. To do what you say, you have to know what you want to say.

Model the Way is the first of The Five Practices of Exemplary Leadership we discuss in this book; one of the commitments you must make to effectively Model the Way is to Clarify Values. In beginning your leadership journey, it's essential that you:

- **Find your voice**
- **Affirm shared values**

Becoming an exemplary student leader requires you to fully comprehend the deeply held values—the beliefs, standards, ethics, and ideals—that drive you. You must freely and honestly choose the principles you will use to guide your decisions and actions. Then you must express your authentic self, genuinely communicating your beliefs in ways that clearly represent who you are.

Moreover, you must realize that leaders aren't just speaking for themselves when discussing the values that should guide their decisions and actions. When leaders passionately express a commitment to learning or innovation or service or some other value, those leaders aren't just saying, "I believe in this." They're also committing on behalf of an entire group. They're saying, *"We all* believe in this." Therefore, leaders must not only be clear about their guiding principles, but also make sure that there's agreement on a set of shared values among everyone they lead. Furthermore, they must hold others accountable to those values and standards.

FIND YOUR VOICE

What would you say if someone asked, "What is your leadership philosophy?" This is the belief system (your core values, principles, and perspectives) that guides your decision-making and actions. Are you prepared right now to say what it is? If you aren't, you should be. If you are, you need to reaffirm it daily.

In order to become a credible leader—one who connects "what you say" with "what you do"—you first need to find your authentic voice, the most genuine expression of who you are. If you don't find your voice, you'll end up with a vocabulary belonging to someone else, sounding as though you are mouthing words written by some speech-writer or mimicking the language of some other leader who is nothing like you. If the words you speak are not your words but someone else's, you will not, in the long term, be able to be consistent in word and deed. You will not have the integrity to lead.

To find your voice, you must discover what you care about, what defines you, and what makes you who you are. You need to explore your inner self. You can only be authentic when you lead according to the principles that matter most to you. Otherwise, you're just putting on an act. Consider Angel Accosta, who worked for an organization called College for Every Student (CFES), a nonprofit that raises the academic aspirations and performance of low-income kids so that they can prepare for, gain access to, and succeed in college.

Angel is the fifth of six children, raised by a single mother from the Dominican Republic. His mother worked multiple jobs and saved enough to bring her whole family to the United States to pursue the American Dream. "I was the first one in my family to graduate from high school, let alone go to college," Angel told us. "And it wasn't easy."

> I had always loved to read, but I was part of the hip-hop culture and intellectual pursuits were laughed at. My friends made fun of me if I talked about the books I was reading. There was a lot of pressure to just stay down.

He also faced a lot of pressure from his family. They were so excited about his potential that they thought they knew what path he should take. When Angel decided to major in anthropology, there were some long and hard conversations, but in the end, Angel's family supported him, and he kept going. "My family's values have always been never say 'never,'" Angel said, "and I found my way. So now I am helping my nieces find theirs. It's tough, but I've been there, and I know what they are facing. When I tell them my story, they seem to listen a little more. They believe me."

Michael Gibler found himself in a somewhat similar place to Angel while working part-time at a laser tag arena and arcade during college. Told at his first performance review that he was a good example for the rest of his peers, Michael was promoted to an assistant manager's position. He was thrilled, but this feeling of excitement soon evaporated because he found that his coworkers didn't really respect him as their leader, and "it seemed like there was nothing I could do to make them work. No amount of threats, begging, or pleading would make them budge."

Michael quickly realized that "I had to determine what kind of manager I wanted to be, to be clear about my values, and to be true to them." High on the list was his commitment to cooperation, collaboration, and camaraderie. He decided he wouldn't order his coworkers around nor ask them to do anything he wasn't willing to do himself. For example, "I wouldn't go sit in the office while everyone else cleaned at the end of the night. I never made demands, and I helped my coworkers even when it wasn't part of my job." Within just a matter of weeks, Michael found that "everyone was back on board," as his coworkers saw that his behavior consistently reflected the congruence between what he said and how he acted.

Leading others begins with leading yourself, and you can't do that until you're able to answer that fundamental question about who you are. When you have clarified your values and found your voice, you will also find the inner confidence necessary to take charge of your life. Take it from Tommy Baldacci, who reported having many leadership experiences throughout college and realizing that too many people don't take the time to reflect, and hence, lack an understanding of their values and philosophy. He told us:

> To know how to lead, you need to know where you are going.
> To know where you are going, you have to know who you are.

Knowing yourself truly means that you have to be honest with yourself. By understanding myself, I was able to figure out professionally where my passions were aimed. Without knowing myself, I would have had no baseline to refer to.

Our research backs up Tommy's observations. There was a dramatic relationship between how student leaders assessed their leadership skills relative to their peers and how often they indicated "talking about their values and the principles that guided their actions." Only about one in ten student leaders who *seldom or only once in a while* talked about their values and principles claimed to have well-developed leadership skills compared with their peers A bit less than three in ten student leaders who reported *sometimes* talking about values and principles felt their leadership skills comparatively well-developed. More than six in ten student leaders who *often to very frequently* spoke about their values and principles felt their leadership skills were well-developed compared with their peers.

Let Your Values Guide You

Values influence every aspect of your life: your moral judgments; your responses to others; your commitments to your family, friends, school, and community; and your personal goals. Values set the boundaries for the hundreds of decisions and choices you make every day, consciously and subconsciously. And believe us: you make hundreds of decisions every day. Usually, people only consider choices that are within their value system. But sometimes, a "whatever" attitude kicks in, and you make poor choices. The question is, can you recognize when that attitude is kicking in? Can you stop yourself from giving in to it and instead listen to your inner voice that knows "this doesn't feel right"? The best chances of this happening are when your internal voice is loud and clear.

Values constitute your personal "bottom line." They serve as guides to the actions you take. They inform the priorities you set and the decisions you make. They tell you when to say yes and when to say no. They also help you explain the decisions you make and why you made them. If you believe, for instance, that diversity makes things better, then you should know what to do if people with differing views keep getting cut off when they offer up fresh ideas. If you value working together over individual achievement, then you'll know what to do when your teammate goes for the shot and ignores the better pass. If you value independence and initiative over conformity and obedience, you'll be more likely to challenge what a good friend or someone of authority says if you think it's wrong. All of the most critical decisions that you will make involve values. You will seldom consider or act on options that run counter to your value system. If you do, it's generally with a sense of compliance rather than commitment.

Alan Yap was hitting a wall trying to balance all his interests—and not making the most of any of them—until he took time to think deeply about his values. Doing so helped clarify his priorities, leading him to eliminate some activities and commit more fully to others. For example, he decided to run for a leadership position in the business fraternity Alpha Kappa Psi. Upon being elected, Alan said he struggled to find an approach to leading the organization. He had to find his voice and figure out, "How do I want to be known as a leader?" He decided "that the best way to lead was through what I valued." Alan's experience illustrates how values are the signposts in your leadership journey. They supply you with a compass by which to navigate the course of your daily life. Clarity of values is essential to know which way is north, south, east, and west. The clearer you are about your values, the easier it is for you and for everyone else in your group to stay on the chosen path and commit to it. This kind of guidance is especially needed in difficult and uncertain times. When there are daily challenges that can throw you off course, it's crucial that you have some signs that tell you where you are and direct you back on the path.

Sophia Bloom identified her personal values early in her life; growing up, she said her family modeled a passion for social justice. But growing up with someone else's values doesn't necessarily mean they are your own. In high school and college, Sophia began throwing herself into social justice work—for example, participating in and starting clubs and movements on campus, like a food bank and an anti-rape education organization. "I realized I tend to feel happiest when I feel like I'm doing something worthwhile and making the world closer to the way I want it to be," Sophia said.

With her values as a guide, Sophia consciously pursued unique opportunities through her university to find ways to develop her capacity to make the difference she craved. For example, she interned at the United Nations, where she thought she might want to work someday in either easing and eradicating poverty globally or in advocating for women's rights. Sophia completed a summer internship in Barcelona, Spain, that worked with local hotels, hostels, and apartments to provide housing for homeless people. Once people were housed, the organization also worked to do empowerment-based training on job skills and functional life skills. Besides this internship, Sophia joined her school's International Scholars program to focus more on learning how to be a better global citizen and engaging in international community work.

By identifying the issues about which she felt most passionate, Sophia was able to find opportunities that could further her skill set and move her toward her ultimate goal of making a difference in the world. Sophia had this to say about how having a strong grasp on her values helped guide her in the opportunities she seeks out:

> I think because it's what I like doing the most, I'm naturally drawn to a lot of organizations where I feel like I'm hopefully making a difference. I feel like my life, personally, is really great, and I'm really lucky to have been born into the life I was born into it—but it was very much luck. If I'd happened

to be born in a different place, I wouldn't have had all the opportunities that I'd been given. I feel like it's really important to me to help other people be able to have any opportunities that they would want. But I think the world would be a better, happier place if that happened—and it would make me happier if the world was like that, too.

Personal values drive commitment. Clear personal values drive motivation and productivity. People who are very clear about their values are more likely to stick around and work harder than those who don't have an internal compass to guide them through uncertainty. It's how you determine if the work you are doing, the group or organization you are in, fits you. You won't stick around (a place, a project, or a team) when you feel in your heart and soul that you don't belong. This is a major reason some people don't stay long in groups they've joined. Commitment is based on alignment with personal values. People who are clearest about personal values are better prepared to make choices based on principle—including deciding whether the principles of the organization fit with their own.

It is also true that the most effective student leaders "talk about their values and the principles that guide their actions." Consider the fact that four out of five students evaluate their leader as effective when they are seen as *often* or *very frequently* talking about their values and principles, as shown in Figure 1.1.

Say It in Your Own Words

People can only speak the truth when speaking in their own true voice. If you only mimic what others say, people are unlikely to commit to you because they don't know who you are and what you believe in.

The techniques and tools that fill the pages of leadership books— including this one—are not substitutes for knowing what matters to

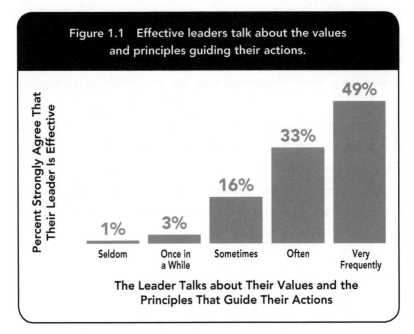

Figure 1.1 Effective leaders talk about the values and principles guiding their actions.

you. Once you have the words you want to say, you must also give voice to those words. You must be able to express yourself so that everyone knows that you are the one who's speaking and not someone else.

You'll find much scientific and empirical data to support the importance of each of The Five Practices of Exemplary Leadership. However, remember that leadership is also an art, and just as with any other art form—whether it's painting, music, dancing, acting, or writing—leadership is a means of personal expression. To become a credible leader, you have to learn to express yourself in ways that are uniquely your own. Jacob Philpott provides a helpful example.

After his first year in college, Jacob applied for a residential advisor (RA) position for the Upward Bound Program (UB). UB is a federally funded educational program created for high school students from diverse, low-income families who are the first generation to go to college. Jacob had participated in the program as a high school student. When asked during the interview process why he wanted to work in the program, he answered from his own experience: "My experience was so enriching I knew I wanted to come back and serve as an RA. I wanted to help prepare the participants for college and provide them with an even better experience than my own while working on a great team."

Jacob's motivation, he told us, was "heavily tied to my core values." Being clear about your values helps you find your voice and be able to express yourself in your own unique way. Genuineness comes through when you can hear yourself using language and words that are your own rather than someone else's. For example, Jacob found that on the very first day of the program:

> I was given an opportunity to find my voice. We got everyone together for an introduction and to discuss our goals. I took that opportunity to share a story about my experience in the program, the values I learned, and the skills that were reinforced which helped me get through college.

All the participants had a chance to share their stories. Although each of these stories was unique to its teller, they carried common themes around building connections with people, growing, learning, and stepping outside one's comfort zone. "I had clarified my values and found my voice," said Jacob, "which enabled me to share my story and gave others the courage to share their own stories. The common values that came from this experience guided us through the rest of the program."

When a close friend and sorority sister of Bella Rovere passed away in an accident just a few weeks into Bella's tenure on her university's student government, she was faced with a tough choice. As one of the few people in student government who knew the young woman who had passed away, Bella could take the lead and release a statement about her friend's death—which had garnered significant attention from the news media—or she could let another member of the leadership team handle it while Bella grieved.

Bella decided she wanted to be the one to handle it—that it was important to her as both a leader and a friend to make sure she acted to offer a statement from the heart. Bella realized that having someone else speak about her friend wouldn't have felt right. She had known her friend well, and she was in the unique position of having held multiple leadership positions on this southeastern university campus that would inform her thoughts on what the institution should do in the wake of the tragedy: "What am I going to do as a leader to honor my friend? I have a position that will allow me to do something—I need to be the one to do it."

Bella spent days drafting a statement about her friend's death. She pledged to work with her campus to improve safety measures, including hosting student focus groups to discuss what they felt the campus needed to do to improve safety.

> It was a very odd leadership turning point because no one would have blamed me if I had opted not to be the one to handle it. But I thought to myself: Did I want someone else to handle this? Or did I feel confident enough in myself as a leader—and in my knowledge of what my friend would have wanted—to step up to the best of my ability? It was hard to find the right words—to know what I should say—but I'm so glad I did it.

Like Jacob and Bella, you cannot lead out of someone else's values or words. You cannot lead out of someone else's experience. You can only lead out from your own. Unless it's your style, your manner, your words, it's not you—it's just an act. People don't follow your title or your technique. They follow *you*. If you're not the genuine article, can you honestly expect others to want to follow? To be a leader, you have to awaken to the fact that you don't have to copy someone else, you don't have to read a script written by someone else, and you don't have to imitate someone else's style. Instead, you are free to choose what you want to express and how you want to express it. You have a responsibility to others to express yourself authentically in a way they would immediately recognize as yours.

AFFIRM SHARED VALUES

Leadership is not solely about *your* values. It's also about the values of those you lead. Just as your values drive your commitment, the personal values of those you work with drive their commitment to the organization, club, or team. They will be significantly more engaged when staying faithful to their beliefs. Although clarifying your values is essential, understanding the values of others and building alignment around values everyone can share is equally critical.

Our research shows that the frequency with which their leader "makes sure that people support the values that have been agreed upon" influences the extent that people are proud to tell others they are working with this leader, as shown in Figure 1.2. Very few people strongly agree with this sentiment when they indicate that their leader *sometimes*, at best, engages in this behavior. Nearly nine in ten people strongly agree that they are proud to be associated with a leader who *often* or *very frequently* makes sure that people support the shared values.

Bethany Fristad felt there was something important inside her pushing to come out. In high school, she hadn't been very involved, felt little sense of purpose, and didn't think she had much direction in life. Halfway through her first year in college, something began to change. As she made friends at her new school and around the local small-town community, she started recognizing that she could serve a

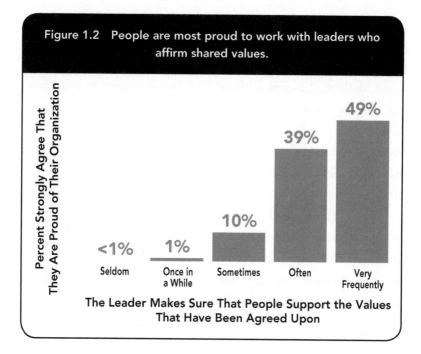

Figure 1.2 People are most proud to work with leaders who affirm shared values.

greater purpose. She brought together a small group of classmates who helped establish a nonprofit organization focused on helping underprivileged children. They called it Firefleyes to symbolize its ability to ignite a fire in people's hearts and eyes. Bethany then recruited an even larger group interested in helping children in need.

Firefleyes members believe that underserved children can flourish in an environment where they can find their voices through music, sports, arts, books, and crafts. The group promoted this belief by collecting enough resources to travel to Sierra Leone and start the first of what Bethany calls Creation Nations, which are essentially playrooms where children explore their creative side with all sorts of arts, crafts, and music.

By giving voice to her convictions, Bethany found many supportive and willing participants who shared her beliefs about how to help children do well and who saw the value in what she wanted to do.

Had she not been clear on what she was trying to accomplish and why, particularly in such a new and large endeavor, others could have easily cast aside her ideas as impractical. Bethany persisted and appealed to the ideals she believed others shared about the need to help those less fortunate. She knew that the people she spoke with understood the value of creativity in helping children discover their dreams. Ultimately, she said, it was relatively easy to help fellow students see how they could transform their values into specific actions that would benefit others.

Shared values are the foundation for building productive and genuine working relationships. Exemplary student leaders, like Bethany, honor the uniqueness and individuality of everyone in the group, and they also stress common values. They don't try to get everyone to be in accord with everything. That goal is unrealistic, perhaps even impossible. Moreover, achieving it would negate the real advantages of diversity.

Nevertheless, leaders build on finding agreement because to take the first step, and then a second, and then a third, people must have some common core of understanding. After all, if there's no agreement about values, then what exactly are the leader and everyone else going to model? If disagreements over fundamental values continue, the result is intense conflict, false expectations, and diminished capacity.[1] Leaders ensure that through affirming shared values, everyone is aligned—uncovering, reinforcing, and holding one another accountable to what "we" value. Once people are clear about the leader's values, their own, and the shared values, they know what's expected of them and can count on others.

Give People Reasons to Care

Although it's vital that leaders forthrightly articulate the principles for which they stand, the values leaders espouse must be consistent with the aspirations of those who follow them. Leaders who advocate values that aren't representative of the group won't be able to get people to act as one. There must be a shared understanding of mutual expectations. Leaders must gain consensus on a common cause and a common set of principles. They must be able to maintain a community of shared values. In this way, a leader's promise is also an organization's promise, regardless of whether the organization is a project team of two, an intramural slow-pitch softball team of ten, a fraternity of one hundred, a campus of seven thousand, a company of twenty thousand, or a town of two hundred thousand. Unless there's agreement about which promises to keep, the organization, its members, and its leaders risk losing credibility.

Recognition of shared values provides people with a common language. That unity generates tremendous energy when individual, group, and organizational values are in sync. Commitment, enthusiasm, and drive intensify. People have reasons for caring about what they are doing. When individuals care deeply about what they are doing, they are more effective and satisfied. They stay committed to the group, are more engaged in what's going on, and are more likely to participate actively. They experience less frustration with the task or the group.

Exemplary student leaders spend time talking about values with the people in their group. Too few groups in classrooms and teams devote enough time doing this. Too often it happens as a one-time occurrence, at the beginning of the school year, when a group is first formed, or new members are brought in. Frequent and continuing conversations reminding people why they care about what they are doing renew commitment and help people feel connected and part of the same team.

Having frequent and ongoing conversations with the people in your group reinforces what is important to the group and the specific individuals in it. Think about a time when you joined an organization as a new member. Did anyone talk to you about what the group stood for? Did you ask the question, "What is important to this group?" If you did, was the answer very clear? If you didn't, how did you know what the group was all about? The group's values will guide everything it does, so it is essential to spend time regularly talking about those values. We know this can be initially challenging for any leader.

Consider Kara Koser's experience as a resident assistant (RA) at a major urban university, trying to figure out how she could best meet the needs of her diverse resident population. She was unsure about proposing any activity that would be of sufficient interest to everyone. She realized that first, she had to listen to her inner voice and then take the time to listen to others. Kara understood that some people find it intimidating to talk about what is important to them, and it takes time for them to become comfortable sharing. Kara adopted an approach she called "leading out front and leading from the back." What this meant to her was both sharing her viewpoints *and* intently listening to what others were saying, hearing firsthand what was important to them. "The difference in this type of leading was subtle," Kara said, "but both approaches were important because they were done with the interests of the group—in my case, my floor residents—in mind."

Kara continued having conversations with her residents about what they needed and wanted. The more they talked, the more they became comfortable sharing. Kara regularly worked to create an environment where people could freely and easily contribute. She encouraged her residents to speak out, knowing that the best solution for all would emerge if she could be respectful of the values of others while at the same time not minimizing her voice. These conversations enabled the residents to develop a greater sense of community and discover their shared values as they got to know each other better and how they wanted to spend their time together.

In another context, consider Grant Hillestad's experience when he joined an organization called Students Today Leaders Forever (STLF), and soon found himself on a "Pay It Forward Tour," one of STLF's community service road trips that go from city to city doing different service projects. Students travel on a chartered bus to visit cities large and small to learn about a variety of social issues; the idea is that in the process they will discover more about themselves, their own community, and the world.

In arranging their first road trip, Grant said that the group's planning for each city had been assigned to different people in order for them to learn and grow from the experience. Even though they were nervous that not enough preparations had been made in some locations, they had to let it play out because the organization valued learning by doing so deeply. "We were really worried that we'd get to a certain city and nothing would be ready," Grant said. "If that happened the whole trip might be remembered for that aspect of the event. It really took a lot for us to say, 'No, our mission is to *reveal* leadership through service. We have to trust that it will work out and that each of us will learn how to make it work out, not just a select few.'"

Grant's and Kara's experiences illustrate that you have to tap into the values of those you are working and interacting with. People become more committed when they can find alignment between their values and those of the group. The quality and accuracy of communication within the group, along with the integrity of the decision-making process, increase when people feel part of a team with the same values. Confidence in one another grows; stress and worry are reduced. People work harder and are more creative because they become fully engaged in what they are doing.

Forge Unity, Don't Force It

When leaders seek consensus around shared values, those who follow them are more positive and productive. You cannot mandate unity; instead, you forge it by involving people in the process, ensuring that they feel you are genuinely interested in their perspectives and that they can speak freely with you. To be open to sharing their ideas and aspirations, others must believe you'll be caring and constructive in searching for common ground.

By encouraging ongoing discussion about the group's common values, leaders avoid the pitfall of people wasting time and energy trying to figure out what they're supposed to do. When people are unsure about their roles, they tend to lose focus or draw the group off-topic; they may stop participating or even leave the group altogether. The energy that goes into dealing with incompatible values, through arguments or misunderstandings, takes its toll on both the leader's effectiveness and the group's engagement. "What are our core principles?" and "What do we believe in?" are far from simple questions. Even with commonly identified values, there may be little agreement on the meaning of values statements. For example, one study reported 185 different behavioral expectations about the value of integrity alone.[2]

Yi Song told us about one of her class projects at a Chinese university, where she was randomly assigned to a team of people she did not know. Judging from their introductions to one another, Song felt that they had few things in common. They didn't all have the same major, were from different states or countries, and had diverse hobbies and interests. Song suggested that they identify what they valued the most from this team: "Let's each grab a pen and paper and write down five characteristics that we see as most important for working together as a team." After they finished writing, they shared what they had written and the reasons they had chosen those values, along with examples showing why they were important. Song told us how this action and discussion affected her and the team:

> Through the individual value-sharing process, we found some common characteristics—responsibility, punctuality, efficiency, good quality of work, and a sense of humor—and these shared values guided our actions for the rest of the semester.

It was a great way to integrate individual values into the group's shared values. Since the shared values were decided by our entire group, everyone understood them, felt like they fit in, and were more willing to follow the shared values.

As Song's experience demonstrates, shared values emerge from a process, not a pronouncement. Leaders can't impose their values on the group's members; instead, they must actively involve people in identifying shared values. Values ownership increases exponentially when leaders actively engage a broad range of people in their development. Shared values result from listening, appreciating, building consensus, and resolving conflicts. For people to understand the values and agree with them, they must participate in the process. Unity can never be forced.

Fervently shared values are much more than advertising slogans. They are strongly supported and broadly endorsed beliefs about what's important to the people who hold them. People must be able to enumerate the values and have common interpretations of how to practice those values. They must know what their values will look like in action and how their efforts directly contribute to the group's success. On Song's team, for example, *being a responsible team member* meant that each person would put in the best effort on all the work they were assigned to do. *Being punctual* meant not being late for team meetings, and thus, showing respect by not wasting their teammates' time.

Having everyone on the same page regarding values has many benefits. It ensures consistency in what the group says and what it does. The result is high individual credibility and an excellent reputation for the group, further preparing people to discuss values and expectations when recruiting, selecting, and orienting new members. Whenever new members join your group, whether at the beginning of a term or in the middle of the year, knowing what the group stands for and talking openly about it helps everyone make more informed decisions about their engagement with the group. Having everyone aligned about shared values builds commitment and community, which is precisely what leaders ultimately hope to do as everyone pursues a common purpose.

REFLECT AND ACT: CLARIFY VALUES

The first step on the journey to exemplary leadership is clarifying your values—discovering those fundamental beliefs that will guide your decisions and actions along the path to success and significance. This becomes your leadership philosophy. That journey involves an exploration of your inner self, where your true voice resides. You must take yourself on this voyage because it's the only route to being a credible leader and because your personal values drive your commitment to the organization and the cause. You can't do what you say if you don't know what you believe. And you can't do what you say if you don't believe in what you're saying.

Although being clear about personal values is essential for all leaders, that by itself isn't good enough. Leaders don't just speak for themselves; they also speak for their followers. There must be agreement on the shared values that everyone will commit to upholding. Shared values give people reasons to care about what they do, which significantly and positively affect their work attitudes and performance. A common understanding of shared values emerges from a process, not a pronouncement; unity and commitment emerge through conversation and debate.

Student leaders must also hold themselves and others accountable to shared values—a topic explored more thoroughly in the next chapter.

Reflect

Model the Way begins with the commitment to *clarify values by finding your voice and affirming shared values.* What are the most important ideas or lessons about exemplary leadership that you learned from this chapter?

_____

_____

_____

_____

Here are some actions you can take to solidify your commitment to **Clarify Values:**

- Reflect on the values that guide your actions and be able to express what they mean in your own words.
- Ask others to describe why they choose to be involved in their current activities and organizations and why they care about them.
- Create opportunities for people to discuss individual values with others in the group.
- Ask the group to identify the shared values revealed in discussions of individual values.
- Find ways to make the shared values visible, which helps ensure that people adhere to them.
- Periodically review the group's shared values to make sure that they are still salient; adjust and reconfirm as necessary.
- Be clear about how you will communicate what the group stands for when someone new joins the group and ensure that others are on the same page.

Act

After you have reflected on what you learned, what you can improve, and the preceding suggestions, record your plan here for taking at least one action that will help you become a better leader:

_____

_____

_____

_____

_____

_____

2

Commitment #2: Set the Example

Tyler Iffland thought he'd play football in college because he'd been the captain of his high school team. That aspiration soon changed when he realized that committing to football would take too much time away from academics. Nevertheless, Tyler wanted to find a way to be part of a team. "I realized that I still wanted that leadership experience," Tyler told us, "and that a good way for me to find a new team was to join a fraternity. Fast-forward to his junior year. Just elected president of his fraternity, Tyler faced a daunting challenge: helping realign his local chapter with the values important to them as a national fraternity. For example, the academic rank of Tyler's chapter was sixth out of seven fraternities on campus, and the chapter needed to address this situation. To do that, Tyler knew he had to take radical action.

First, he understood that he had to exemplify the values that his fraternity held dear. Tyler spent time reflecting on the goals and mission of his fraternity and decided that its most significant values centered around doing good for the community and achieving academic excellence, all while building strong friendships and relationships among the fraternity members. So, Tyler got more involved in the philanthropic aspects of the organization, creating new opportunities for his fraternity brothers to engage in the community. Tyler made sure that he attended every event, sometimes skipping other social commitments, to demonstrate to his fraternity brothers that he was actively committed to the group's mission. He also searched for ways to become more visibly involved on campus academically. Tyler hosted study groups at the fraternity house, led by himself or other executive team members, which emphasized how important it was to be motivated and engaged in their studies. He took on extracurricular academic activities—for example, helping mentor other students at the school. Tyler became involved in a leadership fellowship that met outside of classes and reinforced ways to achieve excellence both in the classroom and extracurricular pursuits. Tyler pushed himself to become the type of brother he wanted to see throughout his fraternity.

At the same time, Tyler knew that to effect lasting change in the fraternity, he needed the support and reinforcement of strong leadership from his fraternity brothers. As a junior, Tyler had to engage the class of outgoing seniors, many of whom were more focused on their futures beyond college and didn't want to participate fully in all the chapter's activities. Tyler believed it was important for the seniors to act as leadership models for the rest of the fraternity, helping promote strong leadership beliefs and behaviors in the underclass members. He said he could've written them off and focused on the brothers who were already more engaged with the values of the fraternity, but he believed in his fellow brothers' potential. Even though it might be hard for them to continue to focus on the fraternity when their time at the university was ending, Tyler didn't want to give up on the idea of having them be actively engaged.

He came up with the idea to sit down with all the seniors and show them why they should remain involved. He brought in alumni brothers who helped demonstrate why getting on board and staying engaged in the fraternity was important. "I wanted to show everyone that this was their chance to leave a legacy, to get involved in something bigger than themselves. I wanted them to see that these alumni were the brothers they'd looked up to when they first joined the fraternity, and now they had a chance to be the same type of leader for our underclassmen brothers," Tyler said. At the meeting, Tyler also laid out what he expected of his fraternity brothers to help uphold the organization's values. He explained:

> I made sure we were very clear on what had brought us together in the first place and what we needed to do to get where we wanted to go—focus on our academics and work hard on our philanthropy.

The strategy worked. By the second semester of Tyler's junior year, the seniors had all assumed the lead-by-example model he'd hoped for. Moreover, by the end of his term as president, his fraternity had moved up from its sixth-place academic ranking on campus to third place, based on overall fraternity GPAs. "We were still not where I'd have liked for us to be, but it was a huge jump," Tyler said.

Student leaders like Tyler realize and appreciate that what you do speaks more loudly than what you say. His experience illustrates the second commitment of Model the Way: leaders Set the Example. They take every opportunity to show others, by their example, that they're deeply committed to the values and aspirations they espouse. No one will believe you're serious until they see you doing what you're asking of others. Either you lead by example, or you don't lead at all. This is how you provide the evidence that you're personally committed. It's how you make your values known and shown.

Our research has consistently revealed that *credibility is the foundation of leadership*. People want to follow leaders whom they can believe. But what makes a leader credible? When asked to define credibility behaviorally, people told us it meant "do what you say you will do." This chapter on Set the Example is all about the *do* part. It's about practicing what you preach, following through on commitments, keeping promises, and walking the talk.

Being an exemplary student leader requires you to live the values you and your organization hold. You must put into action what you and others stand for. You must be an example for others to follow. And, because you're leading a group of people—not just leading yourself— you also must make certain that the actions of others in your group are consistent with the organization's shared values. An essential part of your job is to educate people on what the team or organization stands for, why this matters, and how others can authentically serve the organization. As the leader, you teach, coach, and guide others to align their actions with the shared values because you're also held accountable for their actions, not just your own.

To Set the Example, you need to:

- **Live the shared values**
- **Teach others to model the values**

In practicing these essentials, you become an exemplary role model for what the group or organization stands for, and you create a culture in which everyone commits to aligning themselves with the agreed-upon shared values.

LIVE THE SHARED VALUES

Leaders are their organizations' ambassadors of shared values. Their mission is to represent these values and standards to the rest of the world. It's their responsibility to serve the values to the best of their abilities. Our research shows quite clearly that students evaluate the leadership skills of their leader in direct proportion to how they set an example for others, as shown in Figure 2.1. Four out of five students indicate that leaders who *often* and *very frequently* "set a personal example of what they expect from other people" have the most well-developed leadership skills compared with their peers.

Della Dsouza's leadership challenge was probably not that different from that of most college students who share an apartment with other people: keeping the kitchen clean. From trash piling up to utensils accumulating in the sink, more often than not, the place was a mess, which often led to disputes and finger-pointing about the kitchen's state. The arguments only added to a "cold war" atmosphere among the roommates. "I always had to remind them to do their bit," Della told us, "and in the beginning, no matter how many times I said it, it didn't work."

So, Della decided to take the initiative in making sure the kitchen area was clean, if not all the time, at least whenever she used the area.

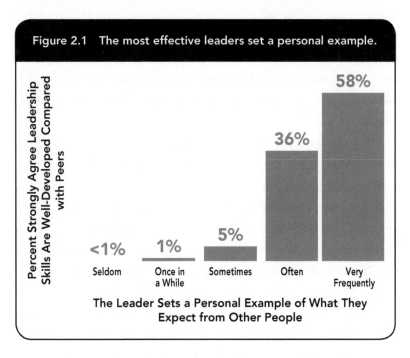

Figure 2.1 The most effective leaders set a personal example.

This meant that even if things were lying around that didn't belong to her, she would put them in the right place. She would take out the trash containers when they were full, and whenever she had time to spare, she cleaned up the place. What did she notice after a month of doing so? "I realized the arguments got fewer, and there were fewer utensils in the sink. Some days, the trash was already taken out before I could do it. Everybody in the house began to do their part. No instructions, no rules laid down. Just my simple actions produced this outcome!" For Della, this is what it meant to live the shared values:

> I had to lead by example. I had to be the doer, not the preacher. I realize that people are constantly observing us. When they see your actions are in sync with your words, you are a more effective leader. And perhaps that is why it was only when I did those things myself that my room-mates followed.

As a leader, you always have influence. People watch your every action, determining whether you're serious about what you say. You need to be conscious of the choices you make and the actions you take because they reveal your priorities and whether you're doing what you say.

Sam Beskind joined the basketball team at his Division I school as a walk-on. Unlike some of his teammates, he hadn't been awarded a scholarship to play, but Sam knew he wanted to be on the team and make an impact. He embraced the team's core values, spelled out in three phrases: be selfless, be invested, and be tough. Sam might not have been as highly recruited as some of his teammates, but he knew that if he invested in living those principles and acted as an example for his teammates, he could positively impact his team.

During the summer between his freshman and sophomore years, Sam traveled with his teammates to Italy to play against global teams. It was there that Sam found out he'd been awarded a basketball scholarship for his sophomore year—a rare occurrence, to be awarded an athletic scholarship after the fact. "I had gone through so much that freshman year—it was so physically demanding, so mentally challenging that it was a really huge reward. It felt like a testament to my hard work. I felt really great about that," Sam said, adding that one of his best friends was the one who presented him with the news, bringing him to tears.

Sam shared how he found ways to embody what otherwise could have just been words to his teammates:

> It wasn't that I worked really hard one day, or that I was performing particularly well all of a sudden. I think it was that I really embodied my role on the team and worked hard to be pretty selfless. I would warm up with my teammates. I'd carry bags through the airport. I knew I was the lowest person on the totem pole. I was trying to read as many books as possible so I could help our team in a different way. I was putting in the work every night, early mornings, trying to improve. I think showing my teammates and coaches that consistency that even if I'd had the best day, I was still in the gym at night shooting, or even if I had the worst day in the world, not being so dejected I couldn't show up the next day. Those were the sorts of things that ultimately earned the respect of my teammates and coaches.

The most significant signal-sending actions you can take to demonstrate that you live your values, as Sam noted, are how you spend your time and what you pay attention to. Also important is the language (words and phrases) you use, the questions you ask, and your openness to feedback about your behavior. Your actions make your commitment to a shared way of being visible and tangible. They provide the chance to show where you stand on matters of principle. Simple though they may appear, you should remember that sometimes the greatest distance you have to travel is from your mouth to your feet.

Spend Your Time and Attention Wisely

How you spend your time is the single most evident indicator of what's important to you. People use this metric to judge whether you measure up to espoused standards. Spending time on what you say is essential; it documents that you're putting your money where your mouth is. Whatever your values are, they must show up consistently. They must show up on your calendar if people are to believe they're significant.

Let's say one of your espoused values is teamwork. You're supposed to meet with your capstone project team on Friday afternoon to go over how everyone's research is coming along, and one of your friends invites you to drive down that afternoon to the family's beach home for the weekend. Do you meet your obligations to your classmates because you are committed to being a good team player, or do you go with your friends because you don't want to miss a weekend at the beach? Or suppose that your club decides to run a fundraising car wash. You have an important exam to study for, and you know there will be no shortage of people there to help. What do you decide to do? Choices like these are not clear-cut or easy, but ultimately, the things you spend your time on reflect your priorities. Are your decisions based on how they reflect your values or indicate that you're distracted or engaged in conflicting interests?

These questions apply to groups as well. Think about the meetings you attend and what's on the agenda. What do you spend most of the time discussing? Being present and consistently aligning your actions with your behaviors say more about what you value than any other message you share, whether on social media, in a text, or passed along by someone else. How you behave as a leader signals to others what's important to you and what's merely lip service.

With an undergraduate student body of nearly 30,000, running for student body president was a highly competitive endeavor.

Students campaigned for months and spent thousands of dollars to boost their visibility. It was an atmosphere designed to foster student competition—and not always healthily. As Lizzie Shaw told us, "When you have a campaign cycle as crazy as ours was, fighting was inevitable because it was always me versus you."

Lizzie felt she needed to focus on her campaign and the good she could do if elected. But that wasn't always easy. It could be hard to shut out negativity being flung at candidates from other students or rival campaigns. A social media app called YikYak allowed students to anonymously connect with—and post about—anyone within a five-mile radius. During the election campaigns, the YikYak comments turned nasty. And at first, Lizzie let the negativity affect her. But Lizzie knew getting entangled in social media slurs wouldn't help her win or focus on positive change at her school—the real reason she wanted to run for student government in the first place. With support from her friends on the campaign, Lizzie found the strength to tune out the negativity. "I just deleted the app and tried not to let it bother me," Lizzie said.

When people working on her campaign approached her about comments from YikYak, Lizzie would say, "I don't want to hear about this. This doesn't help me or anyone. I cannot concern myself with what others are doing or saying about me." Her decision to ignore negative comments stretched beyond her personal choice about social media: she also refused to allow other members of her campaign to focus on it, either. "I was pretty firm on setting expectations. Every meeting, I would add a slide at the end of our PowerPoint deck making it very clear that I wouldn't let someone remain affiliated with us if they participated in any of this behavior," Lizzie said. If someone on her campaign tried to focus negatively on what their opponents were doing, Lizzie would ask them to redirect their focus to their actions. What could they do to use their time more productively for the campaign or their responsibilities rather than focusing on other people's negativity or spreading negativity themselves?

Lizzie's focus paid off: She won the election and demonstrated to her team and her school that she was more interested in what she could do to serve them than getting involved in social media drama.

You can make your commitment to your group and its values visible and tangible to others when you seize the kind of signal-sending opportunities that Lizzie did. Simple though they may appear, actions like just showing up are evidence of where you stand on matters of principle. Leaders like Lizzie are mindful of how they focus their time and what they pay attention to, to show others they are serious about their dedication to the group, the task, and the shared values. You can't just talk the talk. You have to walk it, which generally means rolling up your sleeves and being part of, not apart from, the action.

Watch Your Language

Exemplary student leaders understand and are attentive to language because they appreciate the power of words. Words don't just give voice to one's beliefs; they also evoke images of what people hope to create with others and how people expect others to behave. The tradition within fraternities and sororities of members referring to each other as "brother" or "sister" is an excellent example. It reinforces the sense of family and loyalty valued in the fraternal system. The words you choose have a powerful effect on how others see themselves, those around them, and the events you all share.

Researchers have documented the power of language in shaping thoughts and actions. Just a few words from someone can make a difference in the beliefs that people articulate. At an East Coast university, there was a publicized incident of hate mail sent to an African American student. In a study at that institution, researchers randomly stopped students walking across campus and asked them what they thought of the occurrence. Before the student could respond, a research partner impersonating another student would come up and answer with a response like, "Well, that person must have done something to deserve it." As you might expect, the first student's response was more often than not like the student impersonators. The researchers then stopped another student and asked the same question. This time the impersonator gave an alternative response, such as, "There's no place for that kind of behavior on our campus." Again, the student being questioned replicated the impersonator's response.[1]

This classic study dramatically illustrates how potent language influences people's responses to what's happening around them. Language helps frame people's views of the world, so being mindful of your choice of words is essential. Think about how the phrase "gun control" versus "gun safety" frames political rhetoric. Frames provide the context for thinking and talking about events and ideas and focus the listeners' attention on specific aspects of the subject. "Watch your language" takes on an entirely new meaning from when your teacher scolded you for using an inappropriate word. It's now about setting an example for others of how they need to think and act.

Consider, for example, the intriguing impact of language on people in experiments in which researchers told participants they were playing either the Community Game or the Wall Street Game.[2] In both scenarios, people played the same game by the same rules; the only difference was that experimenters gave the same game two different names. Of those playing the Community Game, 70 percent started out playing cooperatively and continued to do so throughout. With those told they were playing the Wall Street Game, just the opposite occurred: 70 percent did not cooperate, and the 30 percent who did cooperate stopped when they saw that others weren't cooperating. Again, remember: the name, not the game itself, was the only thing different!

This experiment powerfully demonstrates why you must pay close attention to the language you use. You can influence people's behavior simply by giving the task or the team a name that evokes the kind of behavior implied by the name. If you want people to act like members of a community, use language that produces a feeling of community. If you want people to act like citizens of a village, you need to talk about them that way, not as subordinates in a hierarchy. If you want people to appreciate the rich diversity in their organizations, you need to use inclusive language. If you want people to be innovative, you need to use words that spark exploration, discovery, and invention.

Ask Purposeful Questions

Asking questions sends people on mental journeys. Your questions chart the path people follow, and focus their search for answers. The questions you ask send messages about the group's priorities, and they indicate what is on your mind. They're one more tangible indicator of how serious you are about your espoused beliefs. Questions draw attention to the values that deserve attention and how much energy should be devoted to those values.

Questions also develop people by helping them escape the trap of their mental models. They broaden people's perspectives and enlarge their responses, enabling them to take responsibility for their answers to your questions. Asking relevant questions forces you to listen attentively to what those around you are saying, and in doing so, demonstrates your respect for their ideas and opinions. If you are genuinely interested in other people's opinions, you need to ask them, especially before giving your own. By asking what others think, you facilitate their participation in whatever decision will ultimately be determined, increasing support for that decision.

Reflect on the questions you typically ask in meetings, one-on-ones, telephone calls, emails, and texts. How do they help clarify and gain commitment to shared values? What would you like each group member to pay attention to daily? Be intentional and purposeful about the questions you ask. The questions you routinely ask are examples of the questions they should be asking themselves in your absence. What information do you need from the group to show that people live by shared values and make decisions that are consistent with their values? What questions should you pose if you want people to focus on integrity, trust, community service, safety, or personal responsibility?

Whatever the shared values are, come up with questions that will routinely get people to reflect on those values and what they have done daily to act on them. Be clear in the first place about how you would answer any of your questions.

Seek Feedback

You should use questions to challenge others to connect their actions with the team's values and elicit feedback from your colleagues and team members on how your actions impact the feelings of others and their performance. You will never know how you are doing if you don't ask for feedback. You can't match your words and actions if you don't know how aligned they are. There's substantial evidence that the best leaders are very aware of what's happening inside them as they are leading and are attuned to what's happening outside them with others. They are self-aware, and they're very socially aware. They can pick up clues that tell them whether they've done something that has enabled someone to perform at a higher level or whether they have diminished motivation.

It's your responsibility as a leader to keep asking others, "How am I doing when it comes to [whatever]?" If you don't ask, no one is likely to tell you. It's not always easy to get feedback. It's not generally asked for, and most people aren't used to providing it. Skills are required to do both. You can increase the likelihood that people will accept honest feedback from you if you make it easier for people to give you feedback. The most effective feedback has these characteristics: it is specific and not general, focused on behavior rather than on the individual (personality), solicited rather than imposed, timely rather than delayed, and descriptive rather than evaluative. For example, instead of asking, "How was that meeting?" you might say, "One thing I am trying to do as a leader is to encourage others to contribute ideas. I tried to do that during our meeting today. How do you think it went? What could I have done differently?" Although you might not always like the feedback you get, it is the only way to know how you're doing as a leader.

People's reported productivity levels increase dramatically as a result of working with a leader who "seeks to understand how their actions affect the performance of other people." As shown in Figure 2.2, the more frequently their leader solicits feedback, the more people report that their productivity increases when working with that leader. People's satisfaction with their leader demonstrates a similar

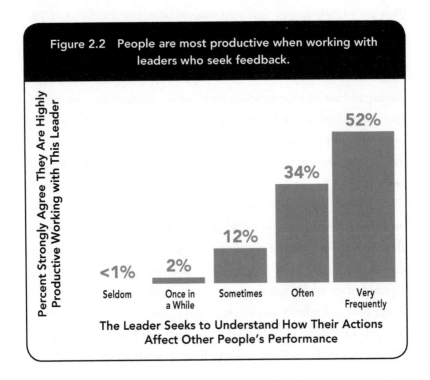

Figure 2.2 People are most productive when working with leaders who seek feedback.

relationship, with satisfaction increasing as a function of how diligently their leader finds ways to obtain feedback.

You invite feedback; you don't demand it. Better yet, couch your request in terms of asking for advice. Creating a receptive climate for feedback and advice is critical. Reviewing past behavior shouldn't be seen as an opportunity to assign blame but to stay curious about what happened and what it says about how you can move forward in line with the group's goals and values. Regularly ask for feedback about "what happened," focusing on "what can we learn?" so that mistakes are not repeated. Keep in mind, however, that if you don't do anything with the advice you receive, people will stop giving it to you.

A classroom project formed the basis of Alex Golkar's personal-best leadership experience. His group initially wasn't on the same page about the project, and there was a lot of infighting, with people being personally critical of each other. "I was forced to find my voice and act as an exemplar of the values that I wanted my groupmates to emulate," Alex told us. As the group found its way, developing mutual respect and dialogue, Alex asked his colleagues if they had feedback for him regarding his role in the project: "I realized that a good leader accepts feedback just as readily as he or she distributes it." Following this up, they turned to Alex and asked him for his opinions on how the group was progressing and what they could do to work even more productively together on the project. Alex indicated that when conflicts arose, "We established an informal system of feedback with one another to make sure we didn't revert to unproductive arguments."

Often people fear the exposure and vulnerability that accompanies direct and honest feedback. Those giving the feedback can feel a bit exposed and may even fear retribution, hurting someone's feelings, or damaging a relationship. It's a risk, but the upside of learning and growth is far more beneficial than the downside of being nervous or embarrassed. Learning to be a better leader requires great self-awareness and making yourself vulnerable. Learning to be a better leader requires feedback. Asking for feedback signals your openness to do what's right and makes it easier for others to be receptive to learning about what they can contribute to the common good.

TEACH OTHERS TO MODEL
THE VALUES

You're not the only role model in your group, team, or organization. Everyone, at all levels and in all situations, should be setting an example that aligns their actions and words. Your role is to make sure that everyone keeps the promises that have been agreed on. How you hold others accountable for living the shared values and how you reconcile deviations from the chosen path are being watched. It's not just what *you* do that demonstrates consistency between word and deed. Every team member, partner, and colleague sends signals about what's valued. Therefore, you need to look for opportunities to lead by your example and by taking on the role of teacher and coach.

Kenzie Crane was responsible for the sorority recruitment program at a large university in the southern United States. She guided nearly two dozen recruitment counselors from sixteen different chapters in this capacity. Their job was to recruit students and help them find the best fit in a sorority. Still, because all the recruitment counselors were already members of one of the sororities, it was sometimes challenging for them to be unbiased. Therefore, Kenzie had to model what it meant to be neutral, and she also needed to hold others accountable for doing the same and teach them how to do that. One action she took each week was to get everyone together and do role plays about how they would handle, in an unbiased fashion, various questions from the women being recruited.

She also worked with them on changing the perception of sororities as simply social entities to organizations focused on community engagement, intellectual enrichment, and personal growth. To make this shift credible, they would all have to be able to share examples of positive experiences sororities offered for personal development. A top priority for Kenzie was making sure that the recruitment counselors knew how to talk about this. "This meant," she told us, "that I always and consistently used this perspective and fostered it in others, not just during the training and role-play sessions."

Exemplary student leaders also know that people learn lessons from how leaders handle the unplanned events on the schedule as well as the planned ones. They know that people learn from the stories circulating on campus, in classes, in dining halls, and on social media. Just as Kenzie's frequent role plays helped prepare the recruiters for any circumstance, attitude, or questions they might encounter, you need to find ways to show others what's expected and ensure that they hold themselves accountable. You do this by confronting critical incidents, telling stories, and finding every opportunity to reinforce the behaviors you want others to repeat.

Confront Critical Incidents

You can't plan everything about your day. Even the most disciplined leaders can't stop the intrusion of the unexpected. Stuff happens. Critical incidents—chance occurrences, particularly during a time of stress and challenge—are a natural part of every leader's life. They offer significant moments of learning for leaders and others in the group. Critical incidents present opportunities for leaders to teach valuable lessons about appropriate behavioral norms and what genuinely matters.

Devin Murphy was working as a resident assistant (RA) when a devastating tornado hit a nearby town, leaving death and widespread destruction in its path. She immediately reached out across campus to see how she could help. "When we realized the extent of the damage," she said, "we wanted everyone to go into action." The university had already decided to help by opening student apartment housing to survivors of the storm. Many of the apartments were empty because most students had already left for the summer, but all the units needed to be cleaned and readied before families could occupy them. Devin contacted her friend Taylor Tyler in Student Life, and together they hatched a plan. "We knew there were a lot of students still on campus, and we knew they would want to help," Devin told us.

> This is a campus with a lot of students who study the arts. People in theater know how to pull together to get ready for a show; fine arts people know how to put in the long hours and do what it takes to get their projects done; music majors are used to long hours of rehearsal. This is not a group of people afraid of hard work. We are a campus with a "pull together, work hard, and get it done" attitude, so we looked for ways to tap into that.

Devin and Taylor created a Facebook page asking volunteers to help clean apartments. In just twenty-four hours, they had enough people to clean sixty-nine apartments and prepare them for the exhausted citizens. "The support didn't stop there," Devin told us. Another student friend, Kelissa Sanders, interned at the state capital over the summer. She persuaded a popular barbecue restaurant chain there to donate food for a Memorial Day picnic for the tornado survivors. In the process of initiating and continuing assistance to the community, they exemplified the values of pulling together to get things done that they see on their campus.

Critical incidents are not always as dramatic as an EF5 tornado. They are simply those events in the lives of leaders—and the groups they are a part of—that offer the chance to improvise while still staying faithful to the script. Although these incidents can't be explicitly planned, it's helpful to remember that how you handle them—how you link your actions and decisions to shared values—speaks volumes about what matters to you most. During critical moments, you must put values on the table and in front of others so they can return to them as common ground for working together. In the process, you make clear how shared values compel your actions. You set an example of what it means to act on values. By taking a stand, you show that having shared values requires a mutual commitment from everyone to align our words with our actions.

Tell Stories

Stories are powerful tools for teaching people what's important and what's not, what works and what doesn't, and what could be. Through stories, leaders define culture, pass on lessons about shared values, and get others to work together.

Rana Korayem had just completed her undergraduate degree in Egypt. She was aware that many women in her country would face significant challenges in pursuing an education, and she was compelled to try to inspire those she could reach. Rana found that opportunity in a public elementary school for girls.

In Egypt, public schools serve the poorest young people in society. The amount of education they get is limited, and many girls stop school at an early age to marry or to care for the family. Rana was determined to help the girls see there were other choices and that they could achieve anything they set their minds to. "I came from a family of means," Rana told us, "and when I began to talk about my education, you could tell that they were not relating to me. They saw me as wealthy, and therefore, not like them. So, I told them stories to show that I was not so different from them."

Rana shared stories with them about the risks she had taken to pursue her education and follow her dreams. As she told each story, the girls began to be drawn in, thinking about times they had been scared or lonesome, and recognized Rana as someone not unlike them.

"I told them about going to the United States to study and leaving my family and my country for the very first time," she said. "I told them how homesick I was and how nervous to be in a totally new place, not knowing a soul." She talked about how scary it could be to reach out to new people and how she was determined to be brave and believe in herself. She shared with them the prejudice she faced and how frightening that was. She talked about how, by overcoming her fear and reaching out, she had learned so much and gained many new friends and rich experiences. She asked them about times they had been lonesome or afraid and how they had found courage. "The stories were different for each of us," Rana said, "but the human emotion is the same, and by sharing these stories we got closer."

Each week for several months, Rana visited the school and shared her stories with the young girls. "The theme was always the same," Rana said.

> The stories always had to do with how my education had shown me that the sky was the limit if you decided to learn and work hard. I wanted them to see their potential, that no matter what their circumstances, or gender, or how much or little money their family has, they could achieve anything they put their minds to if they were determined and willing to learn. I told them that my college education helped me feel strong, that as a woman I was strong and so were they.

Sharing stories is a powerful way for leaders to make values and visions come alive. Rana's stories reinforced the values of self-reliance and independence that she held dear and hoped to inspire in the young girls she chose to spend time with. Storytelling offers a bridge for people to connect their experiences with your message and provides an opportunity to lead through example rather than to come across as lecturing or preaching.

Telling stories has another lasting benefit. It forces you to pay close attention to what is happening around you. When you can write or tell a story about someone your listeners can identify with, they will likely see themselves doing the same thing. People seldom tire of hearing stories about themselves and the people they know. These stories get repeated, and the lessons of the stories spread far and wide.

Reinforce through Systems and Processes

All exemplary student leaders understand that they must reinforce the fundamental values essential to building and sustaining the kind of culture they want. Think about how you recruit new group members, how you make certain selection decisions, when and how you share information, what kinds of assistance you provide, how you measure performance, how you provide rewards, and how you recognize someone when they do a great job. These actions and processes all send messages about what you value and what you don't, and they must align with the shared values and standards that you're trying to instill.

Team sports are full of great examples of this. Consider the stickers added to football players' helmets to indicate the number of tackles made, or the tradition for every team member to suit up in full uniform, even if all they'll be doing is warming the bench. Practices like these speak to the values of being part of a team and evoke a sense of group identity.

Or think about the way different organizations approach new-member recruitment and orientation. When Makana Lin took over as head coach for his university's esports club during his senior year of college, it was the height of the COVID-19 pandemic. The Esports Club—a video gaming club—had moved all team involvement online, communicating primarily through Discord. While the move to Discord allowed the club to continue during the pandemic—and even grow—it created an additional challenge to bringing the group together as a team. "Because this situation was so important to my peers, I felt that because I was in a position of leadership, I was responsible for delivering on expectations for a competitive and professional workplace," Makana said.

To that end, Makana focused on creating a structure for his teams to develop and improve their competitive skills and prepare them to compete in a national championship. To reinforce these goals, he treated the online club like any in-person sporting event. He divided his members into a varsity and a sister team (similar to how a AAA baseball team functions in Major League Baseball), created after-school practice sessions, and held video reviews. Even though the esports club had moved entirely online after COVID-19, that didn't mean they were any less of a team—or that they could take the practice and gaming sessions any less seriously than any other competitive club.

Finally, based on his experience playing baseball in high school, Makana knew a team uniform had great psychological benefits. "In high school, I remembered feeling a psychological motivational force in the locker room while 'suiting up' for an upcoming game—I wanted my esports team to experience this feeling as well as we competed," Makana said.

REFLECT AND ACT: SET THE EXAMPLE

As a student leader, you're always on stage. People are watching you, talking about you, and assessing your credibility—whether you are aware of it or not. That's why it's essential to be mindful of how you Set the Example.

Leaders send signals in a variety of ways, and followers read those signals as indicators of what's okay and what's not okay to do. How you spend your time is the single best indicator of what's important to you, and if you invest your time wisely, you can earn significant returns. What you pay attention to, the language you use, the questions you ask, and the feedback you seek are other powerful ways of shaping accurate perceptions of what you value.

But it's not just what *you* do that matters. You are also measured by how consistent your followers' actions are with the group's shared values, so you must teach others how to set an example. Critical incidents—those chance occurrences in the lives of all groups, teams, and organizations—offer significant teachable moments. They provide you with the opportunity to pass along lessons in real-time. How critical incidents are handled often becomes stories of dedication to shared values, and stories are among the most influential teaching tools you have. And remember that what gets reinforced gets done. You need to align systems and processes to strengthen and reward behavior consistent with shared values if you expect that behavior to be repeated. Keeping people informed about how they're doing also provides guardrails to keep them moving forward on the proper path.

Reflect

The second commitment of the leadership practice Model the Way encourages leaders to *set the example by aligning actions with shared values*. What are the most important ideas or lessons about exemplary leadership that you learned from this chapter?

_____

_____

_____

_____

Here are some actions you can take to act on your commitment to **Set the Example:**

- Be clear about your commitments and follow through on your promises.
- Examine your past experiences to help identify and confirm the values you use to make choices and decisions.
- Request feedback and advice regarding your actions' impact, and make changes and adjustments based on the information you receive.
- Ask purposeful questions that keep people focused on the values and priorities that are the most important.
- Broadcast examples of exemplary behavior through memorable stories that illustrate how people are and should be behaving.
- When you have examples of times when individuals or the entire group have strayed from the shared values, bring those instances up and determine what is needed to return to living the values.
- Reinforce the behavior you want repeated in every way you can.

Act

After you have reflected on what you learned, what you can improve, and the preceding suggestions, record your plan here for taking at least one action that will help you become a better leader:

_____

_____

_____

INSPIRE
A SHARED
VISION

Leaders look toward the future. They imagine what can be. They have a sense of what is uniquely possible if everyone works together for a common purpose. They also help others see the exciting future possibilities. Leaders breathe life into visions. They communicate hopes and dreams so that others clearly understand and share them as their own.

In the following two chapters, we explore how you, as a student leader, must:

➤ **Envision the Future** by imagining exciting and ennobling possibilities.
➤ **Enlist Others** by appealing to shared aspirations.

INSPIRE A SHARED VISION
Reflections from the *Student Leadership Practices Inventory*

1. My overall score from the *Student Leadership Practices Inventory* for Inspire a Shared Vision was:

   _____

2. Of the six leadership behaviors that are part of Inspire a Shared Vision, the statement that I indicated engaging in most frequently was:

   _____

   _____

3. The leadership behavior statement that I engaged in the least often was:

   _____

   _____

   Based on your self-assessment with the leadership practice of Inspire a Shared Vision, complete the following two statements. As you read and review the following two chapters, keep in mind these reflections and observations.

4. Of the leadership behaviors associated with Inspire a Shared Vision, the one(s) I feel most comfortable engaging in is/are:

   _____

   _____

   _____

5. The leadership behaviors that I feel I could engage in more often and be more comfortable with doing are:

   _____

   _____

   _____

Commitment #3: Envision the Future

Divya Pari was in the third year of her biotechnology degree program in India when she volunteered to work as one of the editors of *Nucleo*, an annual magazine published by the Biotech Department. The magazine was created, designed, and managed by the members of Biotikos, the biotech students' association, and was very popular among the university's more than twelve hundred biotech students.

In addition to managing the various aspects of magazine content creation and editing that year, Divya initiated the sale of one hundred unsold copies by marketing them in other universities with biotech courses. In total, about six hundred copies were printed and sold. As a result of her experiences, Divya was asked to be the editor-in-chief for the next edition. "I had about eight months to lead a team of about thirty biotech students to accomplish this," she told us.

But Divya had a broader future in mind for the magazine than simply getting the next edition created and published in the same fashion as the last. "I saw an opportunity to serve the biotech student community both in my university and the country at large," she said.

I envisioned a single student magazine immensely popular among all the biotech students in India, a tool that presented opportunities to foster collaboration among all biotech students and a means to raise funds for student biotech projects by generating advertising revenue. The more I saw what was possible, the more I became excited.

I could clearly see all the possibilities end to end, the people who would benefit from this project, and how my unique role fit into the whole equation. Every aspect of it excited me, and I looked forward to each new day with enthusiasm. I became intensely inspired by my vision and committed to this goal.

Divya's first challenge was to convince the team of thirty students that this dream was indeed achievable. To do that, she got the team to take stock of what needed to be done to improve the reach and quality of the magazine. To improve the reach, they would have to build their network and enlist students from other universities to aid in marketing. To improve the quality, the magazine's content needed to be more student-focused—a direction the team would determine by surveying the magazine's student audience. In addition to soliciting donations from sponsors, selling ad space could help increase revenue. Print quality could be improved by avoiding some of the mistakes made in earlier editions. "By sketching a detailed plan in my mind," Divya said, "I mustered the necessary confidence to talk to my team and take things forward."

Divya organized a meeting with the entire team to share her vision for the magazine: a top-notch biotech magazine for students that would be read nationwide. "I explained what we had done so far, what it would take to make this dream happen, and why it mattered," she told us.

Many reacted, "More than two thousand copies? Sell ad space? Sell *Nucleo* in other universities? You are crazy!"

When your group wonders if you could be crazy, it could make you doubt yourself and your plans. I managed to overcome this with heartfelt persuasive and motivational talk. I said things like, "Only in doing things never done before do we push boundaries, grow in the process, and gain new skills," and "We could either be like all other student magazine teams or do something incredible that we feel truly proud of when we look back."

Divya detailed each step of the plan and said it was not her logic, but the fact that the team "wanted to be a part of a passionate work bigger than them" that inspired them to join in her vision. "They signed up despite knowing that we did not have all the answers to all the problems because we could not foresee all the problems and challenges ourselves," Divya explained. She also believed that her sense of purpose, passion, and excitement, which the team seemed to exhibit with equal intensity, convinced them to subscribe to the new direction for the magazine. "Their sustained motivation for the next eight months ensured that they put in their very best efforts," Divya said.

When the magazine came out the following spring, it was praised by various university officials; students said *Nucleo*'s quality was excellent, its price reasonable, and it could have been priced higher! "We sold close to two thousand copies," Divya told us. "The team was beyond glad and happy. We felt truly satisfied and fulfilled."

Divya's story illustrates how a new initiative—whether a single project, a campus-wide program, or a student movement—begins with one person's imagination. Call it what you will—vision, purpose, mission, legacy, dream, aspiration, calling, or personal agenda—the intent is the same. If you are going to be an exemplary leader, you must be able to imagine the future you want for yourself and others. When you do that and feel passionate about the difference you want to make, you are much more likely to take that first step forward. But if you don't care about the future or don't have the slightest clue about your hopes, dreams, and aspirations, the chance is slim that you will lead others anywhere beyond where they currently are. In fact, you may not even see the opportunity that's right in front of you.

Exemplary leaders are forward-looking. They envision the future and gaze across the horizon, seeing greater opportunities to come. They imagine that noble feats are possible and that something extraordinary can emerge from the ordinary, benefiting their entire group, team, organization, or larger community. Their vision is an ideal and unique image of the future for the common good.

But such a vision doesn't belong only to the leader. It must be a shared vision. Everyone has hopes, dreams, and aspirations, wanting tomorrow to be better than today. Shared visions attract more people, sustain higher levels of motivation, and withstand more challenges than those exclusive to only a few. You need to ensure that what you can see is something others can see and embrace.

The first commitment of Inspire a Shared Vision is to Envision the Future for yourself and others by mastering these two essentials:

- **Imagine the possibilities**
- **Find a common purpose**

You begin with the end in mind by imagining what might be possible. Finding a common purpose inspires people to want to make that vision a reality.

IMAGINE THE POSSIBILITIES

"*The human being is the only animal that thinks about the future,*" writes Daniel Gilbert, professor of psychology at Harvard University (italics his). "The greatest achievement of the human brain is its ability to imagine objects and episodes that do not exist in the realm of the real, and it is this ability that allows us to think about the future."[1] Being forward-looking is an essential characteristic that people seek in their leaders, and in our studies, a majority of student leaders selects it as a quality they desire in someone they would *willingly* follow. People don't generally expect this characteristic from their peers. Yet, our global data on leadership characteristics indicates that the quality of focusing on the future most differentiates people who are seen as leaders from those who are not.[2]

Leaders are dreamers. Leaders are idealists. Leaders are possibility thinkers. As Divya's experience illustrates, all ventures, big or small, begin with the belief that what today is merely a yearning will one day be a reality. It's this belief that sustains leaders and their constituents through difficult times. Turning exciting possibilities into an inspiring shared vision ranks near the top of the list of every leader's most important responsibilities.

When we ask people where their visions come from, they often have great difficulty describing the process. When they provide an answer, it's typically about a feeling, a sense, or a gut instinct. There's often no explicit logic or rationale to it. Clarifying your vision, like clarifying your values, is a process of self-exploration and self-creation. It's an intuitive, emotional process.

When Kirstyn Cole reflected on her personal-best leadership experience, she noted that "being a leader often means going out on a ledge; it means being scared sometimes. But you shouldn't be afraid to see things differently because sometimes your perspective is the one that is necessary and enables you to lead." It can seem difficult, as a leader, to know where you want to take others. You may want to wait for the "right answer" to appear. Yet the correct answer, as Kirstyn points out, may well reside within you already. Finding it requires trusting yourself and that gut feeling about an idea you can't seem to let go of. You just feel strongly about something and compelled to explore that sense, that intuition. Visions reflect your fundamental beliefs and assumptions—about human nature, technology, economics, science, politics, art, and ethics.

A vision of the future is much like a literary or musical theme. It's the main message you want to convey; it's the frequently recurring melody that you want people to remember; whenever it's repeated, it reminds the audience of the entire work. Every leader needs a theme, something on which they can structure the rest of the performance. Recall that for Jacob Philpott, it was preparing low-income students for college; for Bethany Fristad, it was helping underprivileged children; for Kenzie Crane, it was enriching the experiences of women joining sororities; and for Divya Pari, it was publishing a first-rate, revenue-producing student magazine. They could see what they wanted to happen, and how something that didn't exist or wasn't happening now could be possible in the future.

There are several ways you can improve your capacity to imagine exciting possibilities and to discover the central theme for *your* life and the lives of others. When you intentionally and consciously focus on where you want to take yourself and others, you get better at imagining the future. This requires you to *reflect* on your past, *attend* to the present, *prospect* the future, and *express* your passion.

Reflect on Your Past

As contradictory as it might seem, you first need to look back into your past in aiming for the future. Looking backward before you stare straight ahead enables you to see further into the future. Understanding the past can help you identify themes, patterns, and beliefs, which both underscore why you care about certain ideals and explain why realizing those aspirations is a high priority for you.[3] Student groups often look at those who came before them to see how things are done and repeat them, finding that the steep learning curve of doing something new themselves is discouraging. But reflecting on the past isn't about repeating prior practices. Leaders don't settle for replicating what was done before. They look to the past as a context from which to learn and a platform from which to spring.

While a student in Ghana, Christian Gbwardo started The Leadership Lab to combat corruption in Africa. The organization was rooted in his reflections about how the dishonesty he saw around him had come to be. As he thought about how this situation had arisen, he realized that those who had come into power had "only been exposed to corruption and greed, and assumed, therefore, that is what government is meant to be."

> My father showed my family that corruption serves few and denies many. I grew up understanding that we are here to help each other, not take from each other. I realized the only way to stop this trend was to expose young people to an alternative as they become young adults, the way I was. They need to see that there is another way.

None of this is to say that the past *is* the future. That would be like driving while looking only in the rearview mirror. It's just that when you look deeply into your entire life's history, even as a young person, you understand things about yourself and about your world that you cannot fully comprehend by looking at the future as a blank slate. It's difficult, if not impossible, to imagine going to a place you've never experienced, actually or vicariously. Taking a journey into your past before exploring your future makes the trip much more attainable and meaningful.

Attend to the Present

The daily pressures, the pace of change, the complexity of problems, and the turbulence in the world can often hold your mind hostage and make you think that you have neither the time nor the energy to be future-oriented. But looking to the future doesn't mean you should ignore what is happening in the present. In fact, it means you must be more mindful of it.

You must get off automatic pilot, believing that you know everything you need to know, viewing the world through pre-established categories, and not noticing what's going on around you. You must be present to increase your ability to conceive new and creative solutions to today's problems. You must *stop, look,* and *listen.*

Christian looked around at the extracurricular programs that high school students were currently attending and explored how he might build The Leadership Lab to have some of the same appeals. He looked at college-age programs at his university and such programs in the United States while studying abroad. He looked at their purpose, offerings, and popularity; took the best of what he saw for Africa; and began to build his program.

Right now, as you listen to the members of your team, club, or group, what are the hot topics of conversation? What are they saying they need and want? What are they saying should be changed? Is there anything that they have suddenly stopped talking about that seems puzzling? What does all this tell you right now about where things are going?

To envision the future, you need to realize what's already going on. You need to spot the trends and patterns and appreciate the whole and the parts. You need to be able to clearly see at the same time both the immediate situation your group is in and the greater possibilities available to them. You need to be able to see the forest *and* the trees.

Imagine the future as a jigsaw puzzle. You see the pieces, and you begin to figure out how they fit together, one by one, into a whole. Similarly, with your vision, you need to rummage through the bits and bytes of data that accumulate daily and notice how they fit together into a picture of what's ahead. Envisioning the future is not about gazing into a fortune-teller's crystal ball; it's about paying attention to the little things going on all around you and recognizing patterns that point to the future.

Prospect the Future

Even as you stop, look, and listen to messages in the present, you also need to raise your head and gaze out toward the horizon. Being forward-looking is different from meeting the deadline for your current project. Leaders have to imagine what the future will hold. They must be on the lookout for emerging developments—changes inside and outside their groups, such as new technologies, and trends on campus and in local, national, and world news. They must anticipate what might be coming just over the hill and around the corner. They must prospect the future.

There is no hard-and-fast rule regarding how far a leader should look into the future. In fact, in school settings, most student leaders might have a time frame that extends only through an entire academic term or perhaps as far out as graduation. Contrast this perspective with corporate supervisors who typically need to see at least a few years ahead; middle managers who need to see five or more years into the future; and the most senior executives who focus on a future horizon that's ten-plus years or even more. What's critical is not losing sight of the bigger picture while working on whatever it is you are currently doing.

The opportunities for greatness reside in the future. Leaders constantly ask themselves, "What's new?" and "What's next?" while adapting to the urgent needs of the present. Like Divya, Kirstyn, and their colleagues, you need to make choices today that are consistent with where you want to be in the future and decisions that set you up for it. Master chess players, for example, study past moves and make moves in the present designed to get their pieces—and their opponents'—into

specific places for a future victory. This kind of thinking also charac-
terizes great scholars, athletes, video game players, and leaders.

Visions are made real over different spans of time. It may take
six months to create a new-member recruitment and orientation process. Building your new group into one of the most respected student
organizations on campus may take a couple of years. Building a company that is one of the best places to work may take a decade. Making
neighborhoods safe for children to walk alone may take a lifetime.
It may take a century to restore a forest destroyed by a wildfire. It
may take generations to set people free. Pursuing meaningful change
is what matters, not how long it will take to make the change.

Consider Sam Beskind. Sam was already a leader on his Division
I basketball team when he got involved with a civic engagement group
geared toward student athletes. When Sam thought about the future
he wanted, he imagined the good that he and his teammates could
do if they were more involved in their communities. Sam believed
that being a good citizen was the best way to impact the future positively, and he wanted to show others that getting involved and making a change was more possible to do than people imagined. "I felt
like it was a real opportunity to not just talk the talk, but walk the
walk," Sam said.

Sam worked with the leaders of an organization called All Vote
No Play (which lobbied to end games and practices on election days,
promoting voting among student-athletes) to create a civic playbook.
"We created a playbook where you could find options to complete
whether you had five minutes, fifteen minutes, or three hours, whether
or not there was an election cycle coming," Sam said. The playbook
was organized into three sections: learning, engaging, or gathering as
a community. Examples of some of the activities included going to
a civil rights museum in your area, inviting a professor to come to a
lunch and learn about a specific topic impacting your community, or

even watching a five-minute video about a local concern, if that was all the time you had.

While this first step was received well, Sam focused on the future and thought they needed to dream really big and put on the biggest, coolest event to get students interested in the citizenship message. "Could we bring together world leaders from across a bunch of different disciplines and have them share their experiences," he wondered, and thought, "If we're dreaming big, why not try and get future NBA Hall of Famer Steph Curry to speak." Sam began planning at the beginning of the calendar year, even though the event wasn't scheduled until the fall. Instead of a summer internship, Sam spent his summer recruiting athletes and speakers and drafting questions for the interviews with them. They created a list of twenty-five dream people to ask and tried to see if they could find any personal connections to them. One of his coaches had a loose connection to Steph Curry and extended the invitation—and Curry agreed. Sam also ended up with programming that included Condoleezza Rice, Cory Booker, and Tara Vanderveer. The event was virtual, and Pizza to the Polls donated pizzas to the more than two thousand student-athletes who joined virtual watch parties across the country.

Sam said the feedback he got was exceptional: dozens of messages from students talking about how fun the event was and how inspiring and heartwarming. "Obviously, the work isn't done," Sam realized. But the point of the event wasn't just to put on one cool event for student-athletes that spoke to the value of leadership and civic engagement, Sam said. He was also looking to the future, to try to find ways to get his peers invested in leadership—so that, together, they could all build a better future.

As a student leader, you have the opportunity to develop the ability to be forward-looking now so that you are experienced with visioning as you move into the workplace. It can seem unimportant to think about the future when you consider the relatively brief time you spend leading others in school. Yet we know that leaders must always be forward-thinking, regardless of the circumstances in which they find themselves. Even if you lead others on a project that might last only a quarter, semester, or academic year, you can still imagine what you want things to be or look like at the end of that period. It takes practice to develop the ability to envision the future, and it's a skill you will apply throughout your life. Why not start now?

Spend significant time thinking about what you will do after you complete the current problem, task, assignment, project, or program. "What's next?" should be a question you ask yourself frequently. As a student, you live in a culture where the goals are short-term; "If I can just get through this paper [or this exam, or this semester]" is often the prevailing mindset. But if you're not thinking about what's happening after completing your longest-term project, then you're thinking only as long-term as everyone else. It is imperative to create time and space to think about the next things in your life, whether for your immediate school experience or those yet to come in your life beyond school.

Whether it's through reading about trends, attending guest lectures on campus, talking with others outside your campus about issues they face, listening to international news sources, reading a variety of blogs, or watching different types of TED Talks, a significant part of being a leader is developing a deep understanding of where things are going. Those who willingly follow you expect you to have that understanding. You need to spend more of today thinking more about tomorrow if your future is going to be an improvement over the present. And throughout the process of reflecting on your past, attending to the present, and prospecting the future, you also need to keep in touch with what moves you, what you care about, and where your passion lies.

Express Your Passion

Passion goes hand in hand with attention. No one can imagine something exciting when they don't feel passionate about the possibilities. Envisioning the future requires you to connect with your deepest feelings. You must find something so important that you're willing to put in the time, suffer the inevitable setbacks, and make the necessary sacrifices. Everyone has concerns, desires, questions, propositions, arguments, hopes, and dreams—core issues that can help them organize their aspirations and actions. And everyone has a few things that are much more important to them than other things. Whatever yours are, you need to be able to name them so you can talk about them with others. You must ask yourself, "What is my burning passion? What gets me up in the morning? What's grabbed hold of me and won't let go?"

This is precisely the thinking you should use to determine what you want to be involved in. Rather than joining groups or seeking experiences because you think it "looks good on your résumé," you should be looking for pursuits you feel passionate about. Leaders want to do something significant, to accomplish something that no one else has yet achieved. What that something is—your sense of meaning and purpose—has to come from within. No one can impose a self-motivating vision on you. That's why, just as we said about values, you must first clarify your image of the future before you can expect to enlist others in a shared vision. As JD Scharffenberger told us about his experience as captain of the baseball team:

> I realized that the easiest way to inspire my teammates
> was to truly embrace and show my passion for the game.
> I believe when others saw my dedication to the future that
> they were also intrigued by what we could accomplish. They
> would not have been so inspired if I didn't openly show my
> excitement on a day-to-day basis.

Researchers in human motivation have long talked about two kinds of motivation—extrinsic and intrinsic.[4] People do things either because of external controls—the possibility of a tangible reward if they succeed or punishment if they don't—or because of an internal desire. They do something because they feel forced or because they want to; to please others or to please themselves. Unsurprisingly, researchers find that intrinsic motivators are most likely to produce extraordinary results. External motivation is likely to create conditions of compliance or defiance; self-motivation generates commitment and far superior results. There's even an added bonus. Self-motivated people will keep working toward a goal even without a reward.[5] You've probably seen examples of this in sports. Even when it's obvious they will lose the game, team members continue to play their hearts out because they are internally motivated. People who are externally driven will likely stop trying once the rewards or punishments are removed.[6]

"You're not going to be a good leader if you're not doing something you're really passionate about. You have to find what you're truly interested in," Sam Beskind reflected. But passion can also be generated by diving into an interest and working hard at it. Speaking to his own experience, Sam recognized that while he had an interest in civic engagement before All Vote No Play, it wasn't something he was completely passionate about—until he got more involved. "I think you generate passion once you get involved in something," he said. Be willing to take a chance on something that interests you, and the momentum and passion will grow in time.

Leadership might also involve a willingness to be perceived as uncool. "A lot of cool things aren't considered cool—until suddenly they are," Sam said. When he first started working on civic engagement, Sam said he received some good-natured teasing from his teammates. He remembered them asking, "Ooh, are we talking about voting *again* today, Sam?" Sam realized that "if you care about something, and you show people why you care and what intrigues you, then eventually it does become cool." Like Sam, if you can get others interested in an event or action, they may very well wind up becoming passionate about it, too.

Exemplary student leaders are passionate about something other than their fame and fortune. They care about making a difference. If you don't care deeply for and about something, how can you expect others to feel any sense of conviction? How can you expect others to feel passion if you're not energized and excited? How can you expect others to suffer through the long hours, hard work, absences from home, and personal sacrifices if you're not similarly committed?

You know you are on to something meaningful and significant when you feel your passion. Your enthusiasm and drive spread to others. Finding something you truly believe in is the key to articulating a vision in the first place. Once you're in touch with this inner feeling, you can look and think beyond the constraints of your current role and view the possibilities available in the future.

The data from both student leaders and their constituents supports this contention. As you can see from the data in Figure 3.1, nearly nine out of ten students strongly agree that when their leader *often* or *very frequently* "speaks about the higher purpose and meaning of what is being done," they feel they are making a difference. The research also shows a similarly strong relationship between students feeling they are making a difference and leaders "who are upbeat and positive when talking about what could be accomplished."

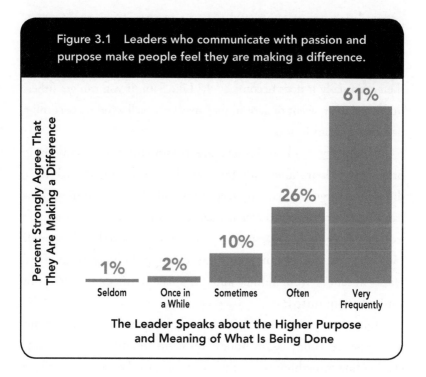

Figure 3.1 Leaders who communicate with passion and purpose make people feel they are making a difference.

FIND A COMMON PURPOSE

It is often assumed that leaders have the sole responsibility to be the visionaries. After all, if focusing on the future is what sets leaders apart, it's understandable that you would get the feeling that it's the leader's job to embark alone on a vision quest to discover the future of their organization.

This, however, is *not* what people expect. Yes, leaders are expected to be forward-looking, but they aren't expected to impose their vision of the future on others. People want to hear more than just the *leader's* vision. They want to hear about how *their* visions and aspirations will come true and their hopes and dreams will be fulfilled. They want to see themselves in the picture of the future that the leader is painting. The crucial task for leaders is inspiring a *shared* vision, not selling their personal view of the world. People in the group want to feel part of the process.[7] This requires finding common ground among the people implementing the vision.

Jade Orth began learning about leadership back in middle school. She believes that the lessons she learned then about giving back drive what is important to her today. Her earlier experiences helped her define a vision for an event she initiated with a small group of students on her college campus to give something back to their community: a Veterans Day ceremony to recognize local veterans. Jade had several family members who served in the military, and she first brought others along in realizing her vision by sharing why she felt so strongly that it was important to have such a ceremony. Nothing was being done in Jade's college town to honor the substantial number of veterans there who had sacrificed much and received very little recognition and appreciation.

In talking with the people around campus who she thought could help make the Veterans Day observance a reality, Jade shared her vision of making the ceremony an annual event. A group of supporters formed around this kernel of an idea, and people started to share their thoughts about how to sustain the program. Some ideas didn't work out, and others did, but the group kept talking through their visions. Jade knew she couldn't just "tell" others what to do. Through this sharing and discussions, they worked to keep the focus on the things that would make the event special rather than being concerned about whose idea was being selected.

Jade discovered something every leader must understand: nobody likes being told what to do or where to go, no matter how right it might be. People want to be a part of the process of developing a vision. The vast majority of people are just like Jade's team members.

They want to walk with their leaders. They want to dream with them, invent with them, and be involved in creating their futures.

This means that you must stop taking the view that visions come from the top down, as Jade realized:

> It doesn't always have to be my idea, nor should it be. The more people we have sharing ideas, the better ideas we will get. We accepted that with five or seven heads in a group, we are going to get differing or conflicting views, but we approached our conversations with a give-and-take attitude, and that worked pretty well.

You must start engaging others in a conversation about the future instead of delivering a monologue. You can't mobilize people to willingly travel to places they don't want to go. No matter how grand one individual's dream is, if others don't see themselves in it, realizing their own hopes and desires, they won't follow freely. You must show others how they, too, will be served by the long-term vision of the future and how their specific needs can be satisfied.

Students were asked about the extent that their leaders "explain how other people's own interest can be met by working toward a common goal." They were also asked about the extent to which "When working with this leader, I feel like I am making a difference around here." The relationship between these two questions was striking. As shown in Figure 3.2, hardly any students strongly felt like they were making a difference when working with a leader who did not help them see how their personal interests were aligned with the goal they were pursuing. In contrast, nearly four out of every five students strongly agreed they were making a difference when their leader *often* or *very frequently* communicated about how reaching a common goal would also serve to meet their own personal interests.

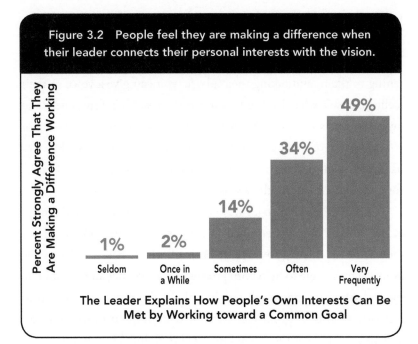

Figure 3.2 People feel they are making a difference when their leader connects their personal interests with the vision.

Percent Strongly Agree That They Are Making a Difference Working

1% — Seldom
2% — Once in a While
14% — Sometimes
34% — Often
49% — Very Frequently

The Leader Explains How People's Own Interests Can Be Met by Working toward a Common Goal

Jade was clear in her mind about what she hoped to accomplish, and she also was careful to make sure that others either shared her ideas or had their thoughts incorporated into the vision for the ceremony. Many people were involved in launching the Veterans Day celebration, from fellow students to campus officials to local veterans. Jade said she knew that she had to trust others and their commitment to the cause, and rather than giving orders:

> I regularly checked with the group to be sure we were all still on board with the project and staying true to what our vision was. If we weren't, I knew that I had a responsibility to keep us focused on our vision. I recognized that each person brought something special to the group, and I wanted to trust in and respect their ideas of where we should be going. It was about collaboration.

Listen Deeply to Others

By knowing the members of your team, group, or organization, listening to them, and taking their advice, you can give a voice to their feelings. That's what Jade did. You can then stand before others and say with assurance, "Here's what I heard you say that you want for yourselves. Here's how your needs and interests will be served by all of us believing in this common cause." In a sense, leaders hold up a mirror and reflect back to others what they say they want most.

One of Jade's challenges was being part of two structured groups at her college: she was enrolled in a leadership class and was also a member of student government, both of which had a stake in the event. She was able to help both groups come together and collaborate by understanding how each saw its role in the program. She talked regularly with both groups about their commitment to the program and also about what they were interested in doing. "I wanted to make sure both groups felt as comfortable as possible and felt that they could play the role they wanted in creating the event," she said. "I did that by listening a lot to others."

You need to strengthen your ability to hear what is important to others. The outlines of any vision do not come from a crystal ball. They originate from conversations with members of your team or club. They come from interactions with other students in classes, at campus events, and over meals. They're heard in the hallways, meetings, and on social media. When Alvin Chen helped launch his university's first international summer academic camp, many things needed to be done, and most of them for the first time in this new venue. Alvin said that "listening is one of the best things any leader can do," and he and his team were, in his words, "learning as we went." His takeaway lesson was an appreciation for how "every stakeholder has a voice, and you should never underestimate or undervalue their opinions."

As Alvin and Jade attest, the best student leaders are great listeners. They listen carefully to what other people say and how they feel. They ask purposeful (and often tough) questions, are open to ideas other than their own, and even lose arguments in favor of the common good. Through intense listening, leaders get a sense of what people want, value, and dream about. This sensitivity to others is no trivial skill. It is a truly precious human ability.

Make It a Cause for Commitment

By listening deeply, you can find out what is meaningful to others. Research finds that people stay committed and loyal to a cause and organization because they like the people they work with and experience the work they are doing as challenging, meaningful, and purposeful.[8] When you listen with sensitivity to the aspirations of others, you discover some common themes that bring meaning to work and life. Students—like people of all ages, it turns out—want to:

- Pursue values and goals congruent with their own
- Make a significant difference in the lives of others
- Do innovative work
- Learn and develop professionally and personally
- Engage in close and positive relationships
- Determine the course of their own lives
- Feel trusted and validated

Indeed, people have a strong desire to make a difference. They want to know that they have done something on this Earth and that their existence has a purpose. The same holds for participating in campus organizations, teams, and clubs. The best student leaders satisfy this human desire by communicating the significance of the group's work and their vital role in creating it. This is true even at the level of a classroom group project—can there be something beyond passing the assignment that motivates you and others to put your best efforts forward? When leaders clearly communicate a shared vision of an organization, they enrich those who work on its behalf. They elevate the human spirit.

Ella Tepper served as one of the Campus Governors at her university, which was developing a program that would inform students about what student government could offer them and how they could get involved. In the past, the publicity for these events mainly highlighted attending because of the free food and giveaways. Ella was determined to make the experience more meaningful; she told us:

> I'm a student too, and I knew that when I attended events like this, I wanted something more. I wanted to leave with more knowledge and have takeaways that were really useful. I wanted to create a way for people to talk about student government, ask questions, and learn.

Ella started by talking to the chief of staff about her ideas. She then quickly went to the larger team with the goal of creating a program where students would leave with a good understanding and appreciation of what the student government did for them. How could they transform the event into a space for meaningful conversations about student government? This focus became the cause that the team was committed to, and they generated many good ideas about giveaways that would last and discussions that would truly inform. They came up with the idea of a safari. Each student got a passport to different areas where representatives from the different parts of the student government were stationed to answer questions. Once the students circled through all the tables, they received a bag of school supplies.

The team, Ella explained, had devised a way to spark significant conversations about the purpose of student government and provide participating students with useful and lasting souvenirs of the experience.

> There is no way I would have come up with all the great ideas they had, and their commitment to design something that gave the students opportunities to ask questions and have meaningful dialogue was amazing. They were all so committed to helping students see the value of the student government they were part of. I may have been the leader, but they were the ones that made the event successful.

People commit to causes, not to plans. How else do you explain why people volunteer to rebuild communities ravaged by a tsunami; ride a bike from Austin, Texas, to Anchorage, Alaska, to raise money to fight cancer; or rescue people from the rubble of a collapsed building after a tornado? People are not committing to the plan in any of these cases. They are committing to something much bigger, something much more compelling than goals and milestones on a piece of paper. That's not to say that executing plans isn't essential in realizing great dreams; they absolutely are. It's just to say that the plan isn't what people are signing up for.

Look Forward in Times of Rapid Change

In a world that is changing at warp speed, students often ask, "How can I have a vision of what's going to happen over the next semester or year when I don't even know what's going to happen next week?" This question gets right to the heart of the role that visions play in people's lives. In this increasingly volatile, uncertain, complex, and ambiguous

(VUCA) world, visions are even more critical to human survival and success than when times are calm, predictable, simple, and clear.

Think about it this way. Imagine driving along the Pacific Coast Highway, heading south from San Francisco on a bright, sunny day. The hills are on your left, the ocean on your right. On some curves, the cliffs plunge several hundred feet into the water. You can see for miles and miles. You're cruising along at the speed limit, one hand on the wheel, tunes blaring, and not a care in the world. Suddenly, without warning, you come around a bend in the road, and there's a blanket of fog as thick as you've ever seen. What do you do?

We've asked this question many, many times, and here are some of the things people say:

- I slow way down.
- I turn my lights on.
- I tighten my grip on the steering wheel with both hands.
- I tense up.
- I sit up straight or even lean forward.
- I turn off the radio.

Then you go around the next curve in the road, the fog lifts, and it's clear again. What do you do? Sit back and relax, speed up, turn the lights off, put the music back on, and enjoy the scenery.

This analogy illustrates the importance of clarity of vision. Are you able to go faster when it's foggy or when it's clear? How fast can you drive in the fog without risking your or other people's lives? How comfortable are you riding in a car with someone who drives fast in the fog? The answers are obvious, aren't they? You're better able to go fast when your vision is clear. You can better anticipate the curves and bumps in the road when you can see ahead. No doubt, there are times in your life when you find yourself, metaphorically speaking, driving in the fog. When this happens, you get nervous and unsure of what's ahead. You slow down. But as the way becomes clearer, eventually you can speed up and continue along the path.

An essential part of a leader's job is to clear away the fog so that people can see farther ahead, anticipate what might be coming in their direction, and watch out for potential hazards along the road. Simply put, to become a leader, you must be able to envision the future. The speed of change doesn't alter this fundamental truth: people want to follow only those who can see beyond today's problems and visualize a brighter tomorrow.

REFLECT AND ACT: ENVISION THE FUTURE

The most important role of vision is to focus people's energy. To enable everyone to see more clearly what's ahead, you must have and convey an exciting, unique, and meaningful vision of the future. Clarity begins by reflecting on the past, moves ahead by attending to the present, and then involves prospecting the future. The guidance system along this path is your passions—the ideals you care about most deeply.

Although you must be clear about your vision before you can expect others to follow, you also need to keep in mind that you can't lead others to places they don't want to go. If the vision is going to attract more than just a few people, it must appeal to all who have a stake in it. Only *shared* visions have the magnetic power to sustain commitment over time and to keep people connected to the group or the cause. Listen to all the voices; listen for people's hopes, dreams, and aspirations.

A shared vision also needs to focus everyone on the future. Doing that must be about more than a single task or job. It needs to be about a cause, something meaningful, and something that makes a difference in people's lives. Whether you're leading a community project, a fraternity or sorority chapter, an athletic team, a campus-wide event, or a national student movement, a shared vision sets the agenda and gives direction and purpose to all those involved.

Reflect

Inspire a Shared Vision requires leaders to *envision the future by imagining exciting and ennobling possibilities*. What is the most important idea or lesson about exemplary leadership that you learned from this chapter?

_____

_____

_____

_____

_____

Here are some actions that you can take to follow through on your commitment to **Envision the Future:**

- Determine what you most care about, what drives you, and where your passions lie.
- When you think about everything you want to accomplish, can you explain *why* these are so important to you? What makes these aspirations meaningful to you and possibly to others?
- Identify the important issues and causes you and your peers are most concerned about. Be curious about what others feel is important to their future.

- When you talk to others in your group about their hopes, dreams, and aspirations for the future, look for patterns and themes in their responses. Determine what these have in common.
- Frame what you and others are doing so that it becomes a cause or calling rather than just an assignment, project, or event.
- Come up with ways to involve others in creating what could be possible; don't make it a process in which you give out orders about what to do.

Act

After you have reflected on what you learned, what you can improve, and the preceding suggestions, record your plan here for taking at least one action that will help you become a better leader:

_____

_____

_____

_____

_____

_____

4

Commitment #4:
Enlist Others

The summer before Emma Bickford's senior year of college, she knew her softball team, of which she was the captain, faced a challenge in the coming season. After years of the COVID-19 pandemic had disrupted regular seasons, the team had lost some of its cohesiveness and drive. "I knew that the results of our games weren't reflecting how good a team we were. And since it was my final year, and my class's final year, I was like, 'Okay, no more excuses. We have to figure this out,'" Emma said.

Even though she had high hopes for her last season, Emma knew it couldn't be a solitary endeavor to build a more cohesive team; she wouldn't get anywhere if her teammates weren't on board. The team needed to believe in the same vision of success Emma had. "Having something to guide us, to give us our why, that felt like it really came from *us*—I thought that would give us confidence and lead us to the team results we wanted to have," Emma said.

Emma gathered her other graduating teammates and explained her thinking: To reach their potential for the upcoming season, the team needed a self-generated set of values guiding their actions and efforts. "We really needed to figure out where we were going to go—because if we just start walking down a path and you don't know where you're going, you're wandering aimlessly, and there's no purpose there," Emma said.

Over the summer, Emma and her teammates collaborated over FaceTime and text messages, and decided on a shared values exercise to create a guiding team ethos. At the first team meeting, the first thing Emma did was share her vision for what the season ahead could look like—the team could be stronger, more dedicated, have more fun, and support each other better. It wasn't just about winning: she painted a picture of her teammates really living their passion for softball each game. What did a great season look like for *all* of them outside of their win/loss record? Emma let herself get passionate and emotional when speaking about her hopes for the season so that her teammates could really *feel* how much she cared—and access their own passion for the sport, too.

Then Emma handed out sheets of paper with the names of personal values on them. Each teammate was instructed to tick off their top ten values, then narrow them down to five, and eventually, their top three values. When Emma reviewed the results, she found three terms consistently came up: excellence, communication, and trust/respect.

But the team's work wasn't done once everyone had identified their personal values. Emma knew it wasn't enough to identify shared values; the team needed to have a common working definition of what those values *meant* to everyone and how they would look in practice so that teammates could execute them. "Everybody has a different definition of *respect* or *excellence*. It's important not only to have the same values, but to have a common definition of them because if we're getting mad at another person for not being respectful when respect means different things to different people, there's going to be a mismatch," Emma said.

As with any large group of people, some teammates were more comfortable voicing opinions than others. Before the next meeting, Emma sent out an anonymous Google form, asking her teammates to submit their own definitions of the values. "Because it was anonymous, anyone could say what they wanted, and it also meant that nobody could copy and paste anyone else's answer," Emma said.

At the next meeting, the group discussed the individual definitions of the values everyone had shared—a long process since there were twenty-five people on the team. "There were a lot of times when somebody would raise their hand and say 'Well, I don't think that belongs there. This isn't what we stand for' because they had a different definition of what the values meant," Emma said. It was a long process, but Emma kept the team engaged by reiterating that their work would bring them closer together as a team, and ultimately, pay off during their season. And through the use of the anonymous Google definition doc, everyone's voice was heard. "It wasn't just the usual ten extroverted people on the team deciding what we wanted our season to look like; it was also the shyest people on the team telling us what they wanted the season to look like," Emma said.

By the end of the exercise, the team had agreed on the following definitions:

- *Excellence*, which meant putting in one hundred percent effort to become the best teammate you can be, whether that's sprinting hard for every base, or asking a teammate to stay late to practice with you.
- *Communication*, which was important not only on the playing field but also in taking responsibility to deal with any team conflicts head-on and respectfully, rather than stewing or gossiping about an issue.
- *Trust* and *respect*, which looked like following through on what a teammate said she'd do and believing that teammates had the team's best intentions in mind during all interactions.

Emma had two posters of the values and their definitions made: a small poster that traveled with the team to games and a larger poster posted in the team dugout. That way, even if her teammates weren't consciously thinking about the values consistently, they had a visual cue to remind them of their goals and help the team live those values on the field. Even if the team lost a game, applying those team goals and values during the course of the competition meant the game had been a success, Emma said.

Going through the experience of evaluating their values brought the team closer together, and Emma explained that "it really built trust between us because we had to be vulnerable and put ourselves out there a bit when talking about our definitions for the values." This experience built empathy, respect, and better communication skills for the team—leading to a more cohesive, fun, and successful season. Thanks to the team's newfound cohesiveness, the season was a success; not only did Emma say the team had more fun than in prior years, but its third-place conference finish was the highest they had ever achieved.

Emma successfully brought the vision for her final competitive softball season to life, but it wouldn't have been possible without her teammates doing the deep work of investigating their values and committing to putting them into practice. "If you just assume that other people have the same values as you, it's probably not going to go very well," Emma said. And in turn, they would not have been willing to do the work to get there without Emma's vision of what might be possible for her final season and her ability to translate that passion for her teammates. Igniting passion in others is the first step toward extraordinary change.

In the personal-best leadership cases we collected, people talked about the need to get everyone on board with a vision and to Enlist Others in a dream, just as Emma did. They talked about communicating and building support for their project, idea, or cause. These leaders knew that to make extraordinary things happen, everyone had to believe fervently in a common purpose and commit to it.

Part of the commitment to Enlist Others is building common ground on which everyone can stand. Equally important is the emotion that leaders express for the vision. Our research shows that in addition to expecting leaders to be forward-looking, people want their leaders to be *inspiring*. Leaders need to tap into people's vast reserves of energy and excitement to sustain their commitment to a distant dream. Leaders are an essential source of that energy because folks aren't going to follow someone who's only mildly enthusiastic. Students actively support those leaders who are *wildly* enthusiastic about what is being pursued.

Whether you're trying to mobilize a crowd in the grandstand or one person with whom you're sharing a class assignment, to Enlist Others, you must act on these two essentials:

- **Appeal to common ideals**
- **Animate the vision**

The commitment to Enlist Others is all about igniting a passion for a purpose and moving people to persist against incredible odds. To make extraordinary things happen, you need to go beyond reason, engaging the hearts and minds of the people in your group. Start by understanding their strongest yearnings for something meaningful and significant.

APPEAL TO COMMON IDEALS

In every personal-best case, student leaders talked about ideals. They expressed a desire to make dramatic changes in the status quo of their environment. They reached for something big, something meaningful and significant, something never done before. This was true even in what might have been the most mundane of classroom assignments.

Visions are about hopes, dreams, and aspirations. They're about the strong desire to achieve something beyond good, something extraordinary. They're ambitious. They're expressions of optimism. Can you imagine yourself being recruited by someone saying, "I'd like you to join me in doing the ordinary, doing what everyone else is doing"? Not likely. Visions stretch people to imagine exciting possibilities for their cause, whether it's simply a new approach to an old event or getting a group of people on board to commit to a shared set of ideals, as Emma Bickford did.

When you communicate your vision of the future to your group, you need to talk about how they will make a difference and how they will positively impact people and events. You need to show them how enlisting in a common vision can realize their long-term aspirations. You need to speak to your group's higher meaning and purpose. You need to describe a compelling image of what the future could be like when people join a common cause. Consider what 5'1" Cameron McCarthy, captain of her college boxing team and National Collegiate Boxing Association champion, says about recruiting people for the sport:

> I convince people to join the team because of what it does for their confidence and how it enables them to stand out after college. I also explain that it is not easy, and it takes courage. Those who are looking for a challenge have stayed.

Connect to What's Meaningful to Others

Exemplary student leaders don't impose their visions of the future on people; they liberate the vision that's already stirring within them. They awaken dreams, breathe life into them, and arouse the belief that people just like them can achieve something meaningful. When they communicate a shared vision, they bring these ideals into the conversation. What truly pulls people forward, especially in difficult times, is the possibility that what they do can make a real difference. People desperately want to know that what they do matters.

Jen Marsh described the time when she volunteered for a special program that helped children learn how to read. On the first day she arrived, as she sat in a child-size chair, a little boy came up to her and asked, "Why are you wasting your summer here?" She was initially surprised by the question but then realized that he just wanted to see if she was going to stay. "I replied by telling him how I genuinely wanted to be there and that I would be his reading buddy for the day. With this reply, his eyes got bigger, and he even let out a tiny smile." Jen realized:

> There was no way I was going to get these second and third-graders to read because I wanted them to; instead, it was something that I had to help them want to accomplish on their own. I had to get the kids excited about reading and show them how important this achievement would be later in their lives. All the children saw reading as a difficult chore, and they would try to avoid it as much as possible. They didn't know how to read, and it is difficult to persuade someone to partake in an activity that requires dedication. Initially, I got frustrated with the kids and they got on my nerves, but I soon realized that it would take time for my vision to become our vision. I needed to better understand the minds of the children, and this could only be perfected by seeing eye-to-eye with them.

Leaders help others see that what they are doing is bigger than they are and bigger even than their instructor, classroom group, school team, or institution anticipates. Their work can be something noble, something that lifts them all up. Leaders believe that their work makes a difference in other people's lives, that it is work done for the greater good, and that it helps make things better for others. "I will never forget my excitement," recalled Jen, "when I witnessed the young child I met on the first day finish an entire book all by himself."

> When he looked into my eyes and saw how happy I was for him, it finally clicked in him why I had come to volunteer at his school. He could instantly perceive how proud I was, and in return, he extended his learning to his classmates. After we had come together in our common vision, the leading was put into the hands of the students. Collectively, we had turned a once impossible chore into a new and enjoyable activity.

Take Pride in Being Unique

Exemplary student leaders also communicate what makes their group, organization, club, team, or project stand out and rise above all others. Compelling visions differentiate, setting "us" apart from "them" in ways that attract and retain group members. People often leave a group because they don't know or understand how the group is different from others that may do similar things. There's no advantage in being just like everybody else. When people understand how they're genuinely distinctive and stand out in the crowd, they're more eager to sign up and invest their energies voluntarily.

You get people excited about signing on to the group's vision by ensuring everyone involved feels that what they do is unique and believes they play a crucial role, regardless of titles or specific task responsibilities. Feeling special fosters a sense of pride. It boosts the self-respect and self-esteem of everyone associated with the group. When people are proud to be part of your group's effort and serve its purpose and feel that what they are doing is meaningful, they become enthusiastic ambassadors to the outside world. When people are proud to be part of the team, they are more loyal and more likely to recruit their friends to be part of it as well. When the campus and community are proud to have you as a member, they will do everything they can to make you feel welcome.

David Chan Tar Wei knows a lot about promoting individual and collective pride. His Singapore college decided to start a new system of "houses" intended to spark greater school spirit and add more diversity to school life. David worked with a committee tasked with exploring various ideas for setting the new house groups apart, thereby fostering greater house unity and pride. "The houses originally did not have unique ways to represent themselves," he explained, "and we felt strongly that things like house shirts and house crests could be used and accepted as formal symbols of identification." David and his committee went on to incorporate house outfits, insignia, and other distinguishing devices into almost every school event, from orientation to Teachers' Day, to "create the house vibrancy and culture that we sought."

David's experience shows how feeling distinctive makes it possible for smaller groups to have their visions and still serve a larger, collective vision. Although every subgroup within a larger organization—be it a religious institution, school, or volunteer association—must be aligned with the overall vision, each can express its distinguishing purpose within the larger whole.

Align Your Dream with the People's Dream

When Tram Dao started telling us about her leadership experiences, she began by explaining, "It is easier for us to share our vision with others when we think about common goals, not our self-interests." With experience as a tutor at her community college, she was asked to train the new tutors for the upcoming semester. She didn't think this would be so difficult; after all, she would show them how she explained the materials to students and answered their questions. When those new tutors went to work with students, however, they found that they weren't ready to help the students needing assistance.

Seeing their difficulties, Tram wondered what she had done incorrectly as a mentor and leader. She thought deeply about why she had become a tutor, which was to help students who were having difficulties and to give back and contribute to the school. "I imagined students returning after their tests telling me that they did a good job, that they were able to understand and complete the test with confidence. That I had made a difference for them."

Tram imagined that the new tutors might share those same beliefs, so she got them all together and asked them why they had become a tutor. She found that "their reasons were similar to mine."

> This was a common purpose for all of us, and I shared my vision with them, wanting them to have the image of successful tutees in their minds. They didn't have to follow my methods if they didn't work for them. I urged them to be creative and follow the methods that were most suitable to their situations. The dream was not about us being great but about how the people we were tutoring would be great and do well in their exams. We were ultimately able to achieve this desired result by working toward a shared vision.

What is it that gets people engaged? How do student leaders like Tram learn how to appeal to people's ideals, move their souls, and uplift their spirits? How can leaders learn to draw people in and speak to their values, visions, and dreams? There is no better place to look for an answer than to the late Reverend Dr. Martin Luther King Jr., whose "I Have a Dream" speech tops the list of the best American public addresses of the twentieth century. This speech is replayed on the U.S. national holiday marking his birthday, and young and old alike are reminded of the power of a clear and uplifting vision of the future. If you have never listened closely to Dr. King's stirring words, take a few moments to do so.[1]

Imagine that you are there on that hot and humid day—August 28, 1963—when on the steps of the Lincoln Memorial in Washington, D.C., before a throng of 250,000, Martin Luther King Jr. proclaimed his dream to the world. Imagine listening to Dr. King as thousands around you clap, applaud, and cry out. Pretend you are a reporter trying to understand why this speech is so powerful and how Dr. King moves so many people.

Over the years, we've asked thousands of people to do just that: listen to his remarks and then tell us what they heard, how they felt, and why they thought this speech remains so moving today.[2] Here's a sampling of their observations:

- He appealed to common interests. Most anyone in the audience or those who heard this speech afterward could find something personal to which they could relate.
- He talked about the traditional values of family, church, and country.
- He used many images and word pictures that the audience could relate to.
- His references were credible. It's hard to argue against the Constitution or the Bible.
- It was personal. He mentioned his own children, as well as struggling.
- He included everybody—for example, different parts of the country, all ages and major religions.
- He used a lot of repetition—for example, saying "I have a dream" and "Let freedom ring" several times.
- He focused on a theme but expressed it in different ways.

- He was positive and hopeful, but also realistic.
- He shifted his focus from "I" to "we."
- He spoke with genuine emotion and passion.

These reflections reveal some keys to success in enlisting others. To get others excited about your dream, you need to speak about meaning and purpose. You need to *show them* how to realize *their* dreams. You need to connect your message to their values, aspirations, experiences, and their own lives. You need to show them that it's not about you but about them and their needs and the communities to which they belong. You need to make the connection between an inspiring vision of the future and the personal aspirations and passions of the people you are addressing. You need to personally believe in what you are saying and have evidence of your commitment. To enlist others, you need to bring the vision to life.

Admittedly, you are not a Martin Luther King Jr. Well, neither is Sheri Lee. Yet, as the editor of her school's yearbook, she needed to get everyone on the same page, motivating them to work hard all year, generally producing smaller pieces of the overall project that would disappear into the yearbook a few days after the work was completed. Think about how many of the same techniques utilized by Dr. King are employed by Sheri in speaking with her peers on the yearbook staff:

> The yearbook is something that I enjoy because we are making something that will be treasured for the rest of our lives. We are in charge of preserving all the memories that occur during this school year, and it is up to us to make sure that there is a yearbook to hand out at the end of the year.
>
> Just think, every time that you look at this year's yearbook, you can see that all your hard work paid off in the pages that you created. When you are older, you can look back at it and be proud that you were responsible for creating something so unique.

Think about how you can communicate using techniques that make a leader's message memorable and inspirational.

ANIMATE THE VISION

Part of motivating others is appealing to their ideals. Another part is animating the vision and breathing life into it. In addition, to enlist others you have to help them *see* and *feel* how they are aligned with the vision. You have to paint a compelling picture of the future, one that enables your group to experience what it would be like to live and work in an exciting and uplifting future. That's the only way they'll become sufficiently motivated to commit their energies to realizing the vision.

Many people don't see themselves as personally uplifting, and certainly few students get much encouragement for behaving this way in most organizations. Despite the acknowledged potency of clearly communicated and compelling visions, our research finds more people uncomfortable with the leadership practice of Inspire a Shared Vision than with any of the other four leadership practices. Most of their discomfort comes from having to express their emotions. Like many people, you may find it hard to convey your emotions, but don't be too quick to discount your capacity to do it.

People's perception of themselves as uninspiring is in sharp contrast to their behavior when they talk about their personal-best leadership experiences or when they talk about their ideal futures—or even when they talk about a vacation they just took or an exciting sports event they just won or witnessed. People are nearly always emotionally expressive when relating extraordinary achievements or major successes. When talking about intense desires for a better future, expressiveness tends to come naturally. When they feel passionate about something, they let their emotions show.

Most people attribute something mystical to the process of being inspirational. They seem to see it as supernatural or a gift others possess, but certainly not them. This assumption inhibits people far more than any lack of natural talent for being inspirational. It's not necessary to be extroverted or charismatic to Inspire a Shared Vision. However, it is necessary to *believe* and to find ways to communicate your belief. If you're going to lead, you must recognize that your enthusiasm and expressiveness are vital assets in your efforts to generate commitment in others. Don't underestimate your talents.

When Emma Bickford wanted her teammates to come together as a team by defining their values, she needed to get them to take the exercise as seriously as she did—not spend five rushed minutes filling out the vision sheets right before the next meeting. "I didn't just hand it out and say, 'Fill this out.' I said, 'We are going to establish team values because we need to find our "why" as a team. We're better than our win-loss record shows,'" Emma said. She tapped into her deep love of softball and her enthusiasm for what defining their values could do to help the team have a successful season and get her teammates excited about the exercise. "I love playing softball and being around my team," Emma said. "My passion [for softball] and explaining why [the values exercise] was important helped the rest of my team receive it positively."

And it wasn't just *what* she said that mattered, but how she made her teammates feel while she was saying it. While speaking, Emma made eye contact with her teammates and practiced deep listening so that she could ask pertinent follow-up questions to her teammates' responses. "I was trying to be the best listener I can be because if somebody who's shy sees that the leader of the meeting is really paying attention and really interested in what someone is saying, chances are, they'll feel a little bit more comfortable speaking up," Emma said.

When we first introduced the values, I said that respect is one of the things that I hold closest to my heart. I opened up about

that to set the stage and show my teammates I was being
vulnerable. I wanted them to know I trusted them so that they
could be vulnerable with me, too, and trust me. I think that really brought us together and helped us understand each other
a lot more and how we can communicate with each other.

Use Symbolic Language

Leaders understand the power of symbolic language to communicate a shared identity and give life to visions. They use metaphors and analogies. They provide examples, tell stories, and relate anecdotes. They draw word pictures, offer quotations, and recite slogans. They enable the group to imagine the possibilities—to hear, sense, and recognize them.

Think about just one type of symbolic language: metaphor. Metaphors are everywhere—there are art metaphors, game and sports metaphors, war metaphors, science fiction metaphors, machine metaphors, and religious or spiritual metaphors. They influence what and how people think, what they imagine and invent, what they eat and drink, what they consume and purchase, for whom they vote and rally behind. Using these figures of speech greatly enhances your ability to enlist others in a shared vision of the future. For example, you can influence people's behavior simply by giving the task or the team a name that evokes the behavior it implies.

Notice how, as mentioned in an earlier chapter, fraternities or sororities use words like *brothers* and *sisters*, and not simply *members*, to evoke the notion of being closely connected, much like members of a family. If you want people to act like a community, use language that awakens a feeling of community—words like *fellowship, neighborhood*, and *citizens*, for example. If you want them to act like Spiderman, "sticking" with things and working for the good of all, use language that cues those images.

In his senior year, Robert Quiles was hired as an assistant resident director in a large residence hall. Move-in weekend for the first-year students was one of the most important events. To get his staff mates on board for the arduous work of move-in preparation, Robert shared this vision about how the residence hall "was to be more than just a room to sleep in. We wanted these residents to feel safe and truly part of a new community." The challenge now was to view this process not merely as checking residents into the "dorm" but as a larger welcoming. Instead of simply going about the standard procedures, the residence hall staff were inspired to make this a bigger, more personal moment. Each resident was welcomed to the building with the phrase "welcome home" to signify how the staff aimed to treat this extraordinary living experience. In addition to calling the building home, the staff also used the language of community when referring to the collective residents.

Create Images of the Future

Visions are images in the mind; they are impressions and representations. They become real as leaders express those images in concrete terms to others. Just as architects make drawings and engineers build models, leaders find ways of conveying collective hopes for the future.

People typically use terms such as *foresight, focus, forecasts, future scenarios, points of view,* and *perspectives* when talking about the future. What all these expressions have in common is that they are visual references. The word *vision* itself has at its root the verb "to see." Vision statements, then, are not statements at all. They are pictures—word pictures. They are images of the future. For people to share a vision, they must be able to see it in the mind's eye.

In our classes and workshops, we often illustrate the power of images with this simple exercise. We ask people to shout out the first thing that comes to mind when they hear *Paris, France.* The replies that pop out—the Eiffel Tower, the Louvre, the Arc de Triomphe, the Seine, Notre Dame, delicious food, wine, romance—are all images of real places and sensations. No one calls out the square kilometers, population, or gross domestic product of Paris. Why? Because most of what we recall about memorable places or events are those things associated with our senses—sights, sounds, tastes, smells, tactile sensations, and emotions.

What this means for leaders is that to enlist others and Inspire a Shared Vision, you must be able to draw on the natural mental process of creating images. When you speak about the future, you need to create pictures with words so that others form a mental image of what things will be like when you are at the end of the journey. When talking about going places you've never been, you have to be able to imagine what they'll look like. You have to picture the possibilities to make them come alive.

Making the possibilities come alive is precisely what David Mullenburg did when he recruited all the members of his senior class to go on an overnight backpacking trip. When we asked how he got people to sign up, David replied, "I told stories of past camping trips I had been on, how great they were, and painted a picture of how much fun we would all have." This is often how the campus crew team will convince people to join up: "Imagine how great it will be to get up in the morning before everyone else does, before the sun even rises, get out on a lake, and start rowing with your friends. If you can see this as fun, exciting, and rewarding, then you're a perfect candidate for the crew team!"

Getting people to see a common future does not require some special power. Everyone possesses this ability. You do it every time you take a vacation, go on a road trip, or have a special celebration and share the photos with your friends. If you doubt your ability to paint word pictures, try this exercise: sit down with a few close friends and tell them about one of your favorite vacations. Describe the people you saw and met, the sights and sounds of the places you went, and the smells and tastes of the food you ate. Show them photos or videos if you have them. Observe their reactions—and your own. What's that experience like? We've done this activity many times, and people consistently report feeling energized and passionate. Those hearing about a place for the first time usually say something like, "After listening to you, I'd like to go there someday myself."

Practice Positive Communication

To foster team spirit, breed optimism, promote resilience, and renew faith and confidence, leaders look on the bright side. They keep hope alive. They strengthen people's belief that life's struggles will produce a positive and more promising future. Overwhelmingly, students reported feeling most highly productive in direct proportion to how frequently they experienced their leaders as "upbeat and positive when talking about what could be accomplished," as shown in Figure 4.1. Nearly every student—more than nine out of ten—felt highly productive when working with a leader who was often or very frequently upbeat and positive about the future.

Alyssa Giagliani was on her college's track and cross-country team and remembers talking with her teammates at the end of their first season. They had won the freshman division title race, and Alyssa asked them what they saw in their future. They said they didn't think they had a future in running; winning the title had probably just been a fluke.

Her teammates asked Alyssa the same question right back, and she told them, "I see a great potential: the potential to be the first women's team in the history of our school to make the championships and win league titles and a division title." These aspirations had never crossed her teammates' minds, Alyssa told us. "I could see that they were enlightened by this idea and that they were willing to put in the hard work to attain those lofty goals."

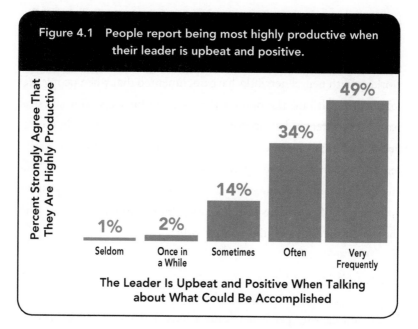

Figure 4.1 People report being most highly productive when their leader is upbeat and positive.

Fast-forward to the varsity team's senior year. Alyssa lies in a hospital bed after a life-threatening auto accident. Her teammates tell her they don't have the heart to finish the season without her. Alyssa is flabbergasted and tells her team in no uncertain terms what she thinks about their quitting. She says that if they finish the season, she will walk with them to the starting line on the day of the championship race. "This way of getting my point across made my teammates realize that I was passionate about the team finishing what we started," she told us. That team didn't quit. Alyssa joined her teammates at the starting line, and they went on to become the first women's cross-country team in the school's history to advance to the championship meet and win a major title.

People look for leaders like Alyssa, who demonstrate an enthusiastic, genuine belief in the capacity of others, strengthen people's will, and help support the group's needs as they take on challenging tasks. They are drawn to leaders who express optimism for the future.

People want leaders who remain passionate despite obstacles and setbacks. They want leaders with a positive, confident, can-do approach. Naysayers only stop forward progress; they do not start it. Researchers working with neural networks have documented that when people feel rebuffed or left out, the brain activates a site for registering physical pain.[3] People remember negative comments far more often, in greater detail, and more intensely than encouraging words. When negative remarks become a preoccupation, a person's brain loses mental efficiency. This is all the more reason for leaders to be positive. A positive approach to life broadens people's ideas about future possibilities, and these exciting options build on each other.

Express Your Emotions

In explaining why particular leaders have a magnetic effect, people often describe them as charismatic. However, *charisma* has become so overused and misused that it's almost useless as a descriptor of leaders. Being charismatic is neither a magical quality nor a spiritual one. Like being "inspirational," it's mostly about how people behave.

Instead of defining *charisma* as a personality trait, many social scientists have investigated how people described as charismatic actually behave. They find that individuals perceived to be charismatic are simply more animated than people who are not.[4] They smile more, speak faster, pronounce words more clearly, and move their heads and bodies more often. Energetic and expressive are also key descriptors of what it means to be charismatic. The old saying that enthusiasm is infectious is undoubtedly true for leaders.

Conveying emotion has another benefit for leaders: emotions make things more memorable. Adding emotion to your words and behavior increases the likelihood that people will remember what you say. Researchers have shown that "emotionally significant events create stronger, longer-lasting memories."[5] No doubt you've experienced this when something emotionally significant happened to you.

The events don't even have to be real to be memorable. They can simply be stories. For example, researchers showed subjects in two groups a series of twelve slides. The slide presentation was accompanied by a story, one line for each slide. For one group in the study, the narrative was quite boring; for the other, the narrative was emotionally moving. The subjects didn't know when they watched the slides that they would be tested, but two weeks later, they returned and took a test on how well they remembered the details of each slide. Although the subjects in the two groups did not differ in their memory of the first few and last few slides, they did differ significantly in the recollection of the slides in the middle. People who had listened to the emotionally arousing narrative remembered details better than the group that listened to the boring or more neutral story.[6]

If you want people to remember your message, you have to tap into their emotions; you have to arouse their feelings about the cause to which you want them to commit. Having your messages remembered requires adding emotion to your words and your behavior. You don't need a complete narrative, and you don't need slides. Just the words themselves can be effective, as demonstrated in another laboratory experiment in which researchers asked subjects to learn to associate pairs of words. Some of the words in the pairs were used because they elicited strong emotional responses. Two weeks later, people remembered the emotionally arousing words better than they remembered the less arousing ones.[7]

Moreover, showing people a concrete example is better than telling them about an abstract principle, which still leaves them on the outside looking in. For example, studies found that a story about a starving seven-year-old girl from Mali prompted people to donate more than twice as much money as the message that "food shortages in Malawi are affecting more than three million children in Zambia."[8]

The dramatic increase in the use of electronic technology also impacts how people deliver messages. More and more people are turning to their digital devices and social media—from podcasts to webcasts, social networking to video sharing—for information and connection. Because people remember things that have strong emotional content, social media has the potential to engage people more than emails, memos, and PowerPoint presentations. Writing a good script's no longer enough; you must also put on a good show. And you've got to make it a show that people will remember.

Whether it's a story, an example, or a word, you're more likely to get people to remember the key messages when you can attach them to something that triggers an emotional response. People are hardwired to pay more attention to stuff that excites or scares them. Keep this in mind the next time you deliver any presentation. It's not just the content that will make your message stick; it's also how well you tap into people's emotions. People must *feel* something to change. Thinking something isn't nearly enough to get things moving. Your job is to enable them to feel moved to change, and expressing emotions helps you do that.

Speak Genuinely

None of these suggestions about being more expressive are of any value if you don't believe in what you're saying. If the vision is someone else's and you don't own it, you'll have a tough time enlisting other people in it. If you have trouble imagining yourself living the future described in the vision, you certainly will not be able to convince others that they ought to enlist in making it a reality. You can't expect others to be excited about the possibilities if you're not. The prerequisite to enlisting others in a shared vision is *genuineness*.

When Bailey Hamm became her sorority's vice president for public relations, she aspired to enhance their image. It was important to communicate to her younger sisters, through her work and words, who she was and her sincere desire to serve the higher principles of their organization. She made it a point to share her personal story with the younger sorority members and explain why she believed the chapter could do great things and become stronger. She felt that the sorority had done much for her and had the potential to make a meaningful difference in the sisters' lives. She explained how important she believed it was for everyone to find a way to contribute to the group.

By being genuine and speaking from the heart about her vision for the chapter, she told us, "I wanted to show the other women that the choices I made were going to be true to who I was and what I thought our chapter stood for." Bailey used her circumstances as an example and spoke genuinely and positively about how her sisters could make a difference even when things were difficult. Bailey told them they might not see results the next day or the next week, but success would eventually come. And through the stories and insights she shared with her sisters, Bailey found the answers for how to talk to people not affiliated with the sorority system:

> Painting a positive picture of who we are and what we could do set me up to speak to people outside the sorority with conviction about what we stood for and what we could accomplish, and it energized people.

The most believable people are the ones, like Bailey, with deep passion. There's no one more fun to be around than someone openly excited about the magic that can happen. There's no one more determined than someone who believes fervently in an ideal. People want their leader to be upbeat, optimistic, and positive about the future. You can be that someone! It's the only way you can get people to willingly follow you to a place they have never been before.

REFLECT AND ACT: ENLIST OTHERS

Leaders appeal to common ideals. They connect people to what is most meaningful in the shared vision. They lift those around them to higher levels of motivation and performance and continuously reinforce that they can make a difference in the world. Exemplary student leaders speak to what is unique and distinctive about the groups, projects, or causes they lead, making others feel proud to be a part of something extraordinary. Exemplary leaders understand that it's not their individual view of the future that's important; it's the collective aspirations of every person that matter most.

To be sustainable over time, visions must be compelling and memorable. You must breathe life into visions, animating them so that others can experience what it would be like to live and work in an ideal and unique future. Use a variety of modes of expression to make abstract visions concrete. Leaders generate enthusiasm and excitement for the common vision through the skillful use of metaphors, symbols, word pictures, positive language, and personal energy.

Above all, leaders must be convinced of the value of the common vision and share that genuine belief with others. They must believe in what they are saying. If you don't truly believe in what you are doing or what you want the group to do, how can you expect anyone else to believe in the cause or task? Authenticity is the key because people will only follow willingly if they sense the vision is genuine.

Reflect

The second commitment of Inspire a Shared Vision is to *enlist others in a common vision by appealing to shared aspirations*. What are the most important ideas or lessons about exemplary leadership that you learned from this chapter?

_____

_____

_____

_____

Here are some actions you can take to follow through on your commitment to **Enlist Others:**

- Clarify with the team what makes this group unique and the points of pride associated with being distinctive.
- Show others why they should persevere because their long-term interests are served by enlisting in a common vision, even if there may be short-term sacrifices.
- Demonstrate that you are listening to what team members are saying by bringing their thoughts and ideas into the vision for the group.
- Generate and share metaphors, symbols, examples, stories, pictures, and words that represent the ideal image of what you all aspire to become.
- Be positive, upbeat, and energetic when discussing your organization's future.
- Be expressive, using gestures, varying your tone of voice, speaking confidently, and don't be afraid to be emotional.

- Acknowledge the emotions of others and validate them as important. Avoid dwelling on emotions that discourage people and cause them to lose heart for the journey.

Act

After you have reflected on what you learned, what you can improve, and the preceding suggestions, record your plan here for taking at least one action that will help you become a better leader:

_____

_____

_____

_____

_____

CHALLENGE
THE PROCESS

Challenge is the crucible for greatness. Leaders seek and accept challenging opportunities and seize the initiative to make something meaningful happen. Exemplary leaders look for new ideas everywhere. They turn adversity into an advantage and setbacks into successes. They take risks with bold ideas and accept and grow from inevitable disappointments. They treat mistakes as learning opportunities.

In the following two chapters, you will see how student leaders:

➤ **Search for Opportunities** by seizing the initiative and by looking outward for innovative ways to improve.
➤ **Experiment and Take Risks** by consistently generating small wins and learning from experience.

CHALLENGE THE PROCESS
Reflections from the *Student Leadership Practices Inventory*

1. My overall score from the *Student Leadership Practices Inventory* for Challenge the Process was:

   _____

2. Of the six leadership behaviors that are part of Challenge the Process, the statement that I indicated engaging in most frequently was:

   _____

   _____

3. The leadership behavior statement that I engaged in the least often was:

   _____

   _____

   Based on your self-assessment with the leadership practice of Challenge the Process, complete the following two statements. As you read and review the next two chapters, keep in mind these reflections and observations.

4. Of the leadership behaviors associated with Challenge the Process, the one(s) I feel most comfortable engaging in is/are:

   _____

   _____

   _____

5. The leadership behaviors that I feel I could engage in more often and be more comfortable with doing are:

   _____

   _____

   _____

5

Commitment #5:
Search for
Opportunities

Ceena Vang and Zora Bowens had never organized a community protest on their own. But when the Atlanta spa mass shooting claimed the lives of eight people, six of them Asian-American women, Zora called Ceena and asked if she wanted to organize an event together protesting the nationwide rise in anti-Asian American and Pacific Islander (AAPI) hate crimes and rhetoric.

"I was taken aback by it. I was like, Okay, if this is something so impactful that my best friend, a Black woman, feels called to do something, then I need to get on board and do something for my community," Ceena, who is of first-generation Hmong descent, said.

Ceena and Zora wanted to move quickly in the wake of the mass shooting, to change the feeling in the community from despair to hope. Ceena reached out to her friends, family, and other AAPI community members to let them know about the protest. Zora created flyers, and the two sent out friends willing to help to put up the flyers in different parts of Detroit.

On the day of the protest, Ceena and Zora expected a few dozen people to show up in support. Instead, more than 500 people came to their protest. "We were thinking it would be something small, but within three days, it turned into something larger than life itself," Ceena said.

Whole families showed up, with generations of people—from grandparents to newborn babies—there to show support for the AAPI community. Attendees came with signs protesting anti-AAPI hate, which had spread since the COVID-19 pandemic, including the attacks on older AAPI people recorded in New York City and San Francisco. Speakers, including Ceena and Zora, shared their feelings and own experiences of racism and discrimination, as well as hopes for a different future. For the two young women, the turnout was a resounding success.

But at the end of the protest, someone approached and asked Ceena and Zora when their next event would be. "I think both of us were just thinking of this doing this one event; we weren't thinking, we're a group, we're going to do more things," Zora said. But as the two talked about it, they realized they both felt called to continue organizing. One march hadn't ended anti-AAPI racism. And plenty of other social justice concerns in their city could use attention.

Ceena and Zora decided to form an organization. They called it Whenever We're Needed (WWN), with a mission statement to provide intersectional support for marginalized communities in their area via organizing events and providing community outreach and education. But they both knew that if their organization was going to last, they needed to learn how to organize more effectively. Even though their first event had had a big turnout, there were things Ceena and Zora hadn't even realized they didn't know until the event.

For example, on the day of the protest, they'd tried to keep people safe by confining activities to the sidewalks—until the fuel of emotion poured protesters into the streets, regardless of whether they had safety clearance. In the future, the group would need to make sure they had the right permits to block traffic. Because the event was taking place during the pandemic, they also brought Purell to keep those who attended the protest COVID-safe, but it was difficult to do that while also making sure no one was gathered in a car or bike lane. "I think a lot of people didn't know that we had leadership capabilities. They were like, 'Who are these girls?' and then suddenly, 500 people show up for our first march," Zora said. For their next event, they needed to master logistics and learn to present themselves as community leaders.

Ceena compiled a list of any Asian American or Asian community-focused advocacy groups in Detroit and reached out to them—about fifty organizations in total—to see if any wanted to collaborate or partner. Ceena and Zora had previously attended protests, but attending as leaders of an official advocacy group allowed them to study how other organizations conducted recruitment and rallying. She also reached out to mutual aid organizations, looking for insight on how to maintain a movement and master logistics for community events successfully. Meanwhile, Zora used her graphic design expertise in creating a logo for WWN, and flyers for future events.

Ceena's networking, and Zora's professional touches, paid off: WWN started being invited to events by other advocacy groups in their state. WWN rallied support for a diverse range of intersectional causes, including Palestinian Youth Resistance groups, Black liberation groups that led the Black Lives Matter movement amidst George Floyd's murder, and reproductive rights groups in Michigan. And Ceena's outreach to mutual aid organizations led to developing best practices for WWN based on what worked for those groups, including best practices for reaching out to the local press to publicize upcoming events and recruit others to your cause by spreading the word.

One march WWN organized alongside the Michigan Coalition for Reproductive Liberation even led to the passage of legislation in Michigan enshrining reproductive rights after *Roe v. Wade* was overturned in 2022. The rally for the bill was the biggest march in support of reproductive rights in the state, with over a thousand activists marching to the state House of Representatives. "I truly don't think without the protest that people would have been so geared up to make sure people turned out to vote and get the law passed," Zora said. "The whole momentum of it felt really crucial."

To help create the impact they wanted to see in the world, Ceena and Zora had to push themselves out of their comfort zone to learn new things—like drafting a mission statement, learning to collaborate as co-founders, and stepping into the spotlight. All came with their own particular challenges. "I struggled with imposter syndrome really badly at first," Ceena said. "The Asian model, in general, is just to be quiet, keep your head down, don't make too much noise, don't draw too much attention to yourself. I had to make that decision to be present in the movement."

When Ceena and Zora decided to organize that first protest, they had no idea they had taken the first steps toward forming an advocacy organization and impacting state legislation. They just knew they felt called to act. "A lot of people say, 'Why do you fight for a group you're not necessarily a part of,' and that's a crazy question to me," Zora said. "We can't move forward as a society until all of us are okay."

The experience of creating WWN after a single successful event taught both Ceena and Zora the power of pushing themselves outside their comfort zones. "A big question that I always like to ask myself is, If not me, then who? If I'm not going to do the work, then who will?" Ceena said. As Ceena and Zora discovered in founding WWN, meaningful change comes about only if you're willing to experience the discomfort of trying new things, learning from your experience, and taking the first step into the unknown.

Challenge opens the doors to making extraordinary things happen. Leaders understand that you don't get to anyplace different if you just keep doing the same things over and over again. Getting out of routines and ruts requires treating every project, assignment, or job as an adventure. Ceena and Zora, like so many other students in their personal-best experiences, illustrate lifting their heads up, looking all around, and being willing to invest time and energy in finding out about other possibilities.

Sometimes challenges find leaders, and sometimes leaders find the challenges; most often, it's a little of each. Ceena and Zora did what all exemplary leaders do. They looked outward, remained sensitive to external realities, and persuaded others to take the challenges and opportunities they faced seriously. They served as catalysts for change, challenging the way things were done. This involved much more than simply complaining about the way things are. It is about proactively looking for options that might lead to a better way of doing things.

The personal-best leadership cases are not about pushing back just to be confrontational or controversial, they are about making changes for a purpose, doing things that have never been done before, and going to places not yet discovered. Change is the work of leaders. In today's world, business-as-usual thinking is unacceptable, and exemplary leaders know that they must transform how things are currently done. Delivering results beyond expectations can't be achieved merely with good intentions. People, processes, systems, and strategies all need to change. In addition, all change requires leaders to actively seek ways to improve things—to grow, innovate, improve, and learn.

Exemplary student leaders embrace the commitment to Search for Opportunities. They make sure they engage in these two essentials:

- **Seize the initiative**
- **Exercise outsight**

Sometimes leaders shake things up. Other times they harness the uncertainty that surrounds them. Regardless, leaders make extraordinary things happen. They actively rely on outsight to seek innovative ideas from beyond the boundaries of familiar experience.

SEIZE THE INITIATIVE

When students recall their personal-best leadership experiences, they always think about times of challenge, turbulence, and adversity. Why? Because personal and organizational hardships have a way of making people come face to face with who they are and what they're capable of becoming. Innovation Adversities challenges and tests people's values, desires, aspirations, capabilities, and capacities. They require inventive ways of dealing with novel and difficult situations. They also tend to bring out the best in people.

Meeting new challenges always requires things to be different than they currently are. You can't respond with the same old solutions. You must change the status quo, which is what students did in their personal-best leadership experiences. They met challenges with change.

We didn't ask students to tell us specifically about change. They could review any leadership experience, yet they chose to discuss the changes they made in response to the challenges they faced. Their electing to talk about times of change underscores the fact that leadership demands altering the present state of affairs. There is a clear connection between challenge and change, and there's a clear connection between challenge and being an exemplary leader.

Leadership is the mechanism through which you guide people through adversity, uncertainty, and other significant challenges. Leadership makes it possible to triumph against overwhelming odds, take initiative when there is inertia, confront the established order, and mobilize individuals and institutions in the face of stiff resistance. In times of constancy and complacency, leaders actively seek to disturb the status quo and awaken others to new possibilities. Leadership, challenge, and seizing the initiative are linked together. Humdrum situations and solutions are not associated with award-winning performances.

Make Something Happen

Alec Loeb joined his fraternity as a freshman. His goal from the start was to hold a leadership position at some point, and he started on that path by accepting the role of philanthropy chair. "I was raised in a family where giving back to the community was a way of life," Alec told us, "so I was well suited to the position. When I took the job, I knew there was a retiring chair who could help me find my way. But then he got an unexpected opportunity to take a semester abroad, and we never got a chance to go over anything. I was left to figure it all out myself."

Several events had been traditions with the fraternity that Alec knew he would be expected to continue. The first up was an annual charity oyster roast. Alec found out that the most they had raised from this event in previous years was $2,000. He thought, "I know we can do better than that."

> I started to talk to the brothers about what makes students come to an event like this and asked about how they got the word out. The answers were pretty vague and definitely not adventurous, with suggestions like "We put flyers up, we use word of mouth, we get our friends to spread the word." I decided to try something new. Why not see if some of the local bars and restaurants would be willing to sell tickets for us or, at the very least, donate food? What if we could get a few of the past brothers or even famous university alumni to donate to the cause? You never know until you ask, right?

These ideas worked out, and as a result, the oyster roast made almost triple what it had made the year before. This experience taught Alec an important lesson: "If you can think of ways to improve the process, you should take them."

If you are going to lead others, you must stop simply going through the motions when it comes to the task, project, or assignment you've been asked to do. It's a lesson all would-be leaders need to learn. Even if you're on the right track, you'll likely get run over if you just sit there. To do your best as a leader, you must seize the initiative to change the way things are.

Being an exemplary student leader necessarily means working beyond your job description and seeing opportunities where others don't. For example, some standard practices, policies, and procedures are critical to productivity and quality assurance. However, many are simply a matter of tradition. In Alec's example, an expectation was set by the title to which he had been elected: "philanthropy chair." Certain events had been done every year and were expected to continue, but the bottom line was that it wasn't the particular event that mattered; the point was to raise as much money as possible for good causes. Keeping that goal in mind allowed Alec to try something new. He also told us that the previous chair was unavailable and how this worked in his favor, freeing his thinking and empowering him to try new approaches.

> There was nobody watching over my shoulder saying,
> "I did it this way; why are you changing it?" There was just
> an expectation to plan an event, and it was up to me to
> make it happen. Once I started thinking about how it could
> be done and talking to people about those ideas, we got
> excited about the possibilities and tried some new things.

New jobs and new assignments are ideal opportunities for asking probing questions and challenging how things are done. They are times when you're expected to ask, "Why do we do this, and why do we do that?" However, don't just ask this question when new to the job or assignment. Make it a routine part of your leadership approach. Ask questions that test people's assumptions, stimulate different ways of thinking, and open new avenues to explore. Asking questions is how you'll continuously uncover needed improvements, fostering innovation. Treat today as if it were your first day by asking, "If I were just starting this responsibility, what makes sense about how we do things, and what might I do differently?" If you don't understand why things are done the way they are, ask questions to determine whether an old routine should stay in place or be done differently. Then act. This is how you'll continuously uncover needed improvements.

And don't stop at what you can find on your own. Ask those around you about what gets in their way of achieving their best. Promise to look into what they say and get back to them, then kick the possibilities around with them some more. Keep looking for things that don't seem right or could be better. Ask questions and then follow up with more.

Leaders want to make something happen and are often frustrated by the "if it ain't broke, don't fix it" mentality. They earn the respect of the people around them when they question the status quo, come up with innovative ideas, follow through with the changes they suggest, get feedback, understand their mistakes, and learn from failures. Leaders don't wait for permission or specific instructions before jumping in. They notice what isn't working, create a solution for the problem, gain buy-in from constituents, and implement the desired outcome. Research shows that students who rate high on proactivity are considered by their peers to be better leaders and are more engaged in extracurricular and civic activities targeted toward positive change. Proactivity consistently produces better results than reactivity or inactivity.[1]

As Alec's experience shows, you also need to give everyone on your team the chance to search for better ways of doing things and

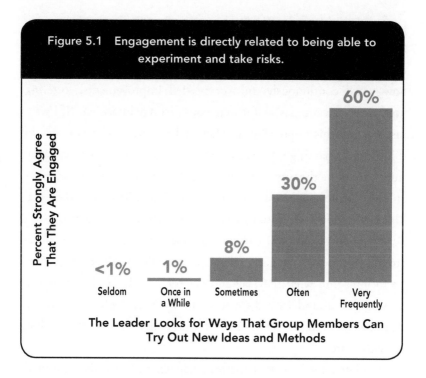

Figure 5.1   Engagement is directly related to being able to experiment and take risks.

Percent Strongly Agree That They Are Engaged

<1%   Seldom

1%   Once in a While

8%   Sometimes

30%   Often

60%   Very Frequently

The Leader Looks for Ways That Group Members Can Try Out New Ideas and Methods

allow them to step forward and take initiative. The data shows that students are significantly more engaged in their organizations (proud, productive, valued, and empowered) when they strongly agree that their leader "looks for ways that group members can try out new ideas and methods." As shown in Figure 5.1, nine out of ten students report being engaged when their leader often or very frequently finds them opportunities to innovate. Analyzed differently, only 10 percent of students in the bottom quartile on the engagement scale reported that their leader *very frequently* promoted this flexibility, compared with 16 percent in the second quartile, 32 percent in the third quartile, and more than half (51 percent) in the top quartile. Everyone performs better when they take charge of change.

Encourage Initiative in Others

Change requires leadership, and every person in the group, not just the leader, can develop creative ideas and suggest improvements. This was certainly Kelly Estes's experience. On the first day as summer interns at a law firm, she and her colleagues took part in an orientation and training session about the work they were to do. Many were disappointed with the type of jobs they were assigned, mostly performing data input and simple office tasks. Their reactions: "This sucks!" "This is going to be one long summer." "We should all just quit now and go on vacation." Kelly was determined to remove herself from all the naysayers, and as she told us, "Right away, I decided that I didn't want to make a waste of my summer and that even in the worst situations, there was always an opportunity to shine."

Kelly walked around the office, introducing herself to anyone she could. She went the extra mile to meet the staff throughout the firm. Kelly started her assignment correlating data for various attorneys and secretaries, but she would ask questions when something didn't seem right. People began to notice her initiative and were happy to have someone on board who would try to resolve issues rather than ignore them, leaving them to turn into bigger problems later.

After a few weeks, the other interns saw that Kelly had developed positive relationships with many in the firm and started asking her what she had been doing. She explained that she asked questions and offered ideas on what they could do better in their departments. Although she admitted that her direct boss wasn't too excited about her taking the initiative to dive more deeply into the firm's business, Kelly said she wouldn't let that undermine her determination to do a good job; and besides, she found others in the firm were very appreciative of her efforts. In fact, many other interns began following suit, and the partners noticed how much work was completed more efficiently and that the "status quo" was quite different in some departments. The interns who followed Kelly's lead enjoyed their work and had a great summer experience. They were not only influenced by Kelly's initiative and her drive to try a different approach, but as a group, they positively influenced the work style within the firm.

Leaders like Kelly take the initiative, and in doing so, encourage initiative in others. They want people to speak up, offer suggestions for improvement, and be straightforward with their perspectives and feedback. Yet when it comes to situations that involve high uncertainty, high risk, and high challenge, many people feel reluctant to act, afraid they might make matters worse.

You can create conditions in many ways so that others will be ready and willing to make things happen in good times and bad. Promote a can-do attitude by finding opportunities for people to gain skills slowly and steadily. Help someone learn and talk things through. Use your time together to build people's ability and confidence so that they feel ready to do something about the situations they face. It's tempting to say, "I don't have time to show someone how to do this! It's easier if I just do it myself," or even "If I want it done right, I'll do it myself," but this short-term thinking will cause problems down the road. The best leaders know that taking the time to help someone learn now can strengthen the group in the long term. People can't be effective when they don't get the knowledge, skills, or tools they need to perform.

Also, find ways for people to stretch themselves. Give people a chance to improve, learn, and grow, but take it one step at a time, at a pace where they feel they can succeed. Give people too much too soon, and they will fail; if they fail too often, they'll quit trying. Increase people's challenges slowly but steadily, and as people get better and build their self-confidence, they will continue moving the bar upward, commensurate with their skills, abilities, and confidence. Leaders encourage initiative by providing access to role models, especially when the role model is a peer who successfully meets new challenges. Seeing others succeed at something new can be an effective way to encourage people to try out new ways of behaving, as long as you put it in a positive and encouraging light, rather than demeaning. Comparing people can turn off initiative in a minute; once it shuts down, it's very tough to restart.

Challenge with Purpose

Doing things differently doesn't necessarily ensure they will be done better, so leaders realize they must approach change with a purpose. When Lizzie Shaw was elected student body president at her university, one thing was immediately clear to her: The campaign process at her institution needed to change. Her school's student government campaign process was notorious throughout their region: students ran on mass tickets of hundreds of people, the process drug out for months, and there was no spending limit, which created a huge barrier to access for many students. But many at her institution regarded the campaign process as a rite of passage, or a tradition, that made their school unique. "It sounds really fun and looks really fun, but as a candidate, it was not fun," Lizzie said.

But even more than being a difficult experience, Lizzie also knew the campaign process overshadowed the good work that student government could do. She said the only time student government felt visible to other students was when they were asking for votes.

Once elected, Lizzie made it her mission to submit revisions to the election code to ensure that future campaigns were better managed for students' mental health and to serve the student body better. Lizzie let her intentions be known to her fellow student government elected officials and asked them for their feedback and ideas of what needed to change in the election code. At a conference for student government in her region, Lizzie asked other student body presidents about their own institutional rules for conducting campaigns and found out that across the region, everyone had lower spending limits than her school.

Lizzie submitted proposed changes to the election code to her school's Senate for review, stressing that the changes were meant to make the campaign process both fairer and more fun—not just to do away with tradition. The Senate approved her revisions, lowering the campaign spending limit by 70 percent, limiting how long campaigns could run, and adding disciplinary sanctions against students who broke the rules.

Lizzie said she's already seen positive progress with the changes. "[The next election cycle] was better. I don't want people coming out of campaigning to hate each other," she said. "Our big elections made our campus think we were really annoying and self-serving, and that's not the point of the work we do at all."

Leaders don't challenge for challenge's sake. They don't try to change things just to shake things up. Students who simply criticize new thoughts and ideas, or point out problems with what others have to contribute without offering alternate options, are not demonstrating leadership. They are merely complaining. Leaders challenge, often with great passion, because they want people to live life *on* purpose and *with* purpose. What gets people through the difficult and scary times—when they don't think they can even get up in the morning or take another step—is a sense of meaning and purpose. The motivation to deal with the challenges and uncertainties of life and work comes from the inside, not from something others hold out in front of you as a reward. Leaders raise challenges to resolve and improve the situation, not simply to complain.

The evidence from our research and studies by many others is that if people are going to do their best, they must be internally motivated.[2] Intrinsic motivators are more likely to produce extraordinary results than extrinsic ones. Recall Jen Marsh's teaching experience: "There was no way I was going to get these second and third graders to read because I wanted them to. Instead, it was something that I had to help them want to accomplish on their own. I had to get the kids excited about reading and show them how important this achievement would be later in their lives." Leaders get people to see beyond the particular task or project and to focus on the meaning that it fulfills. When it comes to excellence, it's not "What gets rewarded gets done." It's "What *is rewarding* gets done." Leaders understand they must find what motivates people internally; they must tap into others' hearts and minds if they want them to do something difficult or novel.

EXERCISE OUTSIGHT

On a visit to the rugged coast of Northern California, we came across a pamphlet describing a stretch of the Pacific Ocean with this warning: "Never turn your back on the ocean." You can't turn and look inland to catch a view of the town because a rogue wave may come along and sweep you out to sea, as many an unsuspecting traveler has discovered. This warning holds sound advice for travelers and leaders alike. When you take your eyes off the external realities, turning inward to admire your team's or organization's beauty, the swirling waters of change may sweep you away. So, too, with innovation: you must constantly scan the external realities. Innovation requires the use of outsight. *Outsight* (the awareness and understanding of outside forces), the sibling of *insight* (the ability to apprehend the inner nature of things), comes through openness. That's because, as researchers have documented, innovations come from just about anywhere.[3]

In his senior year of high school, Logan Hall was elected to serve in the leadership group of his 4-H State Council, whose role was to advance the purpose and vision of 4-H and to promote it throughout sixty-seven counties in the state. They were also to provide various research-based leadership training programs and curricula to local councils and their officers. Logan knew that his council needed help in identifying and meeting the needs of students from across the state. Still, instead of jumping right in and possibly reinventing the wheel, Logan and his team looked around to see how other councils had addressed similar issues. For example, they contacted nearby state councils and reviewed the curriculum and leadership lessons they had created there. They identified speakers they had used and explored what might be adapted to work in their state. Logan explained that they found ways to use many of the ideas they gathered, "And in the process, we began to understand their visions, how they connected to ours, and how we could collaborate. All we had to do was ask."

According to our research, when students indicate that their leader "searches for innovative ways to improve what we are doing," as Logan and his fellow 4-H leaders did, they are significantly more excited and proud about their organization than students who view their leaders as constrained by current and past decisions. As Logan's experience shows, it's by keeping the doors open to ideas and information from outside one's internal boundaries that you become knowledgeable about what is happening around you. Insight without outsight is like seeing with blinders on; you just can't get a complete picture.

Look Outside Your Experience

Studies into how the brain processes information suggest that you must bombard your brain with stuff it has never encountered to see things differently and creatively. This kind of novelty is vital because the brain evolved for efficiency, routinely taking perceptual shortcuts to save energy. You can only get your brain to reorganize information by forcing yourself to break free of preexisting views. Moving beyond habitual thinking patterns is the starting point for imagining truly new ideas.[4]

The human mind is surprisingly adroit at supporting its consistent ways of viewing the world. It is also adept at rationalizing away evidence that contradicts those views. One way to adjust this limiting lens is by expanding your hands-on experiences. While an undergraduate, Courtney Ballagh was employed as an assistant manager in a retail store (where the sales team was not making its numbers), and she grasped the importance of outsight. In retailing, as in many organizations, people often stick to one tactic that works for them until forced to change it. Courtney suggested that each sales associate pick several stores in their area, visit them, and observe how they sold their products. Once they all came back and shared their information, they were able to think outside the box and see that what makes other people successful can work for them, too. Courtney explained:

> These new selling techniques helped our team break out of their rut and get back on track. If you only speak to those around you and do not go out of your way to see new perspectives, you will never come up with anything new. New things are challenging and exciting, and it takes going out of your comfort zone to see that.

Moving outside your usual thinking patterns doesn't have to be as elaborate as Courtney's, and it can occur right where you are today, on campus or off. Find ways to look outside the program, department, or chapter you are in to seek out, and even experience, what other groups like yours are doing. Alec Loeb did this when his predecessor left campus before he could provide any details about the traditional oyster roast. Logan Hall did the same by contacting his counterparts in other states about their processes and experiences.

There's also an example of looking outside one's own experience in Kelly Estes's story. By venturing outside her appointed duties and exploring other departments within the firm, Kelly essentially did, internally, the same thing as the employees who sought firsthand experience with different retailers or 4-H State Council approaches. She found opportunities to make a real difference in the firm's work by lifting her eyes and looking around her larger surroundings.

Student leaders like Courtney, Kelly, Alec, and Logan understand that innovation requires more listening and frequent communication than routine work. Successful innovations take hard work, constant communication, and the willingness to ask, "What if?" You must establish relationships, network, make connections, and be out and about.

Listen to and Promote Diverse Perspectives

Demand for change will come from both inside and outside your group. If everything worked perfectly, there might be no urgency to do things differently. But the truth is that if people are going to realize their aspirations, then some things will have to change, even before they are broken. Standard operating practices keep things going the way they are, but they are often not well suited for dealing with turbulence, uncertainty, or mandates for better results.

You must be receptive to new ideas to challenge the process effectively. You need to appreciate that one person may have a valid point of view about a problem, but individuals from different backgrounds can come up with diverse views on the same problem. Just as Ceena Vang and Zora Bowens learned when founding Whenever We're Needed, or Logan Hall found out from another state's 4-H experiences, the extra information and perspectives can help you formulate better answers and improve outdated systems. Successful leaders need to encourage sharing information from all stakeholders, be receptive to different ideas no matter the source, and use collective knowledge (experience and wisdom) to come up with an effective solution to any challenge.

One of the reasons that people are often afraid to ask around for advice and input from others is that they perceive that doing so means, or at least implies, that they're incompetent, that they don't know something they should already know. However, studies have shown that this fear is misplaced. People perceive those who seek advice as more competent than those who do not seek advice, and this belief is even stronger when the task is difficult than when it is easy.[5] You can enhance others' opinions about your competence by asking questions and seeking advice from people who know what they are talking about. For one thing, doing so makes that other person feel affirmed. Consequently, when you have a particularly perplexing problem, don't hesitate to discuss it with someone who has dealt with similar situations. There is a good chance they will think more highly of you afterward.

What can you do to take a more expansive view of your present circumstances? One way to open yourself to new information is by taking on multiple perspectives. Researchers have suggested three approaches:[6]

- Take the perspective of someone who frustrates or irritates you and consider what that person might have to teach you.
- Listen to what other people say; that is, listen to learn rather than to change their perspective.
- Seek out people's opinions beyond your comfort zone and people you don't typically talk with.

Asking questions and seeking the advice of others lead naturally to knowledge sharing across an organization. This inquisitiveness also strengthens interpersonal relationships. It is imperative that you listen to the world outside and ask good questions. You never know where a great idea will come from, which means that you need to acquire an attitude of treating every job as an adventure.

Treat Every Experience as an Adventure

Leaders personally seize the initiative, encourage others to do the same, and actively look everywhere for great ideas. But that doesn't mean you must wait to be the club president or the team captain to make things better or change the current environment. When we asked students to tell us who initiated the projects they selected as their personal bests, we assumed that most people would name themselves. Surprisingly, that's not what we found. Someone else initiated more than half the cases. If leaders seize the initiative, then how can we call people leaders when they're assigned the tasks they undertake? Doesn't this contradict all we've said about how leaders behave? No, it does not.

The fact that over half the personal-best cases were not self-initiated should be a relief to anyone who thought they were the ones who had to come up with all the new ideas themselves and start all the change themselves. This should encourage an appreciation that responsibility for new ideas and improvement is *everyone's business*. If the only times people reported doing their best were when they got to choose the projects themselves or when they were the elected head of the group, most leadership opportunities would evaporate—as would most social and organizational changes. The reality is that much of what people do is assigned; few get to start everything from scratch. That's just a fact of being part of a group or organization.

People who become leaders don't always seek the challenges they face. Challenges also seek leaders. Stuff happens on campus, in teams, in communities, and in people's lives. Whether you find the challenges or they find you is not so important. It's the choice you make to address those challenges that matter. Are you prepared to answer the door when opportunity knocks? Are you ready to open the door, go outside, and look for an opportunity?

Be an adventurer, an explorer. Treat every day as if it were your first day "on the job." Approach every new assignment as an opportunity to start over. Concentrate on ways to constantly improve your whole team. Consider the leadership journey that Kyle Harvey experienced one summer during an internship at a high-end reseller of printers. One of his responsibilities was working in the warehouse, helping manage the company's inventory.

Historically, the company had simply counted the products in stock and logged them in a book. However, there were always hundreds of parts left over or unaccounted for because they had been mislabeled or stocked in an unorganized manner. Kyle began to think about other ways he had learned to organize bits of merchandise and equipment. He wondered if there might be something he had learned in school and from his various work experiences that would help make his employer's inventory process more efficient and more accurate.

By thinking about how he would approach designing the inventory system from scratch, Kyle came up with the idea of cataloging the parts by their part number and the product they would eventually go into. It took Kyle and his five coworkers a month to set up the system and reorganize the warehouse. Once installed, the brand-new system gave the technicians quicker access to needed parts, and it helped management keep tighter tabs on the company's property. Had Kyle not treated his internship as an opening to apply his experience with other systems to the inventory-management problem, the company would have stayed stuck in the same old way of doing things, and Kyle would have missed a valuable opportunity to develop his leadership skills.

Student leaders like Kyle are always looking for opportunities to use new ideas. If you're serious about trying new approaches and helping others be adventurous, make finding new ideas a personal priority. Encourage others to open their eyes and ears to the world outside the boundaries they know. Collect suggestions from everyone you can, in your organizations or outside them. Use social media to draw ideas from an even wider field.

Encourage your group to spend some time in meetings thinking about new ways you can do some part of a project, task, or event your group does regularly. If you put on annual events or activities, suspend looking at the notebooks and files from past years and treat an event as if it were the very first time you've ever planned it. If you know groups at other schools or organizations that do similar events, as Logan, Ceena, and Zora did, call them to discuss how they do them. Identify groups on your campus with a great reputation and meet with their leaders to get ideas about how they are organized. Find out if they have had challenges or faced difficult situations similar to yours. Search the internet for ideas and experiences that correspond to what you are addressing in your group. Sometimes new ideas spring from things you accidentally come across that aren't even related to your work. Keep your eyes and ears open, no matter where you are. You can never tell where or when you'll come across the next great idea.

REFLECT AND ACT: SEARCH FOR OPPORTUNITIES

Student leaders who make extraordinary things happen are open to receiving ideas from anyone and anywhere. They are skilled at constantly surveying the landscape in search of new ideas. And because they are proactive, they don't just ride the waves of change; they make the waves that others ride.

You don't have to change history, but you do have to avoid the attitude that "we've always done it this way." You need to be proactive, continually inviting and creating new initiatives, and with a purpose greater than just doing something different. Leaders, by definition, are out in front of change, not behind it, trying to catch up. This means that your focus needs to be less on your group's routine and daily actions and much more on the untested and untried. And when you are searching for opportunities to grow and improve, the most innovative ideas are most often not your own. They're elsewhere, and the best leaders look around them for the unexpected places and people where exceptionally useful new ideas are hiding. Exemplary leadership requires outsight, not just insight. That's where the future is.

Change is an adventure, whether you are trying a new approach or taking on a project that's never been done before. It tests your will and your skill. It's tough, but it's also stimulating. The challenge of change introduces you to yourself. To get the best from yourself and others, you must understand what gives meaning and purpose to your work.

Reflect

The first commitment of Challenge the Process is to *search for opportunities by seizing the initiative and looking outward for innovative ways to improve*. What are the most important ideas or lessons about exemplary leadership that you learned from this chapter?

_____

_____

_____

_____

Here are some actions you can take to solidify your commitment to **Search for Opportunities:**

- Have a mindset of always asking: "What's new? What's next? What's better?"
- Make it a daily exercise to reflect on the question, "How can I do better or differently from what I did yesterday or plan to do today?"

- If there is something that you feel is not working well, try a different approach. If something is bugging you, what can you do about it?
- Determine whether you and your colleagues have routines that no longer serve a purpose or ruts you need to get out of. Do something about these.
- Design tasks and projects so that they are meaningful, which means identifying and clarifying the purpose they serve and not just the fact that it's different.
- Get firsthand experiences outside your comfort zone and skill set. Put yourself in new situations where you can learn.
- Talk with people outside your group; get others around you to do the same. Bring back what everyone learned, share it, and discuss how you can apply this outsight to your assignments and projects.

Act

After you have reflected on what you learned, what you can improve, and the preceding suggestions, record your plan here for taking at least one action that will help you become a better leader:

_____

_____

_____

_____

_____

6

Commitment #6: Experiment and Take Risks

When Yijie (Frank) Huang enrolled as an international graduate student at his Ivy League university, he noticed something strange: the school required international students to register for insurance that cost $4,500 per year—much more expensive than what domestic students paid for insurance. Domestic students could opt out of the university insurance, but it was required for international students—and the school didn't recognize any other insurance options.

However, Frank, who grew up in China but came to America at 15 to attend high school in Maryland, had also spent his undergraduate years at a university in the same state. He knew that the state had a program that offered insurance to international students at a much lower, subsidized—or even free—rate. "I was shocked. I thought it was really unfair," Frank said. His university enrolled over 13,000 international students, and Frank thought it was wrong that they faced a financial burden that domestic students at the same school didn't, especially when cheaper options were available. Attending graduate school abroad is often already an expensive endeavor; Frank didn't think it was fair that international students didn't have the option to spend the same amount as their American peers.

Frank felt that he had to do something. He shared his concerns about the insurance policy with a few other international student friends. His passion inspired his friends, who also felt the policy was unfair. They divvied up researching the fine points of the school's insurance policy and benchmarking the policies of other universities that enrolled a similar number of international students. "We were literally looking at fifty-plus pages of insurance contracts. Then we benchmarked [other school's policies against our own] and proposed constructive comments and changes," Frank said.

When Frank first took his concerns to his Student Health Advisory Committee (which oversaw the insurance policy), he was told no one had an issue with the insurance policy. "I asked them if they had any international students on the Committee, and they stopped responding to my questions," Frank said.

But rather than accept that for an answer, Frank decided to double down and show university leaders that there was student support for change to the policy. First, Frank had to translate the petition and the issue behind it into multiple languages to ensure students understood all of his concerns, then upload it to Google Docs for students to access. "American healthcare is particularly difficult for international students to navigate," Frank said.

Frank also made strategic decisions about finding leaders who might back his petition. He reached out to the President of his institution's Law School Student Body, an international student from India, who signed on immediately. He reached out to the local state assembly person, also an alumnus of Frank's institution, explaining why the proposed policy change mattered. That office wrote to the school in support of his proposed changes. "I think it helped that [there was support] not just in the school, but from outside as well," Frank said. "I learned collective force is more powerful than any one person's individual strength."

Frank's efforts paid off: his petition eventually garnered over 800 signatures supporting changes. However, his challenges weren't over. The Student Health Advisory Committee was now willing to consider Frank's concerns seriously, but there were points of contention that required additional research by Frank and his friends. For example, international students require increased levels of coverage in case of fatalities that require repatriation, among other concerns. Frank spent another month researching before returning to the Committee with an updated proposal.

After a full year of research, petitions, and meetings, Frank's proposed changes to the university's international student insurance policy were approved. Students now have the option to stay with the $4,500 policy—which Frank noted provided excellent coverage and many students utilized—or a cheaper option. For Frank, having the opportunity to promote awareness of alternative healthcare options was a huge victory. "I just thought it wasn't fair that students didn't have the choice. That was our main argument: not everyone wants that level of coverage. You should let international students have the option to choose." Now, after his actions, they do.

To achieve the extraordinary, you must be willing, just like Frank, to do things that have never been done before. Every single personal-best leadership experience case speaks to the need to take risks with bold ideas. You can't achieve anything new or extraordinary by doing things as you've always done them. You need to test unproven strategies. You need to break out of the norms that box you in, venture beyond the limitations you usually place on yourself, try new things, and take chances. "Never be afraid to speak up if you see injustice," Frank told us.

Leaders have to be willing to test bold ideas, take calculated risks, and get others to join them on these adventures in uncertainty. It's one thing to set off alone into the unknown; it's entirely another to get others to follow you into the darkness. The difference between an exemplary leader and an individual risk-taker is that leaders create the conditions where people *want* to join them on the journey.

Leaders, as paradoxical as that might sound, make risk safe. They turn new experiences and experiments into learning opportunities. They place a series of little bets, not all-in wagers where everything can be lost in one move. They don't define boldness as primarily go-for-broke, giant-leap projects. More often than not, they see change as starting small, using pilot or test projects, and gaining momentum. The vision may be grand and distant, but the way to reach it is by putting one foot in front of the other and moving forward. These small, visible steps win early victories and gain early supporters. Of course, when you experiment, not everything works out as intended. There are mistakes and false starts. That's part of the process of innovation. What's critical, therefore, is that leaders promote learning from these experiences.

Exemplary student leaders make the commitment to Experiment and Take Risks. They know that making extraordinary things happen requires that leaders:

- **Generate small wins**
- **Learn from experience**

These essentials help leaders transform challenge into an exploration, uncertainty into a sense of adventure, fear into resolve, and risk into reward. They are the keys to making progress that becomes unstoppable.

GENERATE SMALL WINS

Amanda Itliong's personal-best leadership experience occurred when she became vice president of her college chapter of the National

Society of Collegiate Scholars. This organization was, she said, "one of those honor societies that doesn't often do much except induct students with a certain GPA, collect dues from them, and then induct more people the next year." She and her fellow officers quickly realized that the organization had a lot of money from all those years of collecting dues that hadn't been spent on anything.

"We looked to the mission of our organization for ideas about what we could do with the money," she told us. The Society had been founded on the concept of supporting academic and service excellence, so they started to brainstorm ways they might be able to fulfill that aspiration. They decided that there were not many opportunities for students to showcase their work in the arts and that funding for community arts in their city was scarce. They came up with a plan to hold a student-created fashion and arts showcase called "Diversion" to benefit a nonprofit that taught the arts and entrepreneurship to low-income kids in the area. "Even though we were really excited about the plan," Amanda told us, "we knew it was going to be difficult to get other people on board and involved in the process because our chapter didn't usually do anything, and all of a sudden we were planning a huge event."

Planning a large arts event was a significant risk for the chapter because it would require a lot of approvals, support, and volunteers from their school and the community at large. They decided to break the event down into lots of little pieces. First, they started a forum for people to learn about the event's general idea and contribute their perspectives on the project. They literally drew a picture detailing how they envisioned the auditorium during Diversion and described all the possibilities of what would be there and what it could look like. They then started working with people all over campus to find out how to connect to the interests and values of other groups and individuals they would need for support. Little by little, they got people to say yes, again and again. As Amanda told us:

> The Art Department quickly got on board because we included in our idea a small gallery that was open before the show and during intermission and also gave them space to advertise their academic programs to students. The multicultural groups were excited to showcase their music and dance talents while helping a local good cause at the same time. With input and brainstorms from so many people, we were able to create a really amazing vision.

Amanda said from those early small wins, "We went on to host a sold-out event that was fun for everyone! The arts became very visible through the event, and a local charity received significant funding."

Leaders face situations similar to Amanda's all the time. How do you achieve something no one has ever done before? How do you get something new started? How do you turn around a losing team? Or address a campus-wide problem? How do you work to solve even more significant problems, such as human trafficking or global climate change? Challenges can be so daunting that people can become so overwhelmed that they never even get started.

Build Psychological Hardiness

Problems presented too broadly or expansively can appear unattainable and suffocate people's capacity to conceive of what they can do in the future, let alone right now. Leaders want people to reach for great heights but not be overcome with fear of falling. They want people to feel challenged but not overwhelmed, curious but not lost, and excited but not stressed. For example, Bella Rovere was in her second semester when she was appointed Vice President of Marketing for her sorority, which meant she was in charge of all the social media and PR for her chapter. "I was the youngest person in our chapter, responsible for projecting our chapter's image to every other single person outside of it," Bella said. She worried that her more senior sorority sisters thought she wasn't up to the challenge.

Bella was just starting her new role by asking for help and learning everything she could when a new challenge hit: COVID-19. Suddenly, she was faced with an additional challenge: somehow broadcasting an image of her sorority on social media that would make people eager to join even though no one was on campus, and while staying authentic and sensitive to the realities of the pandemic. "That was when I realized I needed to really step it up and get creative," Bella said.

Bella studied what other sororities were doing to engage their followers and set herself to brainstorming possibilities for her chapter. She eventually came up with the idea to create interactive content by asking her sorority sisters to share videos about the things they were most excited to return to when they could get back to campus. She combed through previous pictures of events to post throwback looks at better times. She posted guides to her college campus to get new students excited about going to college. Bella's social media efforts were so successful that other Greek leaders reached out to her and asked if they could use some of the templates she'd created for their chapters. "They were all surprised it was a first-year student behind it," Bella said.

The following year, even though recruitment for the sorority took place virtually, Bella's sorority retained 99 percent of their pledges—a new record for the sorority.

> It was a foundational leadership experience for me. I was figuring out what kind of leader I wanted to be. For the first time, I really needed guidance and help, and I realized it was okay to ask for it. Once I got past that, things started to click.

The tenacious quality that Frank, Amanda, Bella, and other student leaders display in their personal-best stories is referred to by social psychologists as *psychological hardiness*: the persistence and resilience that move them forward against the tide. The circumstances weren't always as long and drawn out as Frank's experience, but the conditions people faced during their personal-best leadership experiences were filled with significant uncertainties and stressors. Although nearly everyone described their personal-best leadership experience as exciting, 20 percent of student leaders called them frustrating, and about 15 percent said they felt afraid or anxious.

Even though the emotions are positive in the overwhelming majority of personal-best cases, we can't overlook the fact that they were also filled with tension. But instead of being debilitated by the stress of a difficult experience, exemplary student leaders said they were challenged and energized by it. The ability to grow and thrive under stressful, risk-abundant situations highly depends on how you view change.

Bryan Johnson was in charge of a junior lifeguard program at a local pool center. Every year, the program was more and more successful, eventually leading to a long waiting list. The pool supervisors felt there was no way to expand the program, given the limited pool space and the cost of adding another lifeguard as an instructor. Not wanting to see kids turned away, Bryan devised a creative way to increase enrollment. If they split the children into two separate groups, one having swim practice in the morning while the other group was doing exercises poolside, more kids could participate. The two groups would meet for lunch and then switch. This arrangement meant the program could potentially add more children to each group. By adding more children, they could increase their profit and make everyone happy.

Bryan was excited by the possibilities and immediately proposed this idea to his supervisor. He listened but quickly dismissed it, saying there was no way it could be done that summer. Instead of feeling discouraged and worrying about the supervisor's reaction to his idea, Bryan decided to work on a way to convince her of the major benefits of increasing their program's enrollment, and he figured he had a year to change her mind. His first task was to research the costs involved in running the junior lifeguard program and the costs of adding another instructor. He learned about the program's financial structure and considered ways to make his idea feasible. He chose not to view his supervisor's rejection as the end of his vision; instead, he was motivated by the challenge of convincing her that they could turn this idea for an expanded program into reality.

After calculating the costs of adding another instructor and more children to the program, Bryan worked out the additional revenue from the enrollment increase. He assembled all the necessary information and approached his supervisor again. He showed that the increased revenue far exceeded the added costs, proving that the program could expand profitably. Once again, the supervisor rejected his idea, and once again, Bryan didn't stress out. He met the resistance with increased enthusiasm, seeing it as an opportunity to develop more ways to convince the supervisor to expand the program. He decided to engage the rest of the lifeguards in the discussion. He asked each instructor what they thought of the idea, getting their input and support so that when he spoke to the supervisor again, there would be a unified voice of the people dealing with the increased workload. It took almost a year, but Bryan's idea was eventually instituted successfully.

Psychologists have discovered that people like Bryan, who experience a high degree of stress, yet cope with it positively, are psychologically hardy.[1] Whether students, corporate managers, entrepreneurs, nurses, lawyers, or combat soldiers, people with a high degree of psychological hardiness are much more likely to withstand severe challenges and bounce back from failure than those low in hardiness.[2] Hardiness is a quality that can be developed.

Commitment, control, and challenge are the three key factors necessary to build psychological hardiness. Think back to what Frank, Amanda, Bella, and Bryan did when facing their challenges. To turn adversity into an advantage, you must first *commit* yourself to what's happening. You need to become involved, engaged, and curious. As you saw in their stories, you must act; you can't sit back and wait for something to happen. When you commit, you'll find the people and the situations much more meaningful and worthwhile to you. You also have to take *control* of your own life, which Frank, Amanda, Bella, and Bryan eventually decided to do. Do what you can to influence what is going on. Even though it's unlikely that all your attempts will be successful, you can't sink into passivity. Finally, you need to view *challenge* as an opportunity to learn from both negative and positive experiences. You can't play it safe, which was the realization experienced in every student's personal-best leadership case.

Your ability to cope with change and stress depends on your viewpoint. To start that new project and take that first step, you must believe that you can influence the outcome. You must be curious about what is happening and look for ways to learn every step of the way. With a hardy attitude, you can transform stressful events into positive opportunities for growth and renewal. What's more, you can help your team feel the same way.

Break It Down and Accentuate Progress

How do you get people to want to move in a new direction, break old mindsets, or change existing behavior patterns in order to tackle significant problems and attempt extraordinary performance? You take it step-by-step, one bit at a time. Just as Amanda and her colleagues did in transforming Diversions from concept to reality, you make progress incrementally. Exemplary student leaders appreciate that they need to break down large undertakings into small, doable actions. They also know that when initiating something new, they need to try many little things before they get it right. Not every innovation works, and the best way to ensure success is to experiment with many ideas, not just one or two big ones. Exemplary leaders help others see how breaking the journey down into measurable milestones moves them forward and small wins promote continued progress.

A small win is "a concrete, complete, implemented outcome of moderate importance."[3] Small wins form the basis for a consistent pattern of winning that attracts people who want to be part of a successful undertaking. Although planting one tree won't stop climate change, planting one million trees can make a difference, and it's that first tree that gets things started. Small wins identify the place to begin. For Frank, the small win was generating 800 signatures for his petition. Gathering that support made his school's administrators take his concerns more seriously, eventually changing the campus's insurance policy for international graduate students. Small wins can make a project seem doable even when time and budget are limited. They minimize the cost of trying and reduce the risks of failing. What's exciting about this process is that accomplishing a small win sets natural forces in motion that favor progress over setbacks.

Exemplary student leaders help people see how breaking the journey into measurable milestones can move them forward. This is essential as the data shows that the more often students reported that their leaders "make sure that the big projects undertaken are broken down into smaller and doable parts," the more they reported being satisfied with that individual's leadership. As shown in Figure 6.1, those leaders viewed as *very frequently* engaging in this leadership behavior were 50 times more likely to have students indicate that they were satisfied with the leadership of their leader, as compared to students who reported that their leaders *seldom* or even *once in a while* demonstrated this leadership behavior. Relationships between small wins and the extent to which students felt they were making a difference are similar.

Leaders certainly have grand visions for the future. They realize those dreams one step at a time, building the momentum, strength, and resolve to continue the journey. Small wins produce visible results

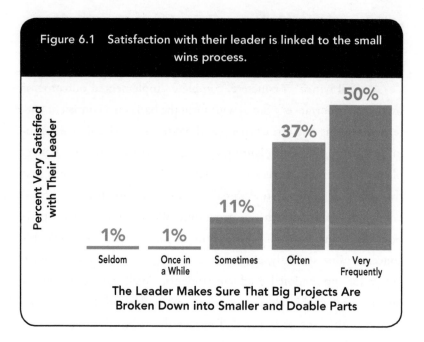

Figure 6.1 Satisfaction with their leader is linked to the small wins process.

that attract people to be connected to a successful group or team. They build people's confidence and reinforce their natural desire to feel successful. A series of small wins, therefore, provides a foundation of stable building blocks. Each win preserves gains and makes it harder to return to preexisting conditions. For example, Sean Dwyer said he heard the word *no* many times when he set out to fundamentally change the way the school's spring dance was traditionally organized:

> Seeing as I had a limited budget and no real respect from my fellow peers in student government as a freshman, I knew I had to work at it. So, I started by getting the vice president of the school to agree to go to lunch. I laid out my plan, and she was very much for it. That was win number one. Then I used her influence to help me get a meeting with the director of student life, which was win number two. I met with the

director, showed her the importance of having a food option at the dance, and a budget, and voilà, win number three.

Upon reflection, Sean realized that the sequence of "small wins was crucial because it allows you to slowly eliminate what is seen as the norms and change things for the better. You have to make the effort to go step-by-step, little by little, to actually get things changed."

Achieving a small win makes people "winners" and subsequently makes it easier for them to want to continue along. If people can see that you are asking them to do something they're quite capable of doing, they feel some assurance that they can succeed at the task. By identifying little ways people can succeed, you create commitment because they see that what they are doing is making a difference. This builds their confidence and creates a positive environment, giving people great reasons to stick around and keep working.

Also, as Sean appreciated from his experience with the spring dance, "You have to be constantly learning from your mistakes. You cannot have one without the other." A common refrain in the personal-best leadership cases was "big things are done by doing lots of small things." When you break a big project down into pieces, you increase the likelihood of making progress by having multiple experiments. Whatever you call your experiments—a practice, dry run, trial mode, demo, rehearsal, pilot project, or test-drive—all are methods of trying numerous little things in the service of something much bigger. These are the tactics that continually generate lots of opportunities for small wins.

LEARN FROM EXPERIENCE

Despite how much you see challenge as an opportunity, how focused you can be, or how driven you are to succeed, there will be setbacks, disappointments, and even failures. Not everything will go exactly as planned. That's what experimentation is all about, and as scientists know very well, there's a lot of trial and error involved in testing new concepts, methods, and practices. People never figure out how to do something new or never done before and get it right the first time—not in the laboratory, the classroom, or the workplace. Yes, it's something that people are told they must do, but it's neither realistic nor useful advice. Some may want and expect you to get it right every time, but when you're doing things you have never tried, doing them perfectly is impossible. When you engage in something new and different, you will make mistakes. Everyone does.

As part of her school's yearbook staff, Kathryn Avila recalled being "confronted firsthand with a major part of challenging processes: failure." At first, she told us, she hated to fail and thought that it meant that all of her hard work was worthless. With time, however, she came to a different realization:

> Just because I failed, or my staff failed, didn't mean that the work we did had no value. If a layout was created that didn't seem to work, it was worth our time to sit down, critique it, and learn what parts of it worked and what parts of it didn't work as well. Failure was just part of our learning process and something that needed to happen for us to grow, create, and learn, as a team and as individuals.

Repeatedly, student leaders in our studies tell us how mistakes and failures have been crucial to their personal and professional success. Without mistakes, they wouldn't know what they can and cannot do (at least at the moment). Without the occasional setback, they say that they would not have been able to achieve their aspirations. It may seem paradoxical, but there is considerable evidence that the overall quality of work improves when people have a chance to fail. This was precisely the lesson from an experiment one ceramics teacher carried out in his classroom.[4]

At the beginning of the semester, the teacher divided the students into two groups. He told the first group they could earn better grades by producing more pots (e.g., thirty for a *B*, forty for an *A*), regardless of the quality. He told the second group that their grades depended solely on the quality of the pots they produced. Not surprisingly, students in the first group got right to it, producing as many pots as possible, while the second group was quite careful and deliberate in how they went about making the best pots. To his surprise, the teacher found that the students who made the most pots—those graded on quantity rather than quality—also made the best ones. It turned out that the practice of making lots of pots naturally resulted in better quality because, for example, these students became more familiar with the intricacies of the kiln and how various firing positions affected the aesthetics of their products.

Failure is never the objective of any endeavor. The objective is to succeed, which will always require some learning. And learning always involves mistakes, errors, miscalculations, and the like along the way. Learning happens when people can openly talk about what went wrong and what went right. Leaders don't look for someone to blame when inevitably mistakes are made in the name of innovation. They ask, "What can we learn from the experience?"

Our research validates the impact of this leadership behavior. From responses about how frequently their leaders "ask what can we learn from this experience when things do not go as expected," the data in Figure 6.2 shows that this behavior is dramatically linked with the extent to which students feel highly productive when working with this leader. The relationship between this leadership behavior and the extent to which students feel proud to tell others they are working with their leader and that they feel their leader values their work mirrors these results.

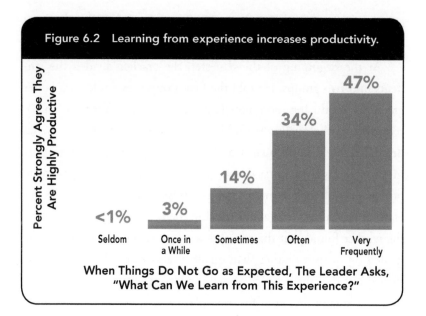

Figure 6.2 Learning from experience increases productivity.

Be an Active Learner

Marie Jones was one of ten representatives from the United States to Insight Dubai. This conference paired sixty young women from around the world with Dubai Women's College students for five days of developing global awareness, intercultural understanding, and leadership skills. The experience was so profound that Marie applied and was chosen to return the following year as a facilitator.

Marie knew from her experience the year before that even though she would be leading a group of sixteen women, eight from Dubai and eight from other countries, she would not be standing in front of them lecturing. Her role was to get her group talking, sharing, and eventually shaping the experience themselves if it was going to be meaningful for each of them. "We all learned so much from each other when I was a participant because we were all actively engaged in the conversations we had," she told us. "I was determined to build that same kind of experience as the facilitator, and the key was active listening and active learning."

Active listening started with Marie herself so that she could understand the women's perspective and experience. "I knew it would take some time to get to know them, so I kept an open-door policy, which led to many late-night talks, but it was worth it," she told us. Marie also knew that each woman brought a unique perspective to the conference based on her personality, background, and life experiences. The key to getting those perspectives into the room, she believed, was to have them actively engaged, drawing on what they knew from their experiences and what they were learning at the conference.

She invited people to form small groups to work on an issue or topic they felt needed attention and discussion. Each group was to come up with a list of concerns and recommendations on ways to address them. Marie told us that she "challenged them all to make sure each voice in their group was heard and to come together as one voice in the end." She also asked the small groups to take time at the end of each session to reflect on what they had learned and their learning process. "The feedback I got was very similar to my own experience as a participant in Insight Dubai. Being fully engaged in your learning helps you understand how you learn. That is so valuable."

Learning is a master skill and is one of the best predictors of future career success.[5] Similarly, our research has found a strong correlation between how engaged a student is in learning and their leadership capability.[6] When you fully engage in learning—when you throw yourself completely into experimenting, reflecting, reading, and getting advice or coaching—you are going to experience the satisfaction of improvement and the taste of success.

More is more when it comes to learning. It's clear that exemplary student leaders approach each new and unfamiliar experience with a willingness to learn, an appreciation of the importance of learning, and the recognition that learning involves making some mistakes.

Building your capacity to be an active learner begins with developing a *growth mindset*. This mindset's foundational belief is that people can learn through their efforts. By contrast, those with a *fixed mindset* believe that people's basic qualities are immutable, carved in stone.[7] Individuals with a growth mindset, for example, believe that people can learn to be better leaders. Those with a fixed mindset think leaders are born and that no amount of training will make you any better than you naturally are.

In study after study, researchers find that when working on simulated business problems, those individuals with fixed mindsets gave up more quickly and performed more poorly than those with growth mindsets.[8] The same is true for students, athletes on the playing field, teachers in the classroom, and partners in relationships.[9] Mindsets, not skill sets, make the critical difference in taking on challenging situations.

You must embrace the challenges you face to develop a growth mindset and nourish it in others. That's where the learning is. When you encounter setbacks—and there will be many—you must persist. You have to realize that your effort, and that of others, is your means of gaining mastery. Neither raw talent nor good fortune leads to becoming the best; hard work is what gets you there. Ask for feedback about how you're doing. Learn from the constructive criticism you get from others. View the success of others around you as inspiration and not as a threat. When you believe that you can continuously learn, you will. Only those who believe that they can get better make the effort to do so.

Create a Climate for Learning

If people are going to grow and thrive, they need to be able to trust one another. They need to feel safe around each other and believe they can be open and honest. They need to support each person's development, have one another's backs, and lift others up when they stumble or fall. They need to be able to collaborate and cheer on everyone. They need to show respect for differences and be open to alternative viewpoints and backgrounds. Studies of top performers strongly demonstrate that people require a supportive environment to become their best. Researchers find that when there are high-quality relationships in a work group—relationships characterized by positive regard for others and a sense of mutuality and trust—people use more behaviors that lead to learning and growth.[10]

As chairperson of the National Society for Black Engineers (NSBE), Matthew Nelson worked with public policymakers, corporate executives, nonprofit organizations, and more than two thousand volunteers to increase the number of engineering degrees granted to black students in the United States. "The leadership philosophy I use within NSBE around culture, trust, and building high-quality connections is the same approach I use with our external partners," he told us. He explained that he began to form that philosophy when he was a college student.

> Leadership doesn't magically appear once you attain a high position. The same philosophy and habits you develop as a student will determine if you get the privilege to lead others as well as your degree of success once you get there. It just so happens that student organizations like NSBE give individuals the opportunity to develop and test their assertions about leadership early in their career.

As an undergraduate NSBE chair at his university, Matthew worked to create a supportive network and learning environment for his board members, believing they would be future leaders in the field of engineering. At the beginning of every semester, Matthew would meet with board members to map out areas of personal development.

Throughout the semester, Matthew helped each person set goals, identify learning opportunities, and track whether or not they felt they were meeting their targets. For example, one individual wanted to improve his skills and confidence in public speaking. "I gave him the opportunity to be the face of NSBE's newly minted partnership with the Biomedical Engineering Society," Matthew said. "That gesture solidified the trust he had in me as a leader and true friend."

Another way that Matthew worked to develop his team was to give them constructive feedback. "I never tell NSBE members that they're not doing a good job," Matthew told us.

> I always ask them if they think they're living up to the example they want to set, and then we have a conversation—a two-way dialogue—about whether or not that's true. I've never had to ask anyone to leave the board. We always have a conversation, and sometimes people concluded on their own that this isn't the right fit for them. But that's because I give them the chance to discuss it first and search their own consciences.

You can't create a climate for learning instantly. "People have learned to trust that I have their best interests in mind," Matthew said.

Appreciate that you won't always get it right the first time you try something and that learning new things can often be intimidating. No one wants to embarrass themselves or look incompetent in front of their peers. To create a climate for learning, you have to make it safe for others to try, fail, and learn from their experiences. As often as possible, make it a habit to ask, "What can we learn?" from each project experience. Build on people's experiences so that mistakes are not repeated but are learned from.

It's a fact of life that failures and disappointments cannot be avoided entirely. It's how you handle them that will ultimately determine your eventual effectiveness and success. You need to be honest with yourself and with others. You need to own up to your mistakes and reflect on your experiences to gain the learning necessary to be better the next time. This is true for you and true for the members of your team.

Strengthen Resilience and Grit

It takes determination and strength to deal with the adversities of life and leadership. Don't let the setbacks get you down or allow the roadblocks to get in your way. Don't become overly discouraged when things don't go according to plan. You can't give up when resistance builds or people criticize your ideas. Nor can you let other tempting new projects divert your attention. You can't lose focus or move on too quickly. You have to stick with it. You must never give up. Neither Frank's nor Bryan's successes would have happened if they had allowed their frustration to shut them down. In both situations, resistance from others spurred them on to do what was needed: to build the teams necessary to make their programs come about.

The ability to recover quickly from setbacks and continue to pursue a vision of the future is often referred to as *resilience*. Others have called it *grit*. *Grit* is defined as "perseverance and passion for long-term goals," and it "entails working strenuously toward challenges, maintaining effort and interest over the years despite failure, adversity, and plateaus in progress."[11] Showing grit involves setting goals, being obsessed with an idea or project, maintaining focus, sticking with things that take a long time to complete, overcoming setbacks, and the like. Empirical studies, whether with students, cadets in the military, working professionals, artists, teachers, and others, document convincingly that people with the most grit are the ones most likely to achieve positive outcomes. The more grit you demonstrate, the better you do.

Like a growth mindset, resilience and grit can be developed and strengthened. People with resilience bounce back, and those with grit don't give up. They interpret setbacks as temporary, local, and change-able.[12] Essentially, resilient people, even in times of considerable stress and adversity, remain committed to moving forward by believing that what has happened isn't going to be permanent and that they can do something about the outcome the next time. As every basketball player knows, 100 percent of the shots *not* taken don't go in. So you'd better keep shooting if you want to make a basket.

When a failure or setback occurs, don't become obsessed with blaming yourself or the people working on the project. Emphasize that the failure or setback is a problem in this instance and not in every case. Even in times of high stress and extreme adversity, resilient people remain committed to moving forward by believing that what has happened isn't permanent and that they can do something about the outcome.

Breed a growth mindset when reaching milestones and achieving success by attributing these to the hard work and effort of the people on your team. Convey a belief that many more victories are at hand and be optimistic that good fortune will come eventually and be with your team for a long time. You can bolster resilience further by assigning people tasks that are challenging but within their capabilities, focusing on rewards rather than punishments, and encouraging people to see change as full of possibilities.[13]

The Personal-Best Leadership Experience cases all involved change and stressful events in the lives of student leaders, and nearly everyone described the experience in terms consistent with the conditions for psychological hardiness, resilience, and grit. They experienced commitment rather than alienation, control rather than powerlessness, and challenge rather than threat. They had passion. They persevered. They didn't give up despite the failures and setbacks. They showed that, even in the toughest of times, people could experience meaningfulness and mastery. They could overcome great odds, make progress, and change the way things were.

REFLECT AND ACT: EXPERIMENT AND TAKE RISKS

Change is the work of leaders. They are always looking for ways to get it done *better*—continuously improving, innovating, and growing. They know that sticking to how things are done today won't get people to the better tomorrow they envision. So they experiment. They tinker. They shake things up. They ask, "What can we change to make things better?"

Exemplary student leaders view change as a challenge that can be successfully met. They believe—and get others to believe—that everyone can influence outcomes and control their own lives. They make sure that the meaning and purpose of change are clearly understood, and they create a strong commitment to the mission.

To get things moving in the right direction, you need to break tasks down into small wins, setting short-term goals or milestones. Take it one step at a time. Create an environment that encourages learning. People need to know that they won't be punished for failure when they experiment and take risks. Instead, it will be treated as a learning experience.

You need to create a learning climate where everyone is encouraged to share successes and failures, and continuous improvement is viewed as a routine way of doing things. Exemplary student leaders make it a practice to create a climate in which others feel strong and proficient, capable of flourishing even under the most adverse circumstances.

Reflect

The second commitment in the leadership practice of Challenge the Process requires leaders to *experiment and take risks by consistently generating small wins and learning from experience.* What are the most important ideas or lessons about exemplary leadership that you learned from this chapter?

_____

_____

_____

_____

Here are some actions you can take to follow through on your commitment to **Experiment and Take Risks:**

- Keep people focused on the tasks or work they all do together and what they can control in their lives, not what they can't.
- Ask yourself what's holding you and your team back and whether there are any obstacles you are putting in the way.
- Emphasize how personal fulfillment results from consistently challenging yourself to improve. How can you use that to motivate yourself and others?
- Break big projects down into achievable steps. What are some of the "little things" in a project that people can do and succeed at and consequently see the difference those make in the bigger picture?
- Remind people of the progress they are making every day, how setbacks are temporary, and the opportunities available for learning.
- Continuously experiment with new ideas. Test them out in a way that will build people's confidence, marking both progress and learning.

- Discuss and reflect on successes and failures; record the lessons learned and make sure that they can be applied in subsequent initiatives.

Act

After you have reflected on what you learned, what you can improve, and the preceding suggestions, record your plan here for taking at least one action that will help you become a better leader:

_____

_____

_____

_____

_____

ENABLE
OTHERS TO
ACT

Leaders know they can't do it alone. They need partners to make extraordinary things happen. Exemplary leaders invest in creating trustworthy relationships, and building spirited and cohesive teams. They make others feel strong, capable, and confident to take initiative and responsibility. Exemplary leaders build the skills and abilities of their constituents to deliver on commitments. They create a climate where people feel in control of their own lives.

In the next two chapters, we explore how student leaders:

➤ **Foster Collaboration** by building trust and facilitating relationships.
➤ **Strengthen Others** by increasing self-determination and developing competence.

ENABLE OTHERS TO ACT
Reflections from the *Student Leadership Practices Inventory*

1. My overall score from the *Student Leadership Practices Inventory* for Enable Others to Act was:

   _____

2. Of the six leadership behaviors that are part of Enable Others to Act, the statement that I indicated engaging in most frequently was:

   _____

   _____

3. The leadership behavior statement that I engaged in the least often was:

   _____

   _____

   Based on your self-assessment with the leadership practice of Enable Others to Act, complete the following two statements. As you read and review the next two chapters, keep in mind these reflections and observations.

4. Of the leadership behaviors associated with Enable Others to Act, the one(s) I feel most comfortable engaging in is/are:

   _____

   _____

   _____

5. The leadership behaviors that I feel I could engage in more often and be more comfortable with doing are:

   _____

   _____

   _____

7

Commitment #7: Foster Collaboration

Soon after Attiya Latif became the chair of the Minority Rights Coalition (MRC) at her university, there was a spate of hate crimes on campus, including spray-painted hate speech and swastikas. For Attiya, the trouble hit home when a racial slur was spray-painted across the door of her passkey-protected, on-campus apartment. It was time to act, she said.

Attiya mobilized the MRC to reach out to other student organizations to create a campaign in response to on-campus hate crimes. Called Eliminate the Hate, the program was envisioned as a way to curb these crimes and provide a united front of peace and tolerance. She brought together members of the MRC, Black Student Lives Matter, Latina Student Alliance, and seven other minority student organizations to figure out what to do. While everyone knew that something had to be done, there was no clear vision of what needed to happen. Each group came with different priorities and solutions for the best way to make a stand against hate crimes. Some students wanted to put together something to launch the next day. Attiya and others figured that to make the most impact, the coalition would have to formulate a longer-range plan.

Attiya wanted to ensure that as many visions and voices as possible were heard and considered. She explained:

> I knew that having an immediate reaction to the hate crimes was important, but I also knew that we needed time to plan something that would gain momentum. Our team was split on how things should be handled, but we came up with a solution that honored everyone's ideas.

By creating a forum in which all the students' concerns would be heard and understood, Attiya encouraged an open exchange of ideas and knowledge, and built a sense of trust among the ten groups with sometimes competing interests. Her approach eventually led to a greater vision for the Eliminate the Hate campaign than the MRC initially had. "I didn't allow my personal opinions to overshadow what other people wanted," Attiya told us.

> There are ten different organizations, all with different needs and priorities, and it's my job to facilitate a conversation that makes sure that we all come to a consensus about what's important. It's essential to be a facilitator and guide people to a mutual decision. If you're not doing that, then you're not leading anyone. You're just doing what you want to do.

Ultimately, the group decided on a combined approach of a quick social media response and a longer, more strategic person-to-person campaign for the school. They would put together an immediate statement proclaiming their mission and what they stood for, which they would post on their social media profiles at noon the next day.

Each organization reached out to other organizations on campus and in the community. By noon the next day, when the statement went viral, one hundred different organizations had posted the statement online in a show of solidarity. At the same time, all ten organizations collaborated to create a single new Facebook page on which the statement would live. On the first day, the Facebook page generated one thousand new likes. By that evening, the page had had thirty thousand views.

"I knew then we had the momentum for our weeklong in-person project," Attiya said. She capitalized on that momentum by forming a committee to organize events for each day of the weeklong campaign. Attiya also created an online forum where everyone involved in the campaign could propose ideas. At the end of a day of planning, the top eight ideas, chosen by everyone on the committee, were each given a day for the Eliminate the Hate campaign.

Each day of the campaign featured a different event on campus, open to participation by anyone and live-streamed on Facebook. The week's first event generated over four hundred thousand views on Facebook. By week's end, the live stream captured close to a million audience members. Attiya attributes this success to the way the group's members had generated a spirit of cooperation. "Everyone felt ownership of the campaign because everyone felt like their ideas could be heard," Attiya said.

The final event of the Eliminate the Hate campaign broke down the walls between the different MRC organizations. Attiya and a planning committee organized a diversity town hall in the university's multipurpose center, where each minority group on campus had its own room for gathering and discussion. In these conversations, professional experts spoke on different topics, and anyone could offer ideas on solutions for diversity-related issues, such as on-campus housing, orientation needs, and transgender bathrooms.

The Eliminate the Hate campaign significantly raised student awareness of diversity issues. "Since the campaign, we have seen less hate crime and increased awareness on campus," Attiya told us.

Moreover, there has been "a cultural shift of how students feel owner-ship over the university space." She explained:

> When we were organizing the campaign, we purposefully
> made it a campaign that anyone could take and feel owner-
> ship of. In the past, students were very apathetic about
> these issues because they didn't feel like it was about them.
> We wanted to make sure everyone knew that this campaign
> was for all students on campus, and I think that started with
> getting so many other organizations involved.

Eliminate the Hate was a bigger success than Attiya and the other members of the MRC had ever imagined. Attiya believes it's because she worked hard to bring together all the minority student organiza-tions on campus. She showed a willingness to incorporate their con-cerns and needs into the MRC's plans. She proved she listened to other people's ideas and handed over the reins of leadership, resulting in a more significant, more inclusive project than if she'd only organized it herself. When you create a climate of cooperation and trust, as Attiya and her team did among the school's minority organizations, you cre-ate an environment that allows people to contribute and innovate freely. You nurture open exchanges of ideas and honest discussions of issues. You motivate people to go beyond compliance and inspire them to reach for the best in themselves. And you nurture the belief that people can rely on you to do what's in everyone's best interests.

Attiya's experience illustrates something that all exemplary leaders know: leadership is not a solo pursuit. It's a team effort. When talking about personal bests and leaders they admire, people speak passionately about teamwork and cooperation as the interpersonal route to success, especially when conditions are extremely challenging and urgent. Lead-ers of all ages, from all professions and economic sectors around the globe, consistently acknowledge that "you can't do it alone."

Exemplary leaders understand that to create a climate of collabo-ration, they must determine what the group needs to do its work and build the team around a common purpose and with mutual respect. Leaders make trust and teamwork high priorities.

Extraordinary performance is only possible if a strong sense of shared creation and responsibility exists. Exemplary leaders make the commitment to Foster Collaboration by engaging in these essentials:

- **Create a climate of trust**
- **Facilitate relationships**

Collaboration is always an indispensable element for success in any extraordinary endeavor. Regardless of age, leaders must find a way to invite and encourage collaboration and teamwork. They must be trustworthy and build relationships with others and between people based on mutual trust and respect.

CREATE A CLIMATE OF TRUST

Trust is the central issue in human relationships. Without trust, you can't lead. Without trust, you can't accomplish extraordinary things. Individuals who cannot trust others fail to become leaders precisely because they can't bear to be dependent on the words and works of others. They end up doing all the work themselves or supervising it so closely that they become micromanagers. Their lack of trust in people results in others' lacking of trust in them. Trust must be reciprocal and reciprocated for you and your group to build and sustain social connections. Trust is not just what's in your head; it's also what's in your heart.

"The achievement of dreams and ambitions is rarely the product of contributions from a single person," says Stephanie Sorg, who went on to tell us:

> Exemplary leaders enlist the help of others and build a team
> to embark upon the path that achieves mutual success.

However, people can only apply themselves to the greatest extent when mutual trust between themselves and the leader is evident.

As captain of her club soccer team in high school, Stephanie admitted that she had not deeply understood the importance of trust. Then, she said, "I had the pleasure of playing college soccer under the leadership of one of the most inspiring individuals I've ever met." That individual was Dani Weatherholt, who now plays professional soccer. Dani was elected to be one of the team's captains, Stephanie says, "because she exhibited the qualities that would bring out the best in each player. The secret ingredient in her recipe for success was trust. Her initial mission as a leader was to let others know what she stood for, communicate her values and goals, and disclose information about herself." For example, one evening early in the preseason, the team took some time to open up and share something about themselves that others would not typically know. Dani was the first to put herself in a vulnerable place and share an aspect of her life with which she was uncomfortable. With each person who shared something about herself, Dani made it clear through her words and actions that she fully supported and appreciated the player for having the bravery and trust to disclose those secrets. "After having that experience with her," Stephanie said:

I felt a greater sense of trust between the two of us, as well as with the rest of the group. It takes a lot of courage to open yourself up to others, making yourself vulnerable, and through the initiatives that Dani took, I learned that the benefits of taking the necessary steps to build trust significantly outweigh the risks and reservations.

With a greater sense of belonging and mutual trust, Stephanie felt that she worked harder on the field and was significantly more invested in the team's goal. "The bottom line," she said, "was that I possessed a greater sense of commitment to both the environment and the people involved."

When trust is the norm, people make decisions and experiment quickly and effortlessly. A climate of trust creates an environment that enables people to contribute freely and innovate. You nurture an open exchange of ideas and an honest discussion of issues. You motivate people to go beyond compliance and inspire them to reach for the best in themselves. You foster the belief that people can rely on you to do what's in everyone's best interests and that you've got their backs. To get these kinds of results, you must ante up first by listening and learning from others, and sharing information and resources with others. Trust comes first; following comes second.

Be the First to Trust

Samantha Malone spent much of her time outside the classroom working with a free SAT prep class for minority students. She understood that building trust is a process that begins when someone (either you or the other party) is willing to risk being the first to open up, being the first to show vulnerability, and being the first to let go of control. She explained:

> If you want your team to trust you, you need to give a little to get anything back, meaning you should trust them before you expect them to trust you. This practice sets reciprocity standards for the group, showing that trust is expected and allowing trust between members to spread as they work toward their collective goal.

Generally, in building a trusting relationship you, the leader, go first, demonstrating your trust in others before asking them to trust you. Going first is a scary proposition. You're taking a chance. When Dani went first, she bet others wouldn't betray her confidence. You're risking that others won't take advantage of you and that you can rely on them to do what's right. This requires considerable self-confidence, but the payoff is enormous because trust is contagious. When you trust others, they are much more likely to trust you. When you choose not to trust, distrust is equally contagious, spreading this virus across the team. It's up to you to set the example and be willing to overcome the need to hide all your vulnerabilities.

When Jordan Goff started working with his classmates on a project, he quickly had to develop the confidence that he could trust his colleagues. As many students know, working on class projects as a group can be stressful, frustrating, and challenging because of individuals' varying commitment levels. Jordan felt he couldn't do the project alone and needed his classmates to complete the task successfully. Even so, he was concerned that they wouldn't meet his expectations.

True enough, Jordan was eventually overwhelmed by the work required, and he decided to take a chance on his classmate Stan and ask him to take over an important piece of the project. Stan did not disappoint Jordan, turning in great-quality work ahead of schedule. That's when it dawned on Jordan that he needed to give up control and create an atmosphere where people could count on others to meet their responsibilities. As Jordan began to trust others with carrying out essential details of the project—considering their individual skills, abilities, needs, and interests—their trust in him grew. By going first and showing that he trusted Stan to succeed, Jordan demonstrated to his classmates that he was confident they could learn from and support one another.

As Dani demonstrated with Stephanie and their soccer teammates, self-disclosure is another way to go first. Letting others know what you stand for, what you value, what you want, what you hope for, and what you're willing (and not willing) to do reveals information about yourself. You can't be sure other people will appreciate your candor, agree with your aspirations, or interpret your words and actions as you intend. But once you take the risk of being open, others are more likely to take a similar risk and be willing to work toward mutual understanding.

Trust is built in many ways, but it can't be forced. If someone refuses to understand you, viewing you as neither well-intentioned nor competent, there may be little you can do to change their perceptions and behavior. However, keep in mind that placing trust in others is the safer bet most of the time. Trust begets trust. It's a reciprocal process. When you are first to trust, others are likelier to trust you.

Show Concern for Others

Showing your genuine concern for others is one of the most unambiguous signals of your trustworthiness. When people know you will put their interests ahead of yours, they won't hesitate to trust you.[1] However, they need to see this in your actions. When you listen to others, pay attention to their ideas and concerns, and are open to their influence, people will be more open to yours.

Fifteen campus fraternity presidents reported to Brock Davenport as Interfraternity Council (IFC) president at his large university in the south. Brock was on a mission to improve the reputation of all Greek life on campus. "We'd been through a lot of challenges. We'd deservedly had a lot of bad press," Brock said.

One initiative was to get the fraternities to clean up after tailgating parties during football season. One chapter was "experiencing challenges at cleaning up," Brock said. He reached out to that chapter's president, sitting down with him one-on-one, and asked what he could do to help. "This guy had a good head on his shoulders, but unfortunately, he was out in the ocean, trying to row the boat single-handedly." That chapter president also frequently had to work on game days, so he couldn't personally spearhead the cleanup efforts for his fraternity.

Typically, the IFC would send a disciplinary letter to the fraternity in this situation. But Brock knew, based on his interactions with the chapter president, that this probably would not impact the rest of the chapter's actions and might make the president look bad to his members. "He was already the one person interested in and trying to do the right thing," Brock said.

Brock needed to think outside of the typical actions of an IC president. He and a few other IFC council members choose to take the lead in demonstrating the importance of cleanup on game days by coming over and assisting with the chapter's efforts. They sought to learn why this was so difficult and listened to what could be done to make this easier. These actions by Brock and his colleagues showed they cared not only about the cleanup idea, but also about helping those in this chapter do their part. Brock admitted, "They still weren't wonderful at cleaning up, but they definitely got better over the course of the season."

The simple act of listening to what other people have to say and appreciating their unique points of view demonstrates respect for them and their ideas and earns their trust. Being sensitive to what others are going through creates a bond that makes people more receptive to another's guidance and advice. Empathy increases trust. Brock's decision to put aside his own interests—partying with his friends on game day—in service of setting an example was a crystal-clear expression of his values, demonstrating that he could be trusted and how he had placed his trust in his fellow fraternity brothers.

Leaders demonstrate how powerful both listening and empathy can be in building trust. See the world through the eyes of others, and make sure you consider alternative viewpoints. Those following you must feel they can talk freely about their difficulties. They need to believe that you'll be caring and constructive in your responses before they will share their ideas, their frustrations, and their dreams with you. They won't do that if they don't feel you are being open with them in return.

More than three out of every four students in the top quartile of engagement reported that their leaders were those who *most frequently* were seen as "actively listening to diverse points of view." There was an astounding gap in this regard, as shown in Figure 7.1, with less than one out of a hundred students feeling most engaged when reporting that their leader failed (*seldom* or *once in a while*) to listen to diverse viewpoints. Not surprisingly, the data also showed that nearly two-thirds of students assessed the leadership skills of their leader as *well developed* for those seen as actively listening *very frequently* versus less than 1 percent of those leaders seen as *seldom* or only *once in a while* listening to diverse viewpoints.

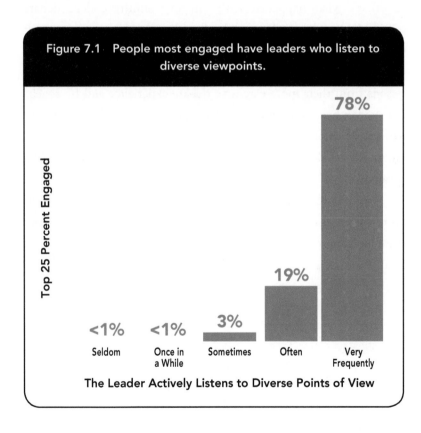

Figure 7.1   People most engaged have leaders who listen to diverse viewpoints.

Share Knowledge and Information

Competence is a vital component of trust and confidence in a leader. As our studies have demonstrated, people want to believe that their leaders know what they're talking about and what they're doing. One way to demonstrate your competence is to share what you know and encourage others to do the same. You can convey your insights and know-how, share lessons learned from experience, and connect team members to valuable resources and people. Student leaders who are knowledge builders set an example for how team members should behave toward each other. As a result, team members' trust in one another and the leader increases, along with their performance.[2]

That's what happened with Gregory Smith's college debate team. Membership had grown so fast that there were not enough coaches to help all the students adequately prepare and compete. Greg and another senior on the team stepped in to assist by sharing lessons from their more extensive debate experience and by coaching the younger competitors. "I led practice every Thursday night, working with anyone who wanted to improve their performance," Greg told us. He also began teaching an undergraduate-level public speaking class.

Greg saw the coaching and teaching as a one-way transfer of his knowledge and skills to the debate team and as a matter of "building communication bridges" within the team. He told us:

> One of the greatest needs I filled on my team was being a sounding board for teammates—whether critiquing an event or just listening and encouraging teammates with their problems because even nonspeech difficulties can distract them from their best performance or infect the team when ignored.

Greg noted that he "was certainly not alone in seeing and acting on this need for the team." Others followed his lead, and team members started opening up with one another and sharing information and insights about what they were learning from their practice and tournament experiences. All this, combined with the team's already high motivation and "willingness to work together," Greg said, "catapulted us from being a mediocre debate team into being one of the best in the country."

Student leaders like Greg know that trust among team members goes up when knowledge and experiences are shared. The fact that performance increases as a result underscores how important it is for leaders to stay focused on the needs of their team. If you show a willingness to trust others with information, they will be more inclined to overcome any doubts about sharing information. However, if you display a reluctance to trust—or if you're overly concerned about protecting your turf and keeping things to yourself—you'll dampen their trust and their performance. And trust, once lost, is very difficult to regain.

FACILITATE RELATIONSHIPS

The importance of relationships is underscored by Samantha Malone's takeaway advice from her personal-best leadership experience: "I would tell them to understand that the experience is not all about you—it is about your followers. Take each person's thoughts into consideration; go out of your way to ask what they think. You cannot lead a team, without a team to lead."

Samantha's lesson was a common refrain. As we noted previously, "You can't do it alone" is the leader's mantra. You can't be much of a leader if no one wants to follow you. What defines leaders, quite simply, is that they have followers. And what makes people willing to follow is, paradoxically, that leaders turn their followers into leaders. Leaders focus first on the best interests of others, which is the foundation of any caring relationship.

Leadership is a relationship that must be nurtured and treasured. When leaders can get the people on their team, in their class, or in their community to trust one another, relationships are strengthened, facilitating the ability of everyone to work together for the collective good. When this happens, asking for help and sharing information comes naturally, and working toward a common goal becomes the norm.

Kerrin McCarthey was a sophomore when she got involved in a peer advisory board for the college's first-generation student mentoring program. She was responsible for helping guide the program and the other mentors who worked with a small group of students throughout the year. The previous boards' practice had been to have all the students attend a retreat to kick off the program and sequentially meet with their mentors regularly to talk about all sorts of things related to the college experience and how to be academically successful. Kerrin noticed that after a few months, students seemed less excited and involved than they had been right after the retreat. She felt that this had a great deal to do with the fact that neither the mentors nor the students they served had developed solid relationships. There was a general lack of trust in the mentoring process and even in the value and worthiness of the program itself.

Kerrin talked with her fellow board members to get their perceptions, and then she started consulting the mentors. "It was very awkward at first to talk with others and get them to open up about what they were feeling and thinking," she told us. "I realized that maybe we hadn't developed much trust yet so that everyone could feel comfortable sharing their thoughts." In her conversations with the board members and the mentors, Kerrin first communicated that she "felt honored to have their trust" and would do whatever it took to help them believe in her and the program.

She often went first in sharing some of her personal experiences, both when she was mentored and when she served as a mentor, thinking that this would help others feel more relaxed in sharing what was on their minds. She felt that if they believed she wouldn't be judgmental or critical, they might open up and talk about what was on their minds. She asked probing questions about their experiences, what they thought the program needed, and how the mentors could better help and work with their mentees. They also talked about what might be keeping other students from getting more involved.

The result of Kerrin's probing seemed to come down to the core issue that folks hadn't taken the time to develop genuine relationships with one another. After the sense of camaraderie from the kickoff retreat wore off, the mentees didn't care about much else because they didn't see their mentors caring. Kerrin continued seeking out stories and ideas of what would help the students and their mentors realize what they wanted from the program and began getting everyone more personally involved in regular gatherings. As a result, the mentors grew more committed to the program because they wanted to be a part of it and make a meaningful difference rather than just going through the motions. Seeing the mentors' newfound dedication, the students grew more enthusiastic and gained more value from the mentoring experience. Soon they became advocates for the program, encouraging their friends and other students to participate.

Leaders like Kerrin understand that facilitating relationships is how leaders build a climate of trust. To collaborate, people must be able to rely on one another. They must appreciate that they need each other to be the most successful. To create an environment where people know they can count on each other, student leaders need to develop cooperative goals and roles, support norms of reciprocity, structure projects to promote joint efforts, and encourage face-to-face interactions. All these practices played a big part in the turnaround of the peer mentoring program.

Develop Cooperative Goals and Roles

For a group of people to have a positive experience, they must have shared goals and a clear reason for being together. Otherwise, why not just let one person do all the work? Have you had a group assignment that caused you to think to yourself, "Holy cow, I could do this whole project by myself and be better off. This is taking forever and going nowhere." That was precisely Tommy Baldacci's thinking when he was assigned to work with two classmates on a yearlong civil engineering senior design project. It didn't take too long for Tommy to find himself not seeing eye-to-eye with one of his colleagues and saying to himself, "I will *never* work with this person again!" Then, he told us, he realized that he still had to work with this person for another six months, and "something needed to change."

> I could not wait for him to change; I had to be the one to adjust. It took every bit of me to swallow my pride and admit that I needed him to succeed on this project. I looked at the aspects of each of my group members and considered what each member did best. By laying out each of our strengths, I made it apparent to the group that we each were a crucial part of the project.
>
> The culture of fighting for who was going to make the decisions was gone. We each saw our roles and worked together toward a common goal. There were many times when the hours were long and adversity was met, but by feeling that we were all in it together, we were able to stay grinding. We ended up finishing first in our section and celebrated this achievement together as a team.

This experience, as Tommy realized, taught him that working toward a common goal is the easiest way to create a collaborative culture, and that trusting others to do what they said they would do is an essential part of the process. "It's that trust which empowers each individual to perform at the best of their abilities," Tommy said. "The energy and power that each member of a group feels from each other are the synergistic strengths of a collaborative culture."

The most important ingredient in every collective achievement is a common goal. Common purpose binds people into cooperative efforts. It creates a sense of interdependence, a condition in which all participants know they can succeed only if everyone else succeeds, or at least they can only be very successful if they coordinate their efforts. Without a sense that "we're all in this together"—that the success of one depends on the success of all—it's virtually impossible to create the conditions for positive teamwork. If you want individuals or groups to work cooperatively, you have to give them a good reason to do so, such as a goal that can only be accomplished by working together.

Keeping individuals focused on a common goal promotes a stronger sense of teamwork than emphasizing individual objectives. For cooperation to succeed, determine how to design roles and responsibilities so that every person's contributions are both additive and cumulative to the outcome. Individuals must clearly understand that the team fails unless they contribute whatever they can. For two people in a fishing boat, one can't say to the other, "Your side of the boat is sinking, but my side looks just fine."

Fostering collaborative goals and roles means ensuring there aren't any in-groups or out-groups, any "us versus them" rivalry, or competition for attention among members. People must identify with the group they are part of to work together. Schools create identity with mascots, uniform colors, unique gestures, and songs. Fraternities and sororities do it with Greek letters, handshakes, special symbols, ceremonies, and rituals. Project teams do it with unique names for product versions, insider jokes, swag, badges, and the like. Make sure you get everyone feeling that they are part of one team. It multiplies the strength of their feeling that it's "all for one and one for all."

Support Norms of Reciprocity

In any effective long-term relationship, there must be a sense of reciprocity. If one party always gives and the other always takes, the one who gives will feel taken advantage of, and the one who takes will feel superior. When this happens, cooperation is virtually impossible. The power of reciprocity has been well-documented in a series of studies involving the Prisoner's Dilemma paradigm.[3] The dilemma is this: two parties (individuals or groups) are confronted with a series of situations in which they must decide whether to cooperate. They don't know in advance what the other party will do.

There are two basic strategies: cooperate or compete. Each party must select without knowing what the other party will do. The maximum individual payoff comes when one player competes and the other party cooperates. In this "I win, but you lose" approach, one party gains at the other's expense. Should both parties choose not to cooperate and attempt to maximize their respective payoffs, they both lose. If both parties decide to cooperate, both win, though the individual payoff for a cooperative move is less than for a competitive one.

Scientists worldwide submitted their proposals for winning in a computer simulation of this test of win-win versus win-lose strategies. "Amazingly enough, the winner was the simplest of all strategies submitted: cooperate on the first move and then do whatever the other player did on the previous move. This strategy succeeded by eliciting cooperation from others, not by defeating them."[4] Simply put, people who reciprocate are more likely to be successful than those who try to maximize individual advantage. Cooperation wins over selfishness in the long run.

The dilemmas this strategy can successfully solve are not restricted to theoretical research. Similar predicaments arise every day: "What price might I pay if I try to maximize my personal gain?" "Should I give up a little for the sake of others?" "Will they take advantage of me if I'm cooperative?" Reciprocity turns out to be the most successful approach for such daily decisions because it shows both a willingness to be cooperative and an unwillingness to be taken advantage of. As a long-term strategy, reciprocity minimizes the risk of escalation: If people know you'll respond in kind, why would they start trouble? If people know that you'll reciprocate, they know that the best way to deal with you is to cooperate and become beneficiaries of your cooperation.

Reciprocity leads to predictability and stability in relationships—in other words, trust. It's less stressful to work with others when you understand how they will behave in response. Treat others as you'd like them to treat you, and they'll likely repay you many times over. Once you help others succeed, acknowledge their accomplishments, and let them shine, they'll never forget it. The norms of reciprocity come into play, and people are more than willing to return the favor and do what they can to make you successful. Whether the rewards of cooperation are tangible or intangible, when people understand that they will be better off by cooperating, they're inclined to recognize the legitimacy of others' interests in an effort to promote their own welfare.

Structure Projects to Promote Joint Efforts

Cooperative behaviors are most likely when the payoffs for working together are greater than those associated with working alone. Many people who grow up in countries that emphasize individualistic or competitive achievement have the perception that they'll do better if each person is rewarded based solely on their individual accomplishments, but they are wrong. In a world trying to do more with less, competitive strategies lose to strategies promoting collaboration.[5]

The motivation for working diligently on one's job while keeping in mind the overall common objective is reinforced when the team's outcome—not simply individual effort—gets rewarded. While each individual within the group has a distinct role, on world-class teams, everyone knows they are unlikely to achieve the best outcomes if they only do their separate parts well.

Cooperative behavior is fostered when people understand that by working together they can accomplish something that no one can achieve individually. You wouldn't necessarily think of fencing as a team sport, but that's what college senior and nationally ranked fencing champion Zachary Chien told us the students he coaches realized from how they organized their practice sessions. "My first and probably most difficult challenge as a coach," explained Zach, "was creating an environment that fostered collaboration amongst all my students. Even though everyone represents the same club, at the end of the day, fencing is an individual sport, so athletes often prioritized their own development."

Although he had personally developed cooperative, respectful, and growth-oriented relationships with all his students, most didn't have that type of relationship with each other. They were quite competitive and didn't socialize and bond as much as other athletes in traditional team sports. To rectify this, Zach created skill games and drills requiring teamwork and cooperation to succeed. For example, students fenced each other, and after each touch, whoever scored told their partner exactly how they set up their point; their partner described what was happening, why it was happening, and how to correct it. These activities brought new energy to practice, and they started fixing each other's form and sharing personal strategies and tactics to help those who were struggling, Zach told us.

Once athletes began showing more support toward one another, I was able to get them to buy in to the larger idea that fostering collaboration and sharing growth is in everyone's best interest. I told my athletes that they couldn't get to the top on their own, and I alone couldn't help get them there. They needed the support from the people they practice with. In order to be the best, you have to beat the best.

That being said, it's incredibly helpful if the people you train with are the best. When your toughest competition is the people you practice with five days a week, tournaments become so much easier. This lesson was understood quickly, and after a few weeks, we created an environment of respect and communal support. Having these types of relationships allows people to compete freely and without worry, which over the last eighteen months resulted in at least one podium finish for all twenty-five of my students.

Joint efforts reinforce the importance of working collaboratively and helping one another. Figuring out how to take as much as possible from others, while contributing as little as possible, has the opposite effect. Make sure that the long-term benefits of joint efforts are greater than the short-term benefits of working alone or competing against others.

Support Face-to-Face and Durable Interactions

While virtual and digital interactions are plentiful, positive face-to-face interactions and durable interpersonal relationships are vital to building collaborative efforts. People trust their friends and work with them more easily and innovatively than they do with strangers or people they never expect to interact with again. This is true not only in the classroom, but also in globally distributed relationships. Getting to know others firsthand is essential to cultivating trust and collaboration. Exemplary leaders ensure frequent and lasting opportunities for people to connect with one another. When Sophia Bloom started an anti-rape culture education group on her Massachusetts college campus, conducting outreach to fraternities on campus to facilitate collaborative training, she knew having tightly knit bonds between people in the group would be important. They were doing difficult, emotionally grueling work; they also needed to be able to lean on each other and talk about the difficulties of what they were trying to accomplish if they were going to persist in their work. "Retention is a common issue," Sophia said. "Even when someone really cares about a topic, it's easy to burn out."

The group regularly held in-person social events and informal meetings where they shared snacks and got to know each other better. Sophia emphasized that these meetings didn't have to be super structured; the point was to gather consistently and informally rather than constantly being focused on their mission. "I really wanted it to be something where the girls all knew each other," Sophia said. "It's an emotionally taxing topic and endeavor. I wanted people to be really close to each other, to be able to rely on each other, and talk to each other about their experiences." Making sure people felt connected to each other and supported was key to getting Sophia's movement off the ground and keeping it going.

Finding the time for everyone to meet in person is often challenging. Technology and social media can undoubtedly enhance communication. Virtual connections abound, and in a global economy, no organization could function if people had to fly halfway around the world to exchange information, make decisions, or resolve disputes. That said, the stroke of a key, the click of a mouse, or the switch of a video doesn't get you the same results as an in-person conversation. There are limits to virtual trust. This is precisely the point Viet Doan made in telling us about his experience working with a group of high school friends to open a bar and grill in Ho Chi Minh City:

> You have to build trust, and the most effective way is to get everyone on the same page as soon as possible. The first

session should not be so much about planning as it should be about getting to know one another. The time "wasted" getting everyone on the same page is still many times better than the cumulative time wasted dealing with frustration among people who don't know each other or feel they don't have anything in common.

For example, talk face-to-face first rather than texting someone across the hall; if necessary, you can continue that communication online. Work as hard as you can to get your group members together in person as often as possible. Firsthand experience with another human being is a more reliable way of creating identification, increasing adaptability, and reducing misunderstandings than virtual connections.[6]

Virtual trust, like virtual reality, is one step removed from the real thing. Humans are social animals; it's in people's nature to want to interact, and bits and bytes or pixilated images make for a fragile social foundation.[7] If you mainly know your group members virtually, you probably don't know them well enough to trust them with extremely important matters. You will have to reconcile the benefits of virtual meeting time and the costs of bringing people together face-to-face with the fact that building trust depends on getting to know one another personally.

People who expect their interactions to be more than a one-time affair, believe they will continue to interact in the future, and like being in a relationship are more likely to cooperate in the present. Knowing that you'll have to deal again with someone tomorrow, next week, or in another class next term ensures that you won't easily forget how you've treated one another. Durable relationships make the impact of today's actions on tomorrow's contacts much more pronounced. Also, frequent interactions between people promote positive feelings about one another. If you want to maximize your leadership effectiveness, begin with the assumption that you'll be interacting in some way with these people again and that these relationships are critical to your mutual success in the future.

REFLECT AND ACT: FOSTER COLLABORATION

"You can't do it alone" is the mantra of exemplary student leaders— and for good reason. You can't make extraordinary things happen by yourself. Collaboration is the key behavior that enables classrooms, clubs, teams, and communities to function effectively. You sustain collaboration when you create a climate of trust and facilitate effective long-term relationships within your group. Promote a sense of mutual dependence—a feeling that individuals are part of a group where everyone knows they need one another to succeed.

Trust is the lifeblood of collaborative teamwork. To create and sustain the conditions for long-lasting connections, you must trust others, they must trust you, and they must trust each other. To build that trust, you must share information and knowledge freely with people in your group, show that you understand their needs and interests, be open and receptive to their ideas, make use of their abilities and expertise, and—most of all— demonstrate that you trust them before you ask them to trust you.

The challenge of facilitating relationships is ensuring everyone recognizes that they are interdependent and need each other to succeed. Cooperative goals and roles contribute to a sense of collective purpose, and the best incentive for people to work to achieve shared goals is the knowledge that you and others will do the same. Structure projects to reward joint efforts. Get people interacting and encourage communication through face-to-face dealings as often as possible to reinforce the durability of relationships.

Reflect

The first commitment of Enable Others to Act is to *foster collaboration by building trust and facilitate relationships*. What are the most important ideas or lessons about exemplary leadership that you learned from this chapter?

_____

_____

_____

_____

    Here are some actions you can take to live out your commitment to **Foster Collaboration:**

- Identify someone you can trust, even if they haven't already shown it to you. Take the initiative and foster reciprocity.
- Share information about yourself—your hopes, strengths, fears, mistakes—the things that make you who you are.
- Spend time getting to know those in your group and learning what makes them tick. Similarly, find ways to engage people in meaningful conversations where they can get to know each other.
- Listen, listen, and then listen some more.
- Share with others what you know, answer their questions, connect them to resources they need, and introduce them to people who might be helpful.
- Clearly and frequently communicate the common goal you are all striving to achieve, the important shared values, and the larger purpose everyone is a part of.
- Structure projects and assignments with a common goal that requires people to cooperate and help each other. Make visible the fact that people are interdependent, relying on one another for success.

Act

After you have reflected on what you learned, what you can improve, and the preceding suggestions, record your plan here for taking at least one action that will help you become a better leader:

_____

_____

_____

_____

_____

_____

8

Commitment #8:
Strengthen Others

"Learning is just information until you put it to use and reflect on it. You have to be able to turn it into something you can use in the future," Amy Lebrecht and Zachariah Karp told us. That was the philosophy of the alternative spring break program they developed as students at a southeastern university.

The alternative spring break was a weeklong trek where all the students were paired up, and each pair had to plan a service learning event, each in a different city along the way. Over the course of the eight days, the group volunteered for three-hour service stops at various service-based organizations, including homeless shelters, a Salvation Army store, and a Habitat for Humanity construction site, all chosen and arranged by the students.

It was up to each team of students to find an organization whose purpose resonated with them and then to coordinate with its leaders to provide a service learning experience for the entire group. Amy and Zachariah assigned the teams the cities where they'd be leading an activity and provided some examples of where to search for service organizations to partner with. The proposal for the specific project and the logistics of each learning experience were left up to the participants. In that way, the entire alternative spring break activity rested on the shoulders of the students themselves.

"We wanted to give them an opportunity to take ownership and find agencies that provided services they were really passionate about," Amy said. She went on to say:

> I don't believe the trip would've had the same impact if we had been arranging every stop and telling them to get involved in different causes—we wanted them to explore the things they really cared about and then find a way to transform that passion into action.

Given the opportunity to take responsibility for one piece of the trip without having to plan the entire trip themselves, each team had a sense of personal ownership over the entire alternative spring break experience.

In addition to taking charge of one of the service learning activities, everyone on the trip was responsible for handling several of the everyday logistics, such as cooking dinner for the group. Even this activity turned into a learning process that evolved throughout the trip. Zachariah recalled that at one stop, only a single microwave was available to prepare food for seventeen hungry people. The team responsible for dinner that night decided to have baked potatoes. "They put together a toppings bar in their room and cycled us in and out, cooking the potatoes in the microwave and allowing us to dress the potatoes ourselves," Zachariah said. "It was a pretty unique solution."

"When we hit the ground running on spring break," Amy said, "there was some learning curve at each stop, but we wanted them to be able to learn from their experiences, so we did our best to keep our hands off. We wanted them to know, this is on you, this is about becoming the leader that you want to be, the leader that we know you can be."

Amy and Zachariah facilitated discussions in which the whole group would sit down after dinner and reflect on the day's successes, talk about its challenges, and celebrate the team's hard work. "We asked them to reflect on the experience that they'd been through and pick out specific ways that each experience made them a better leader," Amy told us. "I actually think that was one of the most important parts of the trip, really solidifying all of the things they'd gone through and what they learned."

At the end of the evening reflection, Amy and Zachariah recognized what behavior and actions had made that day a success, whether it was planning and leading the volunteer activity, handling an unexpected request, grocery shopping, or creatively preparing dinner. They publicly acknowledged each team member, giving specific examples of what they did well. This was a way to help the team develop from their experiences and cement the lessons learned throughout the alternative spring break. Amy said, "We really depended on each other to get through each stop—we're a team, but that team is made up of different people, each of whom had to do their job to get us to the end of a successful day of volunteering."

Exemplary student leaders like Amy and Zachariah make a commitment to Strengthen Others. They enable people to take ownership of and responsibility for the group's success by enhancing their competence and self-assurance, listening to their ideas and acting on them, involving them in important decisions, and acknowledging and giving credit for their contributions. As leaders, Amy and Zachariah gave each team a sense of personal ownership over the entire alternative spring break program in a way that would not have been possible if they had planned each stop and only let the team members execute the work. The team members could explore and try new things, learn new skills, and strengthen their overall capability and self-efficacy.

Creating a climate where people are fully engaged and feel in control of their own lives is at the heart of Strengthening Others.

Exemplary leaders build an environment that develops people's ability to perform tasks and bolsters their self-confidence. In a climate of competence and confidence, people don't hesitate to hold themselves personally accountable for results; they feel profound ownership of their achievements and contribute all they can to make extraordinary things happen.

To Strengthen Others, exemplary student leaders engage in two essentials. They:

- **Enhance self-determination**
- **Develop competence and confidence**

Leaders significantly increase people's belief in their ability to make a difference. They move from *being in control* to *giving over control* to others, becoming more like coaches. They help people learn new skills and develop existing talents, providing the institutional support required for ongoing growth and change. In the final analysis, leaders realize that their responsibility is not to create more followers but to develop more leaders.

ENHANCE SELF-DETERMINATION

Leaders accept and act on this paradox regarding power: you become most powerful when you give away your power. Long before *empowerment* entered the mainstream vocabulary, exemplary leaders understood how important it was for their constituents to feel strong, capable, and efficacious. People who feel weak, incompetent, and insignificant will consistently underperform; they are disengaged, hoping to flee the situation, and are ripe for disenchantment, even revolution. Individuals who are not confident about their power and impact, regardless of their organizational position or place, tend to hoard whatever shreds of influence they have.

We've asked thousands of people to tell us about their experiences of feeling powerless and powerful. Think about this for yourself. First, recall actions or situations that have made you feel powerless, weak, or insignificant, like a pawn in someone else's chess game. Are your recollections similar to what others have reported?

REPRESENTATIVE ACTIONS AND CONDITIONS THAT STUDENTS SAY MAKE THEM FEEL POWERLESS

- "No one was interested in, listened to, or paid attention to my opinion or questions."

- "The leader argued with me in front of my peers—even belittling my contributions."

- "My decisions were not supported, even though people said they would back me up."

- "Someone else took or was given credit for my hard work and results."

- "Information I needed was not forthcoming."

- "I wasn't part of the conversation on things that mattered to what I was doing."

- "I was given responsibility but no authority to actually make decisions or hold others accountable."

- "Our leader played favorites, and I wasn't one of them!"

Now, think about what it's like when you feel powerful: strong, efficacious, like the creator of your experience. Is what you remember similar to what others recall?

REPRESENTATIVE ACTIONS AND CONDITIONS THAT STUDENTS SAY MAKE THEM FEEL POWERFUL

- "All the important information and data were shared with me."

- "I was able to make choices and use my own judgment about how we would handle a situation."

- "People asked for my opinion and listened to what I had to say; in fact, my ideas often carried the day."

- "The leader had my back and supported the decisions that I made."

- "Our leader made time to let me know how I was doing and where I could be improving."

- "I was given the chance to learn new skills and opportunities to apply them."

- "I was appreciated for my accomplishments, especially by people I respected."

One clear and consistent message emerges as you examine what people say about powerless and powerful times: *feeling powerful— literally, feeling "able"—comes from a profound sense of being in control of your life*. People everywhere share this fundamental need. When you can determine your destiny and believe you can mobilize the resources and support necessary to complete a task, you will persist in your efforts to achieve it. However, when you feel controlled by others and believe you lack support or resources, you naturally show little commitment to excel. Even though you may comply, you still realize how much more you could contribute if you really wanted to.

What thousands of students have told us about the actions and conditions that make them feel powerless or powerful is consistent with what Nicholas Scoville told us about a summer job he had as a special programs assistant for visiting faculty at a large public research university in Oregon. Nicholas's role was to create an itinerary for visiting faculty members from Mexico to give them a taste of Oregon and the university community where they found themselves. "I have a lot of pride for my home state, and I was excited to show this group all the amazing things it has to offer," Nicholas told us.

His supervisor gave him an outline that contained details for outings that previous cohorts of faculty had taken—but, crucially, offered him the ability to create his own itinerary. "I was given the outline, and I appreciated that, but I wanted to offer something different as well. I didn't want to just follow the steps given to me without putting my own spin on it," Nicholas explained.

Nicholas's supervisor trusted him, and it was also part of the team culture that his three teammates had to present their ideas, receive feedback, and discuss logistical problems as a group. These conversations led to discussions about why some ideas were good, as well as what the biggest challenges were. "It was figuring out what could work versus what had already been tried and proven in the past," Nicholas said.

Having the opportunity to suggest new outings and get feedback about his proposals was a valuable experience for Nicholas and boosted his confidence in himself as a leader. "I think the best way to convey your idea and give support to your idea is to highlight your thought process behind your idea," he said. Not only did he have to advocate for his outings, but he also had to figure out how to overcome logistical issues that arose. For example, one of his most significant changes was a proposed day trip to Portland, which involved him applying for a new license to drive a bus of faculty himself. Nicholas studied for the permit and received it, and the trip to Portland was widely hailed as the highlight of the faculty's sightseeing around Oregon. "This opportunity motivated me to work as hard as I could to prove myself to my office and gain the respect of my teammates," Nicholas said.

As the youngest member of my team, I was not afraid to ask for support from my superiors. I built a positive relationship with those in my office based on collaborative discussions and personal experiences. The position gave me a lot of independence when determining the group's schedule. I had to follow the preset collaboration periods between the group and the faculty from the university, but besides that, I was in control of the rest of their schedules. The experience resonates with me to this day—it inspired confidence in myself and my ideas.

If Nicholas had been forced to follow the outline, and only the outline, the experience wouldn't have been fulfilling for him. He also wouldn't have gained valuable insights into effective leadership. Sometimes leadership comes directly from being someone's superior and having power over them, but that isn't what makes a good leader, Nicholas said. "I never think of leadership in the sense of commanding. It's important to know what you want to do as a leader. But be aware of the interests of others. Leadership shouldn't be a one-way street. The best way to get results from a team is to garner a two-way street of mutual respect," Nicholas said.

The most effective leaders, as Nicholas's experience documents, exemplify the actions that make people feel powerful.[1] They realize that leadership actions that increase people's sense of self-determination, self-confidence, and personal effectiveness make people more powerful and significantly enhance the energy and commitment they put forward.[2] Self-determination is enhanced when people are given the opportunity to make choices, exercise latitude, and feel personally accountable. Through actions that make people powerful, both figuratively and literally, leaders are not giving away their power but broadening their sphere of influence.

Provide Choices

Freedom is the ability to make choices. People who perceive that they don't have choices feel trapped, and like rats in a maze, when left with no alternatives, they typically stop moving and eventually shut down. By giving people genuine autonomy, leaders can reduce the sense of powerlessness and accompanying stress that people feel and increase their willingness to exercise their capabilities more fully. You want people to take initiative and be self-directed.

What impact do student leaders have when they "give people a great deal of freedom and choice in deciding how to do their work"? Students whose leaders *very frequently* provide this latitude evaluate their leader's skills over fifty times more favorably than those whose leaders *seldom* do so. In addition, as shown in Figure 8.1, the gap in productivity between those students who feel empowered and those who don't is dramatic. Students feel significantly more productive due to their leaders providing an opportunity to use their judgment and have discretion in how their work is completed. Their feelings of self-worth are also directly associated with the chance to exercise their discretion.

Francis Appeadu-Mensah served as director of his school's drama club in South Africa and felt that this organization had great potential for helping his classmates find inventive avenues for personal expression. He gave people choices about participating in any activity they wished, telling them that "this is a place where you can explore and decide where your talent lies." When people were new to the club or simply not sure what part of the club they wanted to explore, Francis would pull them aside, often after rehearsals, and

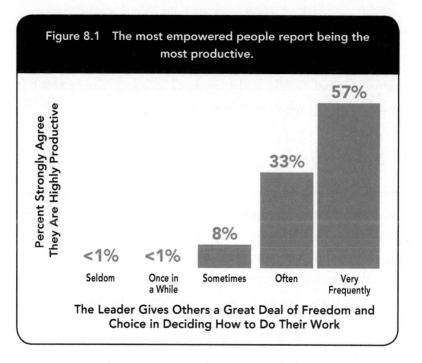

Figure 8.1   The most empowered people report being the most productive.

ask, "What did you think?" or "What would you do if you were directing this scene?" or "How would you have delivered this passage if you were the actor?" Francis left spaces open for people to choose for themselves. In this exploration process, they learned new skills, strengthening their overall capability and confidence, and increasing their commitment to their projects and the overall success of the performance and the club.

Leaders want people to think for themselves and act, not continually asking someone else, "What should I do?" You can't develop this ability if you tell people what to do and how to do it. People can't learn to act independently unless they exercise some degree of choice. The only way to create an efficient and effective group of people who can meet the challenges that are part of trying new things is by giving them the chance to use their best judgment in applying their knowledge and skills. This implies, of course, that you've prepared them to make these choices and that they feel well-grounded and aligned with the group's values and vision.

Structure Tasks to Offer Latitude

Every year, the students in a leadership development program at a large eastern university participate in the annual homecoming week festivities. One of the week's major events is the parade, for which groups across campus build floats based on the theme for the year. Designing and building their parade float had always been a group effort for the students, but the process could have been better planned, and the floats seldom measured up to aspirations.

The year Dan Samuels was cochair, he and his float committee recalled how challenging it had been building the floats in previous years. Conversations at the beginning of previous float projects typically progressed from discussing what had been created in prior years to enthusiastically tossing around new ideas. It was common to start with a high level of energy, Dan said, but then the momentum would quickly wane as confusion set in around who would play what role, who would oversee the work, how the subcommittees would get more students involved, how much time would be required, and on and on.

Dan was determined not to repeat history and set out to make the group's float for that year—and the process of creating it—the best one yet. "I'd been involved in the homecoming float project a couple of times," he told us, "and people getting confused and losing interest didn't make sense to me because as construction on the float progresses, it gets to be even more exciting and fun." When Dan began talking to students who had started strong in years past and then dropped off, he learned that this was because they didn't feel as though they were contributing in a significant way, that there were plenty of others who could do what they had been assigned to do. "That made me realize," he said, "that I needed to help people feel like their unique contribution was valued and that we were counting on each and every one of them."

As in the past, the float committee spent a lot of time brainstorming designs and choosing one they thought best fit that year's homecoming theme. Dan decided that the traditional process needed something else to engage students. He asked some committee members to build a model of the float they envisioned. They could then use the model to encourage students to sign up for specific parts of the float project rather than having people show up night after night and jump right into sawing, hammering, and painting as they had done in years past.

Once the students had signed up for the portion of the float they wanted to work on, Dan led a smaller group to create a list of the specific tasks that needed to be done. The students could then pick the work they wanted to do from the list, factoring in the time they realistically had to contribute and what they thought they'd be good at doing. This strategy made a huge difference in how everyone engaged in the project. With everyone having a choice about what they would do and being asked to be honest about the time they had to contribute, Dan and his committee were able to spread the work out more efficiently and avoid the chaos and disengagement that had characterized their float building in the past. "There was no way people could fade away because they had signed up for the job they wanted and had committed to it," Dan explained. "Students signing up for the float also really liked the fact that they weren't assigned something, but had a chance to provide input on what they wanted to do."

By providing them latitude in the roles they would play, Dan was able to influence the attitude students brought to the project. As a result, most kept their commitments. In addition, because Dan gave people the opportunity to sign up for as much or as little as they could afford, their commitment was stronger. The float committee had far fewer no-shows than in any previous year. People weren't overcommitted, and they knew what they were doing, so nobody bailed. There was much less frustration and much more efficiency and organization in the planning and construction process. "Everyone seemed to simply enjoy their work much more," Dan told us. "The enthusiasm kept on going, and the whole process was fun."

Having latitude in how they do their work strengthens people. They grow when they're allowed to try new things and make decisions that affect how they do their work without having to check with someone else.[3] Effective leaders are not control freaks. Nor are they wedded to a standard set of rules, procedures, or schedules. You need to give people sufficient freedom and choice in deciding how to do their work. The payoff will be significant. Our research shows that student leaders who are observed as *very frequently* "supporting the decisions that other people make on their own" have the most engaged people. They feel valued and productive, and that they know are making a difference.

Foster Accountability

When people take personal responsibility and are held accountable for their actions, their colleagues are much more inclined to work with them and more motivated to cooperate. Individual accountability is a critical element of every collaborative effort. Each person must do their part for a group to function effectively.

Mykell Bates had played soccer from the age of fourteen and was chosen captain of the U.S. Under-17 national team when he was fifteen. When he went on to college, his soccer playing continued, and in his sophomore year, Mykell was chosen captain of his school's team. Being captain entailed many more organizational duties than Mykell was used to, both on and off the field. "At first, I tried to do it all," Mykell told us, "but then it occurred to me, since we depend on each other on the field, shouldn't I depend on them off the field too?"

Mykell began to reach out to his teammates to take on some of the communication duties for the team, he told us.

> We all play an important part in our success on the field, so all I was asking for was that same level of accountability and connection to the team off the field. When I'd ask a player, "Hey, can you text the guys about the team meeting tonight?" they always stepped up.

Slowly Mykell began passing on responsibilities to more members of the team. Ultimately, it became clear that spreading out some of the tasks was a much more efficient way of doing things, and it helped all those who contributed feel accountable for the successful operation of the team.

What Mykell was doing with his team is what student leaders do to foster accountability: they consciously create an environment where team members count on one another to get done what needs to get done. This doesn't mean they are autocratic or controlling. His teammate Brandon Zimmerman told us:

> Mykell was not directive in handing out tasks; he would simply ask for your help, and you would want to help him. He trusted that I could do the job that needed to be done, and I didn't want to break that trust. It was mutual respect, for each other and for the good of the team.

Leaders like Mykell appreciate a fundamental truth about strengthening others: the power to choose rests on the willingness to be held accountable. People understand that with more freedom of choice, they must accept greater personal responsibility. There's also a bonus: the more people believe that everyone else is taking responsibility for their part of the project—and has the competence to do it—the more trusting and cooperative they will be with one another. People will be more confident and committed to doing their part when they believe others will do theirs.

Some students believe that groups, teams, and other cooperative experiences minimize individual accountability. They argue that if their classmates are encouraged to work collectively, they'll take less responsibility for their actions than if they are encouraged to compete or do things on their own. Think about a group project for a class. If there are a lot of individuals in the group, do you think that people are less likely to worry about what happens if they don't do their part? It's true that some people indeed become social loafers when working in groups, slacking off while others do their jobs for them. However, this doesn't last for long because their classmates quickly tire of carrying the extra load. Provided the team has shared goals and shared accountability, either the slacker steps up to the responsibility or the team wants that person removed.[4]

Consider how Brock Davenport strengthened others by fostering accountability in his fraternity chapter at a large southern university. "One of the biggest things I've learned is that the most influential guys [in my fraternity] are the guys who don't have a leadership position," Brock said. Whenever the chapter needed to do something extremely important, he told us that he looked at those guys who sit in the back. If he could get them to care about something, get them to vocalize and advocate for the importance of it, he thought, that would go over a thousand times better than him trying to tell them that they have to step up.

Brock shared an example. In his fraternity, the designated Parks and Rec position—the person responsible for organizing pick-up basketball games or other fun outdoor adventures—had been empty for months. After a chapter meeting, a member approached Brock. The fraternity needed new pool sticks, he told Brock, and asked who was in charge of ordering them. "I was like, well, we don't have anyone in Parks and Rec right now—why don't you order the pool sticks?" Brock said. His fraternity brother agreed and liked the position so much that he slid into the role. "Now he's functioning as Parks and Rec—that's something he never would've volunteered for until I asked him to do it," Brock said.

Crucially, Brock didn't simply *assign* the position to someone in his fraternity; he found a way to offer someone responsibility in an area they were already interested in. As a leader, Brock told us that you need to listen to the interests of the people you're guiding and then match that interest with a responsibility. "You have to empower them to take it from interest to passion. The challenge is to get them from 'go' [as in, I'd go to that event] to 'lead' [I'll lead that event]. If you can get from 'go' to 'lead,' that's where success is."

Enhancing self-determination means giving people control over their lives. It means you need to provide them with something of substance to control and to be accountable for. Define roles broadly—as projects, not tasks—and find ways to ensure that everyone is part of the decision-making process. Make sure that everyone in your group, no matter the task or job, has someone they are serving—someone they feel accountable to. Remember that you also need to provide the necessary resources—for example, materials, money, time, and information—for people to perform autonomously. Nothing is more disempowering than having lots of responsibility for doing something but nothing to do it with.

DEVELOP COMPETENCE
AND CONFIDENCE

Choice, latitude, and accountability give people control over their lives and fuel their sense of feeling powerful. However, as necessary as enhancing self-determination is, it's insufficient. Without the knowledge, skills, information, and resources to do a job expertly, and without feeling competent to execute the choices required, people will be overwhelmed and likely discouraged. Even if they have the resources and skills, there may be times when people are not confident that they're allowed to use them or that they will be supported if things don't go as well as expected. Sometimes, they lack the self-confidence to do what they know they need to do.

When Mykell asked his soccer teammates to step up and take over some of the operational tasks for the team, that action had another benefit beyond fostering accountability. When responsibilities were spread among the group, each teammate could specialize in and perfect one activity, which wouldn't happen if only one person took on all the tasks.

Mykell learned that giving other people responsibilities enhanced their skills and self-confidence. One of his teammates told us that this was precisely what Mykell did for him: "I have a part-time construction job, and Mykell's leadership showed me that one thing I can do is pass on some of the building responsibilities to others. I have always liked doing everything myself, but I am sure the guys I am working with can do just as well as I can, if not better in some cases. I can coach them through it, and that will build their capabilities and confidence, eventually making us a much stronger and more productive work team."

It's no secret that sharing power like Mykell did results in higher performance for the group. Developing competence and building confidence for all members of the group is essential. To make extraordinary things happen, you must invest in strengthening the capacity and resolve of everyone in your group.

Think about a time when the challenge you faced was greater than the skills you had. How did you feel when the challenge was high but your skill was low? If you're like most people, you felt anxious, nervous, and even scared. Now, think of a time when your skill level was greater than the level of challenge in the job. How did you feel? Most likely bored and apathetic. Do you do your best work when you're anxious or bored? Of course, you don't. You do it when the challenge you face is just slightly greater than your current level of skill. That's when you feel stretched but not stressed out. What's true for you is just as true for the other people you work with.

Exemplary student leaders strive to create the conditions that make it possible for people to perform effortlessly and expertly despite the difficulty of the task or project. That means you continuously need to assess the capacity of individuals and the group to meet the challenges they face, which in turn, requires attention to the skill power, and willpower, of each person you lead.

Educate and Share Information

People can't do what they don't know how to do. Therefore, when you increase the latitude and discretion of your team members, you also need to increase training and development opportunities. When people aren't sure about how to perform critical tasks or are fearful of making mistakes, they may be reluctant to exercise their judgment. Developing the competence and confidence of each member in a group is a virtuous cycle that makes everyone involved feel more qualified, capable, effective, and like leaders themselves. It's your job as a leader to instill these feelings. That was the job that Christina Beige took on when she was selected, along with faculty and staff across the campus, to serve on her university's Energy Task Force.

The year before Christina joined this task force, there had been an initiative led by the Student Alliance for a Green Earth (SAGE) to institute a "Green Fee." The university president, however, felt that there was insufficient evidence of overall student support and did not enact the fee. Christina's task force had developed numerous green projects, policy plans, and publicity efforts to make the school more environmentally friendly. "This was a fantastic effort," Christina said, "but I knew it would go nowhere if there was no funding. I had to take action." She wrote a resolution for a $10 Green Fee designed to fund various projects and promotional efforts to boost environmental awareness and responsibility on campus. She presented the Green Fee resolution to the school's student senate with a detailed outline of how the $200,000 assessment would be spent.

The student senate was hesitant and felt that the previous student body survey needed to be conducted again to provide solid evidence of support. Christina, SAGE, and other supportive students across campus reached out again to educate the student body about the fee. They were competing at the time with a proposal from athletics to raise the athletic fee and appeared to be outnumbered and outspent every step of the way. "But we didn't stop," Christina told us. "We had a lot of good information on something we believed the student body really cared about, and we believed that if we could share it with the students, we'd have a fair shot." Their knowledge-sharing paid off big-time. Armed with facts and figures about the impact of the projects the Green Fee would fund, students overwhelmingly supported it, with 75 percent of them eventually approving the fee increase.

Christina's experience demonstrates that sharing information with others is crucial for leaders who want to make extraordinary things happen. Recall that sharing information shows up consistently on the list of what makes people feel powerful, whereas the lack of information makes them feel powerless. For leaders, developing the competence and confidence of the people on their team so they are more qualified, capable, effective, and behave more like leaders themselves reflects their appreciation of the truth that they can't make extraordinary things happen by working alone. Making people smarter is every leader's job. If the people in your group aren't growing and learning from the projects and activities they are involved in, they're likely to leave and find more fulfilling opportunities elsewhere.

Organize Work to Build Competence and Ownership

Exemplary leaders enrich the group members' responsibilities so they experience variety in their tasks and opportunities to make meaningful decisions about how things get done. Do as exemplary student leaders do and organize assignments so people feel their work is relevant to the team's or organization's pressing concerns. Make sure that everyone feels well represented on the committees, teams, and problem-solving groups dealing with the important matters in your organization. Involve them in programs, meetings, and decisions that directly impact what they are being asked to do. Actions like these build competencies and promote a sense of ownership and accountability.

This was another lesson that Dan Samuels learned from his personal-best leadership experience in the homecoming float project. Traditionally, the job assignments had been organized by general tasks: construction, painting, decorating, and so forth. Students would sign up for one type of task, and that was it. Dan had a different idea about how to organize things. "In the past, people were encouraged to sign up for something they felt they knew how to do or had done before, like painting," Dan explained. "The result was that often people just got sick of painting; they felt pigeonholed." Dan thought, why not let people try a new skill? They could do that if they are good at painting, but maybe they want to learn how to do some of the construction. "If we helped people get some new experience and skill," Dan told us, "that would put us in a better position for getting the work done and make it easier in future years too."

This approach increased everyone's ownership of the project. It meant that the subgroups had to coordinate their efforts for the project to be successful. Everyone needed to take ownership of the section of the float they signed up for so that the whole project would come together at the end and look like a coherent construction. By organizing the project this way, the students would depend on each other to complete the final project. This approach also demanded that the quality of each section be consistent, so the groups had to coordinate to meet one another's standards. Altogether, the students' work on the float was done in a way that built their confidence and encouraged ownership; more people were fully engaged in the project than ever before. And there was another payoff: the float took first place in the judging competition.

Student leaders like Dan know how important it is to turn tasks, assignments, and projects into opportunities to increase people's knowledge and skills and to build ownership. For people to feel like owners, they need to understand what is going on to the extent that any "owner" would expect. If your team is going to work together effectively, it needs to be able to know the answers to such questions as: who are the people we serve, and for whom do we exist? How do they perceive us? How do we know whether we're doing what we should be doing for them? How have we done recently? What can we do that is new and better in the next six months?

Foster Self-Confidence

Even if people know how to do something, a lack of confidence may stop them. Without sufficient self-esteem, people won't have the commitment required to take on tough challenges. Low self-confidence manifests itself in feelings of helplessness, powerlessness, and often crippling self-doubt. By building people's belief in themselves, you are bolstering their inner strength to forge ahead in uncharted terrain, to make tough choices, to face opposition, and the like because they believe in their skills and decision-making abilities, as well as yours.[5]

Encouraging self-confidence is what Amy and Zachariah did when they structured the alternative spring break so that the whole experience rested on the participants' shoulders. It's what Francis did when he provided people the opportunity to participate in various parts of the drama club's activities, and what Dan did in letting people work on any part of the homecoming float they wanted to.

And this is precisely what Patrick Quinn's soccer teammate and team captain did for him when he took Patrick aside and empowered him to provide leadership—something he hadn't imagined himself being in a position to do. After all, while playing on his Division III soccer team, Patrick had gotten injured and didn't feel like he had much to offer his team in this condition.

"One game, Rooney—our captain—pulled me aside and said, 'I don't know if you know this, but other people on the team look up to you. What you do and how you act is important.' It made me realize the position I was in and made me want to be a better leader," Patrick told us. Before that moment, he'd viewed himself as nothing special on the team; in other words, replaceable. That was partially because the soccer coach didn't make Patrick or other team members feel important. "If we got hurt, he'd just sub us out and ask us when we thought we'd be healthy again," Patrick said.

But Rooney's wake-up call impacted Patrick's self-esteem and made him feel important and valuable to the team. "It made me feel like, okay, maybe I'm replaceable on the field. But even if I'm physically injured, I can still contribute to the team by being a positive force, by using my personality," Patrick said.

Patrick was one of the team leaders his senior year, and he kept close the leadership lessons he'd learned from Rooney. "I went out of my way to be a leader to the new players and guide them. I tried to teach them the value of working hard and that the effort they're putting in is for the team as a family. I thought about how Rooney had reached me, and I tried to lead with positivity and confidence, the way he did. If you're willing to put your trust in other people, they're more likely to trust you and commit wholeheartedly to your suggestions. These actions build on each other and spiral upwards," Patrick said.

Having confidence and believing in your ability to handle the job, no matter how difficult, are essential in promoting and sustaining consistent efforts. By communicating to your group that you believe it can be successful, you help people push the group members beyond their self-limiting boundaries.

Coach

Although exemplary student leaders communicate their confidence in others, you can't just tell people they can do something if they can't. Leaders need to provide coaching because no one can ever be the best at anything without constructive feedback, probing questions, and active teaching by respected coaches. In strengthening others, you must have high expectations for them and gently guide them by expressing your confidence in their ability to make good choices, backing them up when they make mistakes, helping them learn from experiences, and supporting their decisions. Often, this is incremental, in the fashion of small wins, so people don't feel overwhelmed and stressed out by the gap between their abilities and initial performance.

Anthony Gochenour worked throughout college as one of the building managers of the student union at his mid-western college, eventually becoming the senior building manager and leader of the student employment team. His greatest challenge, he told us, was getting the staff, comprising three different teams of student employees, to appreciate how vital their work was and to be motivated to develop their ability to do their jobs better.

Anthony saw their day-to-day apathetic attitudes and lack of commitment to the job as major problems because the student union was probably the most used building on campus. He began to think about the routine work the staff had to do and looked at these tasks from the perspective of how important they were in serving students who used the building. From there, he began to guide different members of the teams to focus on particular tasks so that the many things they had to do wouldn't seem so overwhelming.

After breaking down the whole job and connecting the student workers to responsibilities that appealed to them, Anthony coached them individually, working alongside them to give pointers and feedback on how they were doing. Over time, team members could see how progress in their smaller assignments contributed to the bigger picture, and they could see the impact each of them had on what happened in the building. With Anthony's support, the student teams came to appreciate that their work didn't just keep the building running but shaped the experience of everyone who came into and used the building.

Student leaders like Anthony never take control away from others. They leave it to their team members to make choices and assume responsibility for them. When leaders coach, educate, enhance self-determination, and otherwise share power, they demonstrate deep trust in and respect for people's abilities. When leaders help others grow and develop, they reciprocate. People who feel capable of influencing their leaders are more strongly attached to those leaders and more committed to effectively carrying out their responsibilities.[6]

Good coaches understand that strengthening others requires paying attention and believing that people are smart enough to figure things out for themselves when allowed to make choices, provided with support, and offered feedback. Coaching stretches people to grow, develops their capabilities, and provides them with opportunities to hone and enhance their skills in challenging assignments.

Good coaches also ask good questions. The benefits of asking questions are numerous. For one, it gives people both the room to think and to frame issues from their perspective. Second, asking questions indicates an underlying trust in individuals' abilities by shifting accountability, and it has the benefit of creating almost immediate buy-in for the solution (after all, it's now *their* idea). Asking questions puts leaders in more of a guiding role, which in turn, frees them up to think more strategically.

The success of every team or undertaking is a shared responsibility. As noted in Chapter 7, you can't do it alone. You need a competent and confident team, and the team needs a competent and confident coach. While you're at it, think about getting a coach yourself. There's no better way to model the behavior you expect from others than by doing it yourself.

REFLECT AND ACT: STRENGTHEN OTHERS

Strengthening others is essentially the process of turning everyone into leaders—making people capable of acting on their own initiative. Leaders need to bring others along *as* leaders. Leaders strengthen people when they make it possible for them to make choices, design alternatives to how things get done, and encourage accountability and responsibility that lead to action.

Leaders develop in others the competence, as well as the confidence, to act on their own and to be successful. They ensure that people have the information they need to understand how the group operates and what is happening. They help build people's abilities and coach them on how to put what they know into practice, stretching and supporting them to do more than they might have imagined possible. Exemplary student leaders use questions to help people think on their own and coach them on how to be at their best.

Reflect

The second commitment of the leadership practice Enable Others to Act requires leaders to *strengthen others by increasing their self-determination and developing competence*. What are the most important ideas or lessons about exemplary leadership that you learned from this chapter?

_____

_____

_____

_____

Here are actions you can follow through on your commitment to **Strengthen Others:**

- Let people make choices about how they do their work.
- Structure tasks so that individuals have opportunities to use their judgment about how their assignments can best be completed.
- Find a balance between people's skills and the work you are asking them to do. Provide opportunities to stretch themselves beyond their comfort zones, but not so far that they lose confidence.
- Promote accountability by ensuring people have the necessary resources to complete their tasks or projects.
- Share your influence and any appropriate organizational authority with others.
- Demonstrate in visible and concrete ways that you believe in the competence of the people on your team.
- Set aside time to coach others. Begin by learning enough about the skills, interests, and aspirations of the people you are working with to determine how you can enable them to make the most of their capabilities.

Act

After reflecting on what you learned, what you can improve, and the preceding suggestions, record your plan here for taking at least one action that will help you become a better leader:

_____

_____

_____

_____

_____

ENCOURAGE
THE HEART

Making extraordinary things happen is hard work, and leaders must encourage those they are working with to continue the quest. Leaders strengthen people's courage and commitment by visibly recognizing contributions to the shared vision. Leaders express pride in the accomplishments of their teams. They make a point of telling the rest of the organization about what has been achieved. They make people feel like heroes. Leaders find ways to celebrate accomplishments and are personally involved with them. They take time out to rejoice in reaching a milestone and moving forward.

In the next two chapters, we see how student leaders:

➤ **Recognize Contributions** by showing appreciation for individual excellence.
➤ **Celebrate the Values and Victories** by creating a spirit of community.

ENCOURAGE THE HEART

Reflections from the *Student Leadership Practices Inventory*

1. My overall score from the *Student Leadership Practices Inventory* for Encourage the Heart was:

   _____

2. Of the six leadership behaviors that are part of Encourage the Heart, the statement that I indicated engaging in most frequently was:

   _____

   _____

3. The leadership behavior statement that I engaged in the least often was:

   _____

   _____

   Based on your self-assessment with the leadership practice of Encourage the Heart, complete the following two statements. As you read and review the next two chapters, keep in mind these reflections and observations.

4. Of the leadership behaviors associated with Encourage the Heart, the one(s) I feel most comfortable engaging in is/are:

   _____

   _____

   _____

5. The leadership behaviors that I feel I could engage in more often and be more comfortable with doing are:

   _____

   _____

   _____

9

Commitment #9: Recognize Contributions

Throughout her college career, Kadesha Zimmerman had been academically successful—earning a place on the dean's list, honor roll, and a leadership award her senior year—but it wasn't always as easy for her as it looked. As a young black woman looking to enter finance, she didn't see many other students like her when she arrived on campus. The support and mentoring of a senior faculty member, who was also African American, significantly contributed to her academic achievements. That experience inspired her as a senior to become what her school called a *success coach* for her peers on campus.

Even though she received good grades, Kadesha often struggled and needed help from others to achieve her academic goals. She told us that she wanted to show other students that:

> Just because it looks like academic success comes naturally
> to some people, sometimes those people are really strug-
> gling too. I learned a lot that I wanted to be able to pass on:
> study habits that worked for me, how to deal with certain
> professors and time management. I think there's a lot that

goes into being successful in your studies that we don't
talk about.

Kadesha had come to understand the importance of coaching and peer support for academic success and wanted to find a way to pass that on to others. Becoming a success coach was her way to demonstrate how students can help each other do well in school and become future leaders.

Success coaches work with students who have been placed on academic probation or have been flagged from placement exams as potentially having difficulty adjusting to college-level academics. Although students in the program are assigned a success coach, it's up to the student to utilize the success coach's services. "I can't force anyone to want to work with me, but I can try to get them excited to work with me," reflected Kadesha.

During her first semester as a success coach, Kadesha convened a meeting for all her assigned students to discuss goals and set up individual meeting times to identify things she could work one-on-one with them on. During that meeting, Kadesha noticed that one first-year student was quiet and attentive, but didn't speak up and did not make a follow-up appointment.

Afterward, Kadesha learned that this young woman (let's call her Akira), a very talented graphic artist, was one of the students flagged as having potential difficulties in college courses. Kadesha reached out to her several times via email, but didn't receive any responses. Finally, she tried one last route: social media. Kadesha sent her a message on Facebook, letting her know how much she liked the art Akira had posted and ways she thought it might be used to enrich the environment and experience of college life for her fellow students. She also suggested several ways that Akira could get more involved in the artistic community on campus, and that did the trick. Akira made an appointment to discuss her artistic ambitions and what she wanted to do with her artwork while on campus. "I think she felt a lot of shame associated with having been assigned to a success coach," Kadesha said, "but I made her feel like she had something valuable to offer to our campus community. Instead of just focusing on things she needed to work on, we were able to build a relationship."

At their meetings, Kadesha outlined the courses that Akira would need to take and explained several career paths she might consider, including becoming a graphic artist. Kadesha told Akira how talented she thought she was and how the other courses that she was taking (e.g., geometry and composition) would be important to her future. She also gave Akira suggestions about organizations she could join on campus that would appreciate and stretch her artistic talent, including a group that displayed their artwork in an on-campus café.

At the same time, Kadesha also clarified her expectations for Akira. They would continue to meet regularly to discuss her schoolwork, and Akira would set academic goals for herself—for example, a grade-point average goal that she and Kadesha would continue to review over the course of the year. Their meetings would also allow Kadesha to give feedback to Akira on her targets.

> Early on, Akira set a goal of just making a 2.0 her first semester, and I thought she could do better. I urged her to aim a little higher; maybe we could set up more appointments if she needed, but I believed she should aim for at least a 2.5 because she was more than capable of achieving that. I asked Akira to consider the more challenging goal from a place of faith and belief in her abilities. I didn't want her to think that I didn't believe her difficulties in her classes weren't real, but I also wanted her to know how much I believed in her academic potential.

Akira earned a 2.8 GPA in her first semester and improved that to a 3.0 in her second semester.

Toward the end of the school year, Kadesha held another meeting with all the students she had worked with to showcase what they had accomplished. Everyone brought something they were proud of having created or worked on during the year, whether it was a paper, a project, or a grade on a final exam. "It was the highlight of the year," Kadesha said, "all of us getting to acknowledge the things we were proud of. For me, I was most proud of all of my students and how hard they had worked together." After the celebration, Kadesha sent thank-you notes to everyone she worked with for bringing in their personal contributions.

Kadesha's year as a success coach showed her the importance of seeing and acknowledging each person's individual talents and contributions and how doing that can help build meaningful relationships. "That experience taught me a lot," Kadesha said.

> It taught me how much it meant to people to be found valuable for what they're good at and how much my experience as a success coach was about the relationship being a two-way street—the students I work with have a lot to teach me, too.

Like Kadesha, exemplary student leaders know how important it is to connect with the people around them, not taking anyone for granted and appreciating folks for who they are and what they do. All exemplary leaders make the commitment to Recognize Contributions. They do it because people need encouragement to function at their best and to continue to persist when the hours are long, the work is hard, and the task is daunting. Getting to the finish line of any demanding journey demands energy and commitment. People need emotional fuel to replenish their spirits.

To Recognize Contributions, you need to utilize these two essentials:

- **Expect the best**
- **Personalize recognition**

By putting these essentials into practice, you uplift people's spirits and arouse the internal drive to strive. You stimulate their efforts to reach for higher levels of performance, and to aspire to be faithful to the visions and values of the group. You help people find the courage to do things they have never done before.

EXPECT THE BEST

Exemplary student leaders elicit high performance because they firmly believe in people's abilities to achieve even the most challenging goals. That's because positive expectations profoundly influence not only the aspirations of the people in your group, but also, often unconsciously, how you behave toward them. You broadcast your beliefs about people in ways you may not even be aware of. You give off cues that say to people either "I know you can do it" or "There's no way you'll ever be able to do that." The highest performance levels cannot be realized unless you let people know—in word and deed—that you are confident that they can attain it.

Social psychologists refer to this phenomenon as the "Pygmalion effect," from the Greek myth of Pygmalion, a sculptor who carved a statue of a beautiful woman, fell in love with the statue, and appealed to the goddess Aphrodite to bring her to life. Aphrodite answered his prayers. Leaders play Pygmalion-like roles in developing others. Ask students to describe the best leaders they've ever had, and they consistently talk about individuals who brought out the best in them. They say, "She believed in me more than I believed in myself," or "He saw something in me even I didn't see." The same is true when students describe why they took on the assignment that became their personal best—"because someone believed that I could do it, even if I had never done something like this before and had doubts that I could."

Exemplary leaders bring others to life, figuratively speaking. If the potential exists within someone, they always find a way to release it. They dramatically improve people's performance because they care deeply for them and have deep faith in their capacities. They nurture, support, and encourage people they believe in.

Consider Arthur Neuhaus's experience. As co-captain of his Division I tennis team, Arthur knew that his example on the court could inspire his teammates to achieve their own personal best. Because tennis at the collegiate level is both a team and an individual sport, Arthur was in a unique position to inspire his teammates during a particularly tough match against a division rival. "Before that match, I would say we'd had a few good matches, but also we'd been struggling. It wasn't the best season ever. We'd lost one player because he wasn't eligible, and the whole team was affected by that," Arthur said. While the team was working hard to step up to the season's challenge, Arthur felt the team lacked the confidence to truly get to the next level.

Going into the big match, Arthur knew it was important for his team to play with heart and not give up—even when the matches were tight. He wound up in a position where he was matched against a highly ranked player—ranked 35th in the nation. Arthur knew that winning his match might inspire his teammates to play hard in their own matches, so the team could come out on top. "It was pretty stressful. I was trying to remain calm and in control of the match, even though in my head I was pretty nervous. But I still had to find a way to show not only my opponent but my teammates that I had everything in control," Arthur said.

Arthur believed his team could win, but he wanted to show them he believed. He chose to do that by getting fired up as he played and audibly yelling on important points, so his teammates on different courts could hear him fighting to win and be fired up themselves.

It can create a momentum shift in the match—not just within your match, but also in the matches around you. I was trying

> to show my teammates that I was gonna compete until the end of the match, no matter what happened. I wanted to show my presence by getting loud, getting fired up so that they could hear me and know that no matter what's going on, there's still gonna be a fight.

Arthur won his individual match—and his team ended up winning the match overall. It was a meaningful moment for Arthur, but not just because he'd won as an individual. "The fact that it was for the team made it even bigger. That's why that moment was so important [to me]—I was able to do something that was bigger than just for myself," Arthur said.

People do respond positively to expectations. Research on the phenomenon of self-fulfilling prophecies provides ample evidence that people act in ways that are consistent with others' expectations of them.[1] When you expect them to succeed, they probably will. If you expect people to fail, they probably will. Think about this from your own experience. Can you recall feeling overwhelmed by something you were asked to do? Perhaps it was a crucial game your team had to win against a team that hadn't lost all season. Maybe it was being asked to take over an assignment about which you knew very little but for which you were to be held accountable. Maybe it was an exam that would earn you the grade you needed to get into college or graduate school. If you were successful, chances are there was someone who let you know in one way or another, "I believe you can do this"—someone who reinforced your self-confidence. Sentiments like these send a powerful message to people's brains, one that helps them step up to match the image others hold of them.

Alex Golkar told us he wasn't initially very excited about the people he would work with for his finance capstone project. After all, he only joined them because they needed one more member, and this team was his and their only option. He was even more skeptical when he found out that one team member, though quite smart, was preoccupied with the rigorous demands of his internship and made it clear that he could not devote his full energy to their project. The other member of the group was an amicable fellow who enjoyed socializing. However, he was in the midst of family issues, so his attention to the project was also compromised. The team performed poorly over the next five weeks, with the teacher rejecting all four of their initial project proposals.

With the deadline looming, Alex decided that he had to take the initiative and enact some changes to redirect the team's focus and restore their sense of optimism and possibility. "The first impediment that I addressed," he said, "was personal. I had to change my manner of thinking about my group mates. Rather than viewing them as unproductive and ineffectual, I decided to have some faith in their abilities."

There's substantial evidence that leaders who create a positive orientation, foster high standards, and focus on achieving outcomes beyond the norm are quite successful.[2] When Alex decided to have confidence in the expertise and motivation of his teammates, he also began to alter his thinking and behavior.

> Initially, I was somewhat withdrawn because I believed that my efforts would be wasted due to the unfocused nature of the group. However, with a renewed interest in the group's success, I openly expressed to them my beliefs in their abilities and what we could accomplish together. By communicating in a way that exhibited confidence, we were able to share information and work cohesively as a unit more effectively.

The best student leaders, like Arthur and Alex, bring out the best in others and themselves.

Show Them You Believe

Tiffany Lee was interning in a major metropolitan city's vice mayor's office. As the youngest and most inexperienced person in the office, she was given much of the grunt work, including taking messages for return phone calls, filing, writing thank-you letters, and responding to the routine correspondence sent to the office. She felt out of place in the office where staff members had close relationships based on a history of working together. "I was not seen as a vital part of the staff," she said, "but just an intern who did everyone's leftover work."

At the end of each week, she was required to sit in on staff meetings during which each member would share an item they were working on. Each week, as her coworkers shared important issues they were a part of, such as helping to author legislative bills or working with the health board, Tiffany's response was always the same: "Correspondence." "I would feel almost embarrassed as I hurriedly stated my 'contribution,'" she told us, "and compared with my coworkers' responses, I felt insignificant and not a very important part of the team."

A short time later, at one of the meetings, the chief of staff praised the team for contributing to another successful week. Then, the chief of staff told everyone that due to how correspondence was handled, the vice mayor's office was now receiving thank-you letters from residents who felt that their concerns and welfare were not being ignored and that the office genuinely cared about them. Knowing that Tiffany was the person responsible for handling this correspondence, her coworkers turned to her and told her what a fantastic job she was doing. The chief of staff went on to say that each person in the office had something valuable to bring to the group and that their joint efforts were the reason the office was so highly respected and valued. In telling us about this experience, Tiffany explained how the chief of staff, and her coworkers, demonstrated that they believed in her and made her feel that she was not the most insignificant person on the team and that this, she said, "is something I will take with me forward into every situation."

That is precisely what Tiffany has done. When she was asked to supervise the other interns, for example, she made it a point to expect the best from them, giving them opportunities to make a difference and watching carefully for their contributions to the team, no matter how small or seemingly insignificant. "I make it a rule to help people see how even the small tasks contribute to our collective success," Tiffany says. "People need to know they matter."

Or consider how Patrick Quinn's soccer team captain, Rooney, helped inspire his team before a competitive season. Patrick and Rooney played on a Division I soccer team together. Before Rooney's senior year, he set the tone of the season by writing everyone on the team—even the first-year recruits, whom he hadn't yet met—a personalized letter to get the team excited about the season. "He signed them "Future League Champion, Rooney," at the bottom. That set the tone for the entire season. We all wanted to win for him," Patrick said. Although the team was good, winning the league would still be an uphill battle. Patrick's school had never won the championships, and it wasn't a favorite to win that year. "We'd come in second a few times, but in all the years we'd been in the league, we'd never won," Patrick said.

Throughout the season, Rooney kept reiterating his faith in his teammates, sending them individual texts before each game and reminding them that he saw them as future league champions. Patrick said that Rooney's visible confidence in the team made all the difference in the team's success that year. "Even when we were stumbling, even when we lost games, even when we were in fourth place going into the tournament—he never lost hope. That spirit of 'it's not over yet' really inspired us to give 110 percent," Patrick said.

Patrick's team made it to their league's championship playoffs, not by winning the league outright but by being in the top four. By placing fourth, they had to play their toughest game first, playing the number one seed in the playoff tournament. The team squeaked out a win in penalty kicks. "Once we won that, we were like, 'We have to do it now. We're in the final; we played the hardest team, and we won. Let's do it!'" Patrick said. The team went on to win the league championship for the first time in the school's history.

"I think good leaders know how to bring the best out of people—not necessarily because they're the best themselves, but they know who is the best for the job, and they can facilitate that and make you perform better than you ever thought you could, just because they believe in you," Patrick said.

Leaders' positive expectations aren't fluff.[3] They're not simply about keeping a positive outlook or getting others psyched. The expectations you hold as a leader provide the framework into which people fit their realities. Expectations shape how you behave toward others and how they behave on the task. Maybe you can't turn a marble statue into a real person, but you can draw out the highest potential of your group members. Patrick's experience, like Tiffany's, is a clear example of how showing people you believe in them, even when they are down, helps them acknowledge that they still have their best to give. Holding positive expectations of high performance and motivation in others, along with recognizing them for their contributions, easily beats the alternative of the "just do what I tell you" approach. People need to feel they belong, are accepted and valued, and have the skills and inner resources needed to be successful.

Believing in others is an extraordinarily powerful force in propelling exemplary performance. If you want people to have a winning attitude, you must do what Tiffany's supervisor did: show you believe that the people in your group are already winners. It's not that they will be winners someday; they are winners right now! When you believe that people are winners, you behave in ways that communicate to them that they are precisely that—not just in your words but also through tone of voice, posture, gestures, and facial expressions. No yelling, frowning, cajoling, making fun, or putting them down in front of others. Instead, it's about being friendly, positive, supportive, and encouraging.

Our research shows that students who work with a student leader who *very frequently* "praises people for a job well done" are most highly engaged. For example, as shown in Figure 9.1, there's a strong relationship between the pride they take in working with their leader and how often that leader recognizes their good work. Similar results are found regarding how valued people feel, as well as their productivity, in relation to how often their leader "expresses appreciation for the contributions that people make."

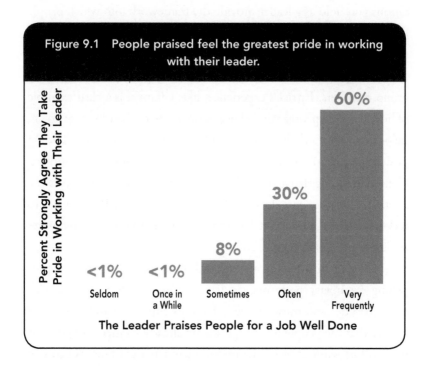

Figure 9.1   People praised feel the greatest pride in working with their leader.

It's a virtuous circle: you believe in your group members' abilities; your favorable expectations cause you to be more positive in your actions; and those encouraging behaviors produce better results, reinforcing your belief that people can be successful. Another virtuous circle begins as people see that they are capable of extraordinary performance; they develop that expectation of themselves.

Be Clear about the Goals and the Rules

Positive expectations are necessary to generate high performance, but that level of performance isn't sustainable unless people are clear about the ground rules and outcomes. You might have read Lewis Carroll's *Alice's Adventures in Wonderland* when you were younger. Do you remember the croquet match? Flamingos were the mallets, playing-card soldiers were the wickets, and hedgehogs were the balls. Everyone kept moving, and the rules kept changing all the time. There was no way of knowing how to play the game or what it took to win. You don't have to fall into a rabbit hole to understand how Alice felt. She was extremely disoriented.

Believing that people can succeed is only part of the equation. If you want people to give their all and put their hearts and minds into their work, you must also ensure they know what they should be doing. You need to clarify what the expected outcomes look like. You must ensure consistent norms govern how to play the game and score points. Have you ever been involved in a class where the learning outcomes and assignments weren't clear? How do you feel when the course syllabus isn't ready until several weeks after classes start? If you have ever found yourself asking, "Why are we doing this?" or "Where is this all going?" you have experienced the frustration, apathy, fear, and resentment that can surface when you're asked to do something but don't know the reasons why.

Liz Eilen was working in the tutoring center when the director suggested to her that greater encouragement might influence the commitment students being tutored would have to their study groups, and as a result, affect their academic improvement. Liz decided to come up with ways to recognize active and involved students for their work at the center. She began by challenging the students to involve themselves more fully in the study-group process, setting high expectations for what each group needed to do. She discovered that setting the expectations was just what the individual members needed to feel motivated and enthusiastic about participating and improving their academic standing. "It was as though the high expectations had a way of creating a self-fulfilling prophecy," Liz said. She also noticed students pushing themselves harder to ensure they wouldn't let their colleagues down. "Students started accomplishing so much, showing improvement in new and different areas," Liz told us. "They surprised everyone, including themselves."

As Liz learned, expectations play an essential role in developing people, drawing out their highest potential and desire to achieve the extraordinary. And as Liz also discovered, expectations can address goals, the level of group participation, and values, such as the importance of academic achievement.

Goals and values provide people with standards that concentrate their efforts. Goals are typically short-term, whereas values (or principles) are more enduring. Values and principles serve as the basis for goals. They're your standards of excellence and your highest aspirations, and they define the arena in which to set goals and metrics. Values mediate the path of action. Goals release energy.

Goals focus people's attention on shared values and standards. They help people keep their eyes on the vision. Goals enable people to choose the actions they need to take, to know when they are making progress, and to see when they need to course-correct. They help people put their cell phones in do-not-disturb mode, appropriately schedule their time, and focus their attention on what matters most.

Goal setting also affirms the person. Whether you realize it or not, goals contribute to what people think about themselves.

But what do goals have to do with recognition? They give recognition context. Goals give people something to strive for, something important to attain—such as coming in first, breaking a record, or setting a new standard of excellence. Goals enhance the significance of recognition because the acknowledgment is for something a person set out to accomplish or exemplify. Recognition is most meaningful when you reward appropriate behaviors and achievement of something everyone knows is highly desirable.

Provide and Seek Feedback

People want and need to know whether they're making progress toward a goal or simply marking time. Their motivation to perform a task increases only when they have a challenging goal *and* receive feedback on their progress.[4] Goals without feedback, or feedback without goals, has little effect on people's willingness or motivation to put discretionary effort into any task.

With clear goals and detailed feedback, people can become self-correcting and more easily understand their place in the big picture. With regular feedback, they can also determine what help they need from others and who, in turn, might benefit from their assistance. Anyone who has been a part of a fundraising event with a set goal knows the power of seeing progress toward that target.

Consider what happens to your self-confidence without feedback. Think how you might feel in a class when you don't receive timely feedback on assignments or receive a grade on a paper without any explanation of why or about what is needed to be more successful in subsequent efforts. Wouldn't you agree that this is frustrating and demotivating?

Saying nothing about a person's performance doesn't help anyone—not the performer, leader, or group. People want useful feedback. They prefer to know how they are doing; no news generally has the same negative impact as bad news. In fact, people would prefer to hear bad news rather than no news at all. Most stressful is not knowing because it leaves the person in a state of limbo, unable to determine what steps to take next.

Moreover, with feedback, there is more learning. Getting feedback about how they are doing is the only way people know whether they're getting close to their goal and whether they're executing properly. Although most people realize intellectually that feedback is a necessary component of self-reflection and growth, they are often reluctant to open themselves to it because feedback can be embarrassing or even painful. People often want to look good more than they want to get good! Researchers consistently point out that developing expertise or mastery requires receiving constructive, even critical, feedback.[5]

Think back to when Nicholas Scoville shared his personal-best leadership story with us in Chapter 8—the one in which he successfully created meaningful experiences for visiting international faculty at his university. Getting useful feedback from his team was an integral part of the experience. When Nicholas wanted to create new itinerary stops for the visiting faculty, he had to pitch his stops to the team for feedback about potential challenges based on their previous experience running the program.

Rather than discouraging him, though, getting feedback on his ideas proved useful in unearthing concerns that he needed to troubleshoot and strengthened his confidence in himself as a leader. It taught Nicholas the importance of building a case before he presented his argument while staying open to the concerns and challenges highlighted by his teammates. The experience pushed him to think more deeply about his ideas and learn how to present his options more convincingly, enabling him to become a more seasoned leader and teammate.

Feedback, as Nicholas's experience demonstrated, should create dialogue. Your goal as a leader is to encourage the best in others and to find out what they need to feel more confident and competent in meeting the challenges they face as a group member. Giving feedback in a way that encourages dialogue will create a learning opportunity for you both.

When leaders provide a clear sense of direction and feedback along the way, they encourage people to reach inside and do their best. Information about goals and progress toward those goals strongly influences people's abilities to learn and achieve, and this applies to leaders themselves. Encouragement is more personal and positive than other forms of feedback, and it's more likely to accomplish something that other forms cannot: strengthening trust between a leader and group members. Encouragement, in this sense, is the highest form of feedback.[6]

PERSONALIZE RECOGNITION

One of the more common complaints about recognition is that far too often, it's highly predictable, mundane, and impersonal. Genuine recognition cannot be industrially manufactured and distributed en masse. There is no cookie-cutter solution or template for effective acknowledgment. A one-size-fits-all approach to recognition feels insincere, forced, and inconsiderate. Over time, it can even increase cynicism and damage credibility. Generalized statements of encouragement fail to produce a significant effect because no one is very certain about to whom the comments are directed or for what actions.

Clay Alm put together an intramural softball team consisting of friends, some coworkers from his job in the student union, and even a faculty member. No matter how well or poorly they played, Clay told us, "I knew this season was going to be extremely interesting purely because of the wide variety of personalities we had on our roster." The season went well, and the day before their first playoff game, Clay invited everyone on the team to his house for a surprise he had organized:

> I had prepared tie-dyed baseball shirts for each of my teammates. We then spray-painted numbers onto the back of everyone's shirt, and they got to choose their favorite number. Finally, I had purchased an iron-on patch for each person on the team. Each patch was different, and each patch had a short story behind it. Some of them ranged from things that each specific teammate was interested in, to personal jokes, to representations of their hometowns.
>
> I took the time to present everyone with their patches individually, and in front of the entire team, I told the story of why I got each of them their specific patches. It was a proud moment for me not only because the gesture was well received, but also because everyone on the team got to see some of the personal bonds we had formed with one another. The single most important part of the uniforms was that they were entirely genuine. It was not an act.

People appreciate knowing that you care about them, and as a result, they are more caring about what they are doing. When recognition is not personalized, it will quickly be forgotten and discounted. The softball team was brought closer together by experiencing a unique mixture of team spirit and individuality embodied in Clay's personalized recognition. Recognition is most effective when it comes from your heart.

When students tell us about the most meaningful recognition they've received, they consistently say, "It's personal." They say that it feels special. You get a lot more emotional bang for your buck when you personalize recognition and rewards. That's why it's so important for student leaders to pay attention to the likes and dislikes of every individual in their group. Step into other people's shoes and ask yourself, "What do I wish someone would do to celebrate and recognize my contribution?" Let your answer to this question guide your thinking about how to acknowledge the contributions of others while also being sensitive to the fact that not everyone is just like you. This means that you must get close enough to others to know what makes recognition meaningful to them.

Get to Know People

Think back to Liz's experience in her school's tutoring center, where she learned that students were more productive when they had a clear understanding of the goals of the program and its expectations of them. That experience also taught her that students were much more motivated and encouraged when they felt someone expected great things from them and was watching to see how they were doing. Liz noted that she couldn't have helped foster those feelings without making a point of getting to know as many students in the groups as possible: "The time spent connecting with each student, sharing our expectations, helped motivate each student to succeed, not just for themselves but for the group as well." That time proved to be well spent when Liz wrote a weekly note of appreciation to students who had met or surpassed expectations, occasionally even finding a special little gift that acknowledged their individual progress or their contribution to the group. By getting close to her students, Liz gained insight into the challenges they faced and the efforts they were putting forth, enabling her to recognize their accomplishments in a genuine and significant way.

To make recognition personally meaningful, as Liz and Clay did, you first need to get to know the people you work with and are involved with. If you're going to personalize recognition and make it feel genuinely special, you'll have to look past the organizational diagrams and roles people play and see the person inside. You need to get to know who they are, how they feel, and what they think. As a leader, this means you need to find a way to get close to people.

Because proximity is the single best predictor of whether two people will talk to one another, you have to get physically close to people if you're going to find out what motivates them, what they like and don't like, and what kinds of recognition they most appreciate. The payoffs are significant. For example, over a five-year period, researchers observed groups of friends and groups of acquaintances (people who knew each other only vaguely) performing motor-skill and decision-making tasks. The results were clear. The groups composed of friends completed, on average, more than three times as many projects as the groups composed merely of acquaintances. In decision-making assignments, groups of friends were over 20 percent more effective than groups of acquaintances.[7] There is an important caveat, however. Friends have to be strongly committed to the group's goals. If not, then friends may not do better. This is precisely why we said earlier that it is absolutely necessary for leaders to be clear about standards and to create a condition of shared goals and values. When it comes to performance, commitment to standards and good relations between people go together.

Another payoff from meaningfully connecting with team members is that it will be reciprocated with loyalty. In other words, paying attention, personalizing recognition, and creatively and actively appreciating others increase their trust in you. If others know that you genuinely care about them, they're more likely to care about you.

People are more willing to follow someone with whom they have a relationship. And the foundation of any relationship is trust. An open door is a physical demonstration of a willingness to let others in. So is an open heart. To become fully trusted, you must be open to and with others. This means telling others the same things you'd like to know about them—talking about your hopes and dreams, your family and friends, your interests, and your pursuits.

Be Creative about Incentives

Can you think of an acknowledgment you received for something you did that makes you smile or feel proud every time you recall at it? It may be a picture of your team celebrating after a major victory, a small gift symbolizing what you did or what you love, or a simple handwritten note. Whatever it is, somehow, it is attached to a feeling of self-worth and being a part of something significant. As a student leader, you can provide that same meaningful connection with the rewards you give. It is not the size or expense of the momento; it's the meaning the recipient associates with it. All it takes is a little thought. If you've done your homework and you know your group members, it doesn't take long at all. Let yourself be creative.

Spontaneous, unexpected acts of recognition are often more meaningful to people than expected ones. The most effective recognition is highly specific and given close to the time the appropriate behavior occurred. An important byproduct of spending time with people on your team, being out and about as a leader, is that you can personally observe people doing things right and then recognize and possibly even reward them on the spot or at your next public gathering.

You can't be a broken record when it comes to recognizing and appreciating others, praising people the same way again and again. People respond better to a variety of recognitions and rewards.[8] That's the beauty of being creative and personalizing your recognition. You have lots of options. You can give out stuffed giraffes, rainbow-striped zebra posters, T-shirts, mugs with team photos, crystal apples, classic car rides, clocks, pens, plaques, and hundreds of other creative expressions of appreciation. You can provide recognition verbally and nonverbally, elaborately and simply. There are no limits to kindness and consideration, as Kara Koser knows. Kara talked to us about how she used what she called "small token surprises" when she was a residence hall adviser at an East Coast urban university. Those "tokens" were all the little things she would do to recognize the students who lived on her floor.

> I tried to surprise people with little things, maybe a small handmade gift. It doesn't have to be a big expensive deal. It's a simple gesture. I liked to do it when it was least expected. That's what makes it fun.

It's important to understand that genuine recognition does not have to include anything tangible. Exemplary leaders also make extensive use of intrinsic rewards—rewards built into the task itself, including factors such as a sense of accomplishment, a chance to be creative, and the challenge of the assignment—all directly tied to an individual's effort.

Often the simple, personal gestures, like Clay's patches and Kara's small surprises, are the most powerful rewards. It's all about being considerate. The techniques you use are less important than your genuine expression of caring. When you genuinely care, even the smallest of gestures reap huge benefits.

Just Say "Thank You"

There are few more basic human needs than to be noticed, recognized, and appreciated for one's efforts. Extraordinary achievements bloom more readily in climates marked with a high volume of positive and appreciative comments. Studies show that work teams in which the ratio of positive to negative interactions is greater than three to one are *significantly* more productive than those teams that haven't achieved this proportion.[9]

"Saying thank you is easy to do, is powerfully important, but often easily forgotten or put off," Cameron McCarthy told us. Growing up, she said she hated it when her parents asked her to write thank-you cards. "I'd argue that I had already said thank you in person." However, as captain of her school's boxing team, Cameron realized:

> I had missed the point, which is common in my generation, especially with the ease of the Internet. It's more than the card, or those two words, but rather it's the sensation of receiving a personal note of appreciation. The key point is to illuminate their individual excellence so they continue to do their best. Praising accomplishments along the way allows individuals to continue to raise the stakes and strive for greatness.

It is always worthwhile to recognize someone's hard work and contributions. All too often, people forget to extend a hand, a smile, or offer a simple thank you. Don't you feel frustrated and unappreciated when you and your efforts are taken for granted? Sometimes these feelings can be set aside because there are deadline pressures, and the mandate to deliver on time overtakes expressing gratitude. However, it's critical that you stick around for that extra minute or two to express your appreciation. Letting people know why you value them and their contributions reinforces the vision, strengthening everyone's commitment.

By the way, don't assume you need to be in a leadership position to provide recognition. Andy Ramans, while an undergraduate at a small private West Coast university, wondered whether he had to be "the person in charge" to Encourage the Heart. He questioned whether he was wasting his time saying, "Good job" or "Thank you."

Would his classmates value these sentiments from a fellow student? We asked Andy how he felt when his classmates thanked or praised him. He thought about this for a moment, smiled, and then had that "aha realization" about the importance of recognizing and appreciating others: "It always made a big difference to me," he said.

Or take it from JD Scharffenberger, who was part of a five-person community-based consulting team in one of his undergraduate classes. He says that a large part of their success was that they celebrated reaching milestones and never failed to praise one another's contributions. For example, throughout the weeks leading up to the due date for their proposal, JD said:

> I went out of my way to text or call my teammates and thank them for their dedication. I figured that praising them for a job well done was one of the easiest ways to keep group morale high. Giving a simple "Thank you" or "Great work today" to my classmates made them feel that their accomplishments were meaningful and not overlooked. This also incentivized them to keep producing quality work, knowing that their contributions were being recognized and celebrated.

Making a point of regularly saying thank you goes a long way in sustaining high performance. Personalized recognition comes down to being thoughtful. It means knowing enough about another person to answer the question, "What could I do to make this a memorable experience so that this individual will always remember how important their contributions were?" As Cameron learned from her experience, "Encouraging my teammates was one of the easiest and most beneficial things I could do to make each person on the team better."

REFLECT AND ACT: RECOGNIZE CONTRIBUTIONS

Exemplary student leaders have positive expectations of themselves and their group. They expect the best of people and create self-fulfilling prophecies about how ordinary people can take extraordinary actions and produce exceptional results. Exemplary leaders have clear goals and standards, helping people fully understand what needs to be done. They provide timely feedback and reinforcement. By maintaining a positive outlook and providing motivating feedback, they stimulate, rekindle, and focus people's energies and drive.

Exemplary leaders recognize and reward what individuals do regarding shared values and contributing to the vision. They don't limit their expressions of appreciation to formal events but seek to be timely and imaginative in saying thank you. Personalizing recognition requires knowing what's appropriate individually and culturally. Though it may be uncomfortable or embarrassing at first, recognizing someone's efforts is not all that difficult. And it's well worth the effort to connect with each person. From many small and often casual acts of appreciation, learn about what works for each person in your group and how best to personalize recognition. Take part in the celebrations yourself. After all, being present is a tangible signal to others that showing up and sharing in the festivities is important for everyone.

Reflect

The first commitment Encourage the Heart requires leaders to *recognize contributions by showing appreciation for individual excellence.* What are the most important ideas or lessons about exemplary leadership that you learned from this chapter?

_____

_____

Here are some actions you can take to follow through on your commitment to **Recognize Contributions:**

- Elevate expectations about what individuals and teams can accomplish.
- Create an environment that makes it comfortable to receive and give feedback, including feedback about your own actions.
- Link recognition and rewards with what your group wants to achieve, and be sure that only those individuals who meet or exceed these goals receive them.
- Connect with people on a personal basis. Find out the types of encouragement that make the most difference to them.
- Be creative when it comes to recognition. Be spontaneous. Have fun.
- Make saying thank you a natural part of your everyday behavior.
- Identify anyone you might be taking for granted and do something that acknowledges who they are and what they contribute.

Act

After you have reflected on what you learned, what you can improve, and the preceding suggestions, record your plan here for taking at least one action that will help you become a better leader:

_____

_____

_____

_____

10

Commitment #10: Celebrate the Values and Victories

While in college, Kevin Straughn and Kaitlyn Morelli spent a summer working together as head coaches for a swim league team in their local community. With swimmers ranging in age from six to eighteen and an eight-week season giving them a relatively short time together, they needed to build bonds and a sense of community on the team right from the beginning. They started the season with a get-together during which they clarified their goals for the summer: improvement of each swimmer on the team and success for the whole team in the Summer Swim League Championship. "The team had won the championship in previous years," Kevin and Kaitlyn told us, "and we wanted to build off of that right from the start, giving swimmers something to set their sights on."

The team's name was the Hurricanes, and the coaches used this name as a metaphor to reinforce its values and the potential victories ahead. At their kickoff get-together, Kevin and Kaitlyn had all the swimmers paint the back wall of the clubhouse with slogans like "Hurricanes—we blow you away" and "Hurricanes—we make waves." All the swimmers signed their names to the wall that day, pledging to come to practice and work on improving their skills to help the team make it to the championship. It was a way to pull the team together on individual development goals and team success. "Swimming is a sport that makes it easy to feel part of something," Kaitlyn explained. "It has both an individual and a collective component. We could celebrate the success of individual swimmers after each meet and also point to the impact this had on the team's success. We made it a point to help them see that connection, to make them feel part of something bigger than their individual success or loss in each race."

As they worked to create a clear set of goals for the individual swimmers and the team, Kevin and Kaitlyn took the time to understand each swimmer's strengths, challenges, and potential for contributing to the team's performance. With this knowledge, they could encourage each swimmer individually and celebrate their accomplishments with the rest of the team. "The first practice after each meet was always a fun game day," the coaches told us.

> We'd talk about the successes of the meet—there were always some, even if we lost the match—and then spend time just having fun in the water, being together, and celebrating the hard work they'd all put in to get ready for the meet and the way they'd supported each other. It was enjoyable and pulled the team together.

Celebrations—from swim teams to work teams; across classrooms, homes, families, communities, and organizations; and around the globe—are an important part of what it takes to make extraordinary things happen. People take time off from classes or work to gather to mark special occasions. They march in elaborate parades down the city's main street to shower a championship team with cheers of appreciation. They set off fireworks to commemorate historical events or the beginning of a new year. They convene impromptu ceremonies to cheer the victories of their colleagues. They attend banquets to show appreciation for individuals and groups who've accomplished an extraordinary feat. They sit down at elaborate feasts to give thanks for the bountiful harvest. They join with classmates at the end of a capstone project, give each other high-fives for a job well done, and make plans to get together and celebrate. And in tragic times, people come together with eulogies and songs to honor those who showed courage, conviction, and sacrifice.

People take the time to gather, tell stories, and raise their spirits because celebrations are among the most significant ways people worldwide proclaim respect and gratitude, renew a sense of community, and remember shared values and traditions. Celebrations are as important in defining a group as the things that make up its daily existence.

Performance improves when leaders on campuses, communities, and corporations publicly honor those who excel and demonstrate to others that "we are all in this together." Leaders make the group a place where people want to be and stay. That is why exemplary student leaders make a commitment to Celebrate the Values and Victories by mastering these essentials:

- **Create a spirit of community**
- **Be personally involved**

When leaders bring people together, rejoice in collective successes, and directly display their gratitude, they reinforce the essence of community and commitment. Being personally involved makes it clear that making extraordinary things happen requires everyone's responsibility.

CREATE A SPIRIT OF COMMUNITY

Too often, teams and organizations operate as if social gatherings were a nuisance, which is nonsense because they aren't. Human beings are social animals—hardwired to connect with others.[1] This is evident all the time on campuses around the world. Students have a desire to connect with other students, so they form and join student governments, fraternities and sororities, honor and service societies, residential learning groups, intramural sports teams, and the like. People are meant to do things together and form communities, demonstrating a common bond. When social connections are strong and numerous, greater trust, reciprocity, information flow, collective action, and happiness are evident.

Katie Szykman and Gianna (Gi) DiMatteo started a queer club at their art institute campus midway through their collegiate careers. During their junior year—the first year they were back on campus in person following the COVID-19 pandemic—Katie and Gi decided to put on a queer prom for their fellow students. "We hadn't been able to see each other since COVID; some of the freshmen at our college didn't get to have a senior prom in high school," Katie said.

Katie and Gi dreamed big for the event they wanted to put on for their peers, and they also knew they wanted the event to be as inclusive as possible, which would represent the values of the queer club. That meant the event should be free, open to all, easy to access for those with disabilities, and offer inclusive activities and catering. Most of all, queer prom was about offering every attendee, regardless of sexual orientation, a safe space to be their authentic self and make connections with new people. "We just really wanted everyone to feel like they had a space to come and just come as they are," Katie said.

The theme of the prom was "Be your most authentic self." Students came dressed in elaborate costumes they had created weeks in advance that they felt best represented their interiority. The queer prom had a dance floor and a raffle—with items donated by local community members—and attendees could visit a quiet space if they were overwhelmed by the music or preferred to talk or play games instead. The catering for the event was allergy- and vegan-friendly.

Instead of having prom kings and queens, the event had prom monarchs. One of the monarchs chosen was a trans woman, who came up to Gi after the event with especially meaningful feedback. "She just said she felt very recognized in her identity—that she could come to queer prom in her prettiest dress and feel accepted and welcomed and celebrated, it was really special," Gi said.

Queer prom was a hit—for weeks after, Gi said, people she only tangentially knew were coming up to her and congratulating her on how the event went. "A lot of people said things like, 'This was the best prom I've ever been to,'" Gi told us. But it wasn't because it had been the most over-the-top party—it was because Katie and Gi had created a way to celebrate their values and those of their friends and peers.

Exemplary student leaders know that promoting a culture of celebration fuels feelings of unity. Whether celebrations, ceremonies, and similar events honor an individual or group achievement or encourage team learning and relationship building, they offer leaders the perfect opportunity to explicitly communicate and reinforce the actions and behaviors vital to realizing shared beliefs and goals. Sometimes, celebrations can be elaborate, but more often they are about connecting everyday actions and events to the organization's values and the team's accomplishments. In the college environment, populated by students eager to have fun and "party down," celebrations can, however, lose their potential for these purposes.

Celebrations are about something other than having a great party. They often contain the same elements as a great party, but an additional ingredient makes them so significant. Authentic celebrations include a proud articulation of the achievements of group members and clearly communicate that "This is what we stand for, this is what we believe in, and this is what we are proud of." Exemplary leaders seldom let an opportunity pass to ensure that everyone knows why they're all together and how they should act in service of the shared values and

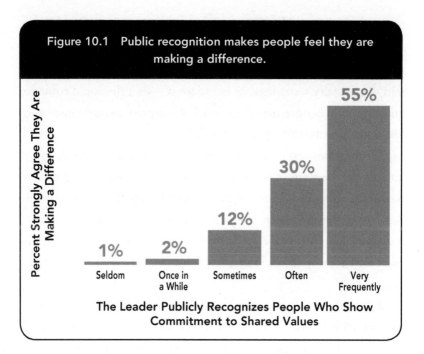

Figure 10.1 Public recognition makes people feel they are making a difference.

vision. Moreover, recognition and celebrations often are not just about what has already occurred and been accomplished; leaders also use these occasions to build the foundation for future contributions.

The data shows that there is a tremendous payoff experienced when student leaders "make it a point to publicly recognize people who show commitment to shared values." Such recognition increases people's sense of self-worth and level of productivity. It also strengthens their belief that their work is making a difference, as shown in Figure 10.1. Visibly recognizing commitment to shared values is integral to creating community and providing social support.

Celebrate Accomplishments in Public

Kaitlyn and Kevin took the opportunity to highlight the successes of individual team members after each swim meet. Swimmers who made personal-best times were recognized on a "Hurricane Heroes" bulletin board for all club members to see. The coaches also took time during the first practice after each meet to highlight the contributions of individual or relay wins and personal bests. "We'd let them know the points each win added to the team's score and give a round of applause for a personal-best time," Kevin said. "That recognition makes a difference; whether it's for a six-year-old who just beat their first time or a senior swimmer who hasn't set a personal-best time in a long while, the recognition reinforces that their accomplishment matters." Kevin and Kaitlyn understood that individual recognition increases the recipient's sense of worth and improves performance. Public celebrations also have this effect, and they add other lasting contributions to the welfare of individuals and teams that private, individual recognition can't accomplish. It's these added benefits that make celebrating *together* so powerful.

For one thing, public events are an opportunity to showcase real examples of what it means to "do what we say we will do." When the spotlight shines on certain people, and others tell stories about what these people did, those spotlighted individuals become role models. These people visibly represent how the organization would like everyone to behave and concretely demonstrate that it is possible. Public celebrations of accomplishment also build commitment among both the individuals recognized and those in the audience. When you tell individuals, "Keep up the good work; it's appreciated," you also speak to the larger group. You are saying, "Here are people like you who exemplify what we stand for and believe in. You can do this. You, too, can make a significant contribution to our success."

Exemplary leaders point out the individual's accomplishment and effectively reinforce that the entire group wins when people excel in this way. They understand that celebrations are not about making people feel as though there are favorites in the group, but about making them feel proud of what they have accomplished because of the contributions of particular members. The secret is in the word *we*. Leaders might point to individual accomplishments, but they connect how one person's excellence contributes to a win for all, pulling the group together and reinforcing the sense of community. Creating community helps ensure that people feel that they belong to something greater than themselves and are working collectively toward a common cause. Public celebrations of accomplishment serve to strengthen the bonds of teamwork and trust.

Some people are reticent or reluctant to recognize others in public, fearing that it might cause jealousy or resentment. Forget these fears. All winning teams present Most Valuable Player (MVP) awards, with the recipients usually selected by their teammates. Public celebrations are meaningful occasions to reinforce shared values and recognize individuals' contributions. They provide opportunities to thank specific individuals for their outstanding performance, and they also provide occasions to remind people of exactly what the organization stands for.

Private recognition is a marvelous thing. It motivates and builds the relationships essential for leading others, but it doesn't have the same impact on the team as public acknowledgment. To generate community-wide energy and commitment to the common cause, you need to celebrate successes in public. Awards ceremonies or banquets are familiar to most people, but there are other ways to celebrate publicly, even when you can't get everyone together in the same room.

Kenzie Crane, for example, created an online "Brag Room." Responsible for overseeing recruitment for all the sororities on her campus, she worked with a team of twenty recruiters, and the Brag Room was the way she provided a mechanism for people to be recognized "publicly" by their peers. Setting it up on the web was easy enough, but the key was ensuring everyone understood the space's intention and participated. The Brag Room's message was: "Here's where we want you to post and share the stories about someone you've seen doing something that made you proud to be associated with that person and with recruiters in general." Tons of stories of appreciation were posted. There was a posting about how someone dealt with a medical emergency in a special way; another acknowledged someone making a valuable introduction; and others gave examples of people going out of their way to stand up for the sorority system. All those stories, Kenzie said, "really made us all feel great and proud of the work we were doing."

Provide Social Support

Ceremonies and celebrations are opportunities to build healthier groups, to enable members of the organization to know and care about each other and offer social support. Research across a broad range of disciplines consistently demonstrates that social support enhances productivity, psychological well-being, and even physical health. Studies have shown that among undergraduate students, social support is the best predictor of their happiness; it is even more important than factors such as GPA, family income, SAT scores, age, gender, or race.[2] Social support enhances wellness and buffers against disease, particularly during times of high stress. This latter finding is true regardless of an individual's age, gender, or ethnic group. In fact, George Vaillant, Harvard professor of psychiatry who directed the world's longest continuous study of physical and mental health, when asked what he had learned from his forty years of research, said, "The only thing that really matters in life are your relationships to other people."[3]

Take it from Angela Close, who started a school club called Letters to Soldiers when she was a high school sophomore. A teacher suggested that students write a letter to a U.S. soldier to show appreciation for their service. When Angela wrote her letter, she included a few facts about herself—some cheesy jokes, events happening around her town, and condolences for the loss of friends in the line of duty.

It took nearly five months before she received a response, but the letter she received was filled with gratitude for her caring and sharing. The reply was from A. J. Pascuiti, a Marine gunnery sergeant who had graduated from her same high school. About the letter, he said, "It was the nicest thing anyone has ever done for me. Although the students may never physically get to see how they change lives, they are doing something that is helping soldiers who are out on the front lines; it validates what we do."

From that moment, Angela knew she had to continue sending letters to soldiers abroad. She started the letter-writing club, and it has been growing ever since. The club members receive very few letters back, but that is not the goal. Their purpose is to offer the support and connection they believe the soldiers serving the nation deserve. As one student explained, "I feel like it's a small way to change the world."

Lorenzo Zamora expressed a similar sentiment about his role as the food pantry director at his large midwest state university, where he was a graduate student. His job was to ensure that the pantry was adequately stocked, that students, faculty, and staff knew about the resources available there, and to keep operations running smoothly. But he also considered that part of his role was to make the food pantry a welcoming, supportive place. Lorenzo always thanked the people who visited the food pantry. Lorenzo told us that the pantry became an unofficial social gathering spot on campus, particularly for international students. A professor who teaches her classes in the same hallway as the food pantry told Lorenzo that she loved being close to it because it was always full of laughter and conversation. "It's really important to me to be encouraging and positive, to always have a smile on my face when people come to the food pantry. I just want to make everyone feel welcome."

Social support is not just good for your physical and mental health. It's also essential to outstanding performance. You have probably heard a class valedictorian's presentation at graduation. You may not remember the exact message, but if you recall the spirit of the speech, it was most likely one of appreciation for the support received along the way, gratitude for the friendships and meaningful relationships that led to the speaker's success, and optimism for the future of their classmates. These sentiments are consistent with what researchers found when analyzing the speeches of baseball players when inducted into the National Baseball Hall of Fame.[4] As elite athletes, they had achieved the highest recognition in a field demanding top physical skills. Yet their words of appreciation were not so much about technical or practical assistance as they were about emotional support and friendship.

What's true at home, in the community, and on the playing field is just as true for student organizations. People with friends at work, on their team, or in their classes are more productive, feel more informed, and are more comfortable sharing ideas. They report not only being more creative but also having more fun in these activities and getting more done in less time.[5]

Think about how these findings translate to the activities you are involved in. Isn't it more fun to work side by side on an event with people you know, trust, and can share and laugh with? Doesn't it feel like you get more done when communicating with people you understand and appreciate? Leaders find every opportunity to strengthen the personal relationships in their teams, not only because it helps get the job done, but also because, in doing so, they boost the people's spirits and well-being.

Our files are full of personal-best leadership cases in which robust human connections produced spectacular results. When people feel a strong sense of affiliation and attachment to the people in their group, they're much more likely to have a higher sense of personal well-being, feel more committed to the organization, and perform at higher levels. When people feel distant and detached, they're unlikely to accomplish much of anything.[6] When people are personally involved with the task and feel connected with their colleagues, they can perform extraordinary feats.

Student leaders understand that celebrations provide concrete evidence that individuals aren't alone in their efforts and struggles, that other people care about them, and that they can count on their support. Celebrations reinforce that people need each other and that it takes a group of individuals with a common purpose working together in an atmosphere of trust and collaboration to get extraordinary things done. Kenzie told us that when the sorority rush ended at her school, everyone met in a large open space on campus to welcome their new members. All the recruiters she had worked with came to this event and had the chance to see the results of their hard work. "I looked around and saw all the recruiters, some in tears, some holding hands, all of them smiling," Kenzie told us. "We had done good work, and so many were benefiting. That event really helped them see that."

Have Fun Together

Every personal-best leadership experience was a combination of hard work *and* fun. Students agreed that without the enjoyment and pleasure they experienced interacting with others on the team or project, they wouldn't have been able to sustain the intensity and diligence required to achieve their personal best. People just feel better about the work they are doing when they enjoy the people they're working with.[7]

Having fun sustains productivity because it lightens the load. And it's not all about parties, games, festivities, and laughter. Leaders who make addressing challenging issues fun are clearly passionate about their purpose, what they believe in, and how they pass this on to others. They understand that the work required to meet the dreams and goals of the group can be difficult and demanding and that people need a sense of personal well-being to go the distance. And leaders set the tone.

John Gray was a resident assistant for the Honors Program at his southwestern U.S. college, where student-created events were held throughout the year to help bring people together as a community. John was responsible for creating and supervising one of these events, which was scheduled to take place late in the academic year. Because the school calendar was issued early in the year, when the details of many events were not finalized, his event was simply listed on the calendar as "John Gray Day."

As the date approached, John wondered what kind of event to create. Many fun events took place at the beginning of the school year, but they tended to focus more on getting everyone off on the right foot. "I felt like it was time to get together just to have fun," John told us. But he still wasn't clear on what he wanted to plan. Then John noticed that people were curious about what was on the calendar, asking one another, "What is John Gray Day?" He decided to build on the mystery and have fun with it.

The whole point of these campus events was to bring people together, so John began to hatch plans to name one "John Gray Day." This wasn't a product of arrogance or self-absorption; it was John's way of playing on people's curiosity and rewarding them with a lot of fun. "It didn't hurt that John already had a reputation as a warm, funny, engaging guy," Michelle Madsen, resident community director, told us. "People were drawn to him. They'd wait outside their rooms when they knew he was doing rounds just to talk with him and laugh. That's the kind of appeal he had, and it meant that people anticipated that John Gray Day would be like him—fun—and it was."

John Gray Day was a big hit, offering many entertaining ways for students to get involved in the festivities. John assembled a bunch of people's baby pictures, including some of himself, and held a contest to "find the real John Gray." He made copies of black-and-white pictures of himself that people could color in. There was a chocolate fountain and lots of food from a local restaurant. "Everyone had a good time," Michelle told us, "but what I remember the most is the laughter."

John created a space for people to come together, be part of a community, and have fun being themselves. John Gray Day spoke to the spirit of the Honors Program: members work hard, but they want to have fun and enjoy each other's company, too.

John Gray Day took on a life of its own and continued for the next three years that John was an RA. People got more excited about it each year, and the energy grew. Students even created a "flat John Gray" and took it to different locations, even over the summer, to capture their adventures with John Gray and then post them for their fellow Honors Program classmates to see. John graduated and went on to medical school, but he has left a legacy as a student leader: John Gray Day continues.

Leaders set the tone. When student leaders openly demonstrate their joy and passion for their organizations, team members, and challenges, as John did, they send a compelling message to others that public displays of playfulness and gratitude are perfectly acceptable. They know that group assignments in and outside the classroom are demanding on today's campuses. Consequently, people must have a sense of personal well-being to sustain their commitment. It works for everyone when leaders show enthusiasm and excitement about the work required.

BE PERSONALLY INVOLVED

Our discussion of exemplary student leadership started with Model the Way, and we've come full circle. If you want others to believe in something and behave according to those beliefs, you must set an example by being personally involved. You must practice what you preach. To build and maintain a culture of excellence and distinction, you must be personally involved in celebrating the actions that contribute to and sustain the culture.

While enrolled in college, Kyle Harvey coached a local high school basketball team. At the end of the first season, he got some feedback from team members and their families that he had been focusing more on the negatives than the positives during games and practices, and that it was affecting the players' enthusiasm and commitment. In his second year of coaching, Kyle was determined to be more upbeat and focus on developing his players on the basketball court and as individuals.

On the first day of practice, Kyle told the team that he intended to be positive and hoped that the team would do the same, keeping an eye out for the things their fellow players did that were helping the team. As a result, Kyle got much more personally involved with the athletes, which helped him discover even more positive qualities in his players. He began recognizing them much more for what they were doing well rather than pointing out what they were doing wrong— and he did it out loud for the whole team to hear.

Over time, Kyle observed the team working harder and holding *each other* to higher standards.

> I could tell that when I was celebrating positive contributions,
> whether or not the individual played in the game, it boosted
> that player's confidence and gave us extremely positive results.

One example was a kid who had really been struggling with the game. Kyle spent time getting to know this player better, made it a point to be patient, and concentrated on applauding the improvements in his game and the successes he was having. As a result, the young athlete's performance improved dramatically and significantly impacted the team's success. This experience proved to Kyle that getting more engaged with his players and recognizing their individual contributions to the entire team resulted in stronger relationships with each player, greater individual development, and notable advancement for the entire team.

If you want to build and maintain a culture of excellence and distinction, you need to do as Kyle did: recognize, reward, reinforce, and celebrate exceptional efforts and successes. And you need to get personally involved in celebrating the actions that contribute to and sustain the culture. If you want people to have the courage to push through tough times, you need to encourage them yourself.

Consider Deus Cuong Do's experience. When Deus volunteered to teach English in a crash-course language school in Mexico, he wanted to create a culture of fun, togetherness, and sharing in the course. At the end of the language learning school, Deus and his group put together a song and dance performance to showcase their mastery of English. Deus knew it was on him as the teacher to create an environment where students could share and feel comfortable—and that failing to do so would make the experience a bad one for him, as well. "If I'm encouraging, and still no one wants to participate, that's not going to make me feel so good, either," Deus said.

Earlier in the language school, Deus had discovered that some of his students were dancers. He recruited them to come up with choreography that the entire group would feel comfortable doing. He fostered discussions so the students could pick a song they felt comfortable with—he also volunteered to participate in the group performance. "It trickled down; it made everyone a little more comfortable and willing to participate," Deus said.

The performance was a success, and afterward, Deus took the entire class out to a long lunch to celebrate the moment. To Deus, the most important part was that his students had put together the performance as a group and enjoyed it together.

Everyone was enthusiastically involved. No one was just *there*; it was like we were celebrating each other onstage. Everyone was dancing, singing along happily and willingly, even if they didn't remember all the English words. It was almost like a celebration during the performance. We were really happy. Everyone had a chance to shine.

Getting personally involved puts the spotlight on connecting what you preach with what you celebrate. If they are not one and the same, your celebrations will come off as insincere and phony—and your credibility will suffer. Recognition events and celebrations must be honest expressions of commitment to key values and to the hard work and dedication of the people who have lived the values. Remember, it's not just another chance to party. Treat it that way and you lose one of the best opportunities you have as a leader to pull people together, help them feel great about being part of the group, and inspire them to keep going. Elaborate productions that lack sincerity or do not connect in some clear way to the values of the group are more entertainment than encouragement. Authenticity is what makes conscious celebrations work.

When sending a message throughout an organization, nothing communicates more clearly than what leaders do. You're sending a positive signal by directly and visibly showing others that you're there to cheer them along. When you set an example that communicates the message that "around here we say thanks, show appreciation, and have fun," others will follow your lead. The group will develop a culture of celebration and recognition when everyone becomes a leader, adheres to the same values and norms, and everyone makes the time to celebrate the values and victories. As Kyle learned with his basketball team, when leaders are encouraging, their example is replicated, and an organization develops a reputation for magnetically holding people together.

Show You Care

People don't care about how much you know until they know how much you care for them. They must believe that you want them to be safe and secure and feel supported and valued; that you want them to be successful, continuously learning and developing themselves; and that you wouldn't ask them to do something where they could intentionally be embarrassed, injured, or hurt. Demonstrating this isn't rocket science. Take it from David Braverman's experience.

Iowa summers can be brutally hot, and before heading back to college, David found himself in an organic tomato field supervising an eclectic group of people. There were two other college students, a teacher interested in learning about organic farming firsthand, an "aging gentleman" who had dabbled at various careers and thought this one might be interesting, and a local health food store employee who had decided to stray from the air conditioning on this particular day to pick tomatoes. However, as the day wore on, the crew became demoralized, and David sensed that they were ready to quit. He realized that they needed someone to care about them; they needed encouragement if they were going to continue. With this epiphany, David said:

> First, I ran from the tomato fields and got all my coworkers an ice-cold glass of lemonade. Next, I explained to them that I knew the work was tough and that the day was hot, but that we needed to finish the tomato harvest so as to eliminate any possibility of tomatoes rotting. I asked them to stay positive.
>
> I then pointed out their strong suits as farm workers. I told them to look and see all of the tomatoes we had already harvested and how close we were to completing our task. We were in this together; we were all sweating as one. I thanked them for their help and explained that we were very

capable of completing the task and that the faster we did
so, the faster we could be by the nearest swimming pool.

They did finish the job that afternoon, and David says that the
lesson from this experience was profound: "When people are down
and demoralized, they need to be picked up and encouraged. Every
person needs to be valued not just for themselves as a person but for
their contribution to the team." As David realized, "Showing that you
care about someone is a simple yet overlooked quality essential to the
success of a leader."

What David says is spot-on. Also true is that one of the most
significant ways student leaders show others they care is to be there
with them—as David was. Thank-you notes and emails expressing
your appreciation are important, but being visible makes you more
real, genuine, approachable, and human. You show you care when you
spend time sweating in the fields yourself, when you are there helping set up for an event and cleaning up afterward, and when you are
attending meetings, work sessions, and organizational functions, even
when you're not directly responsible. Being there also helps you stay
in touch, quite literally, with what's really going on. And it shows you
walk the talk about the values you and others share. Credibility goes
up when leaders show they care.

Spread the Stories

Getting involved personally in showing that you care provides an
opportunity to both find and convey stories that put a human face
on values. The stories you tell give up-close-and-personal accounts of
what it means to put into practice shared values and aspirations. In the
process, you create organizational role models to whom everyone can
relate. You put expected behaviors into a real context. Values become
more than simply rules; they come alive. Through the stories you tell,

you dramatically and memorably illustrate how people should make decisions and act.

Storytelling is how people pass along lessons from one person to another, generation to generation and culture to culture. Stories aren't meant to be hush-hush; they're meant to be told. And because they're public, they're tailor-made for celebrations. The stories that leaders tell have much the same impact as the stories that parents tell their children, in the sense that the stories chosen provide a viewpoint about what is important and what matters. The content of the stories underscores what values are central and the actions that follow from them. They help set both a moral and a practical compass.[8] You can think of stories as celebrations and celebrations as storytelling.

Being part of the action by getting personally involved in celebrating the team's achievements allows leaders to create and find stories to share. First-person examples always have more impact than third-party examples. It's that critical difference between "I saw for myself" versus "someone told me about." Exemplary student leaders are constantly on the lookout for "catching people doing things right," and this is difficult to do if you are not out where the action is. Tell a story if you want to quickly translate information about how people are supposed to act and make decisions.[9]

By telling stories, you accomplish the objectives of teaching, mobilizing, and motivating people more effectively than you can through bullet points in a PowerPoint presentation or text messages. Listening to and understanding the stories leaders tell does more to inform people about a group's values and culture than any organizational handbooks, policies, or operational guidelines. Well-told stories are effective in reaching people's emotions and pulling them along. They make the message stick. They simulate the experience of actually being there and give people a compelling way of learning the most important thing about the experience. Reinforcing stories through celebrations deepens the connections between people.

Make Celebrations Part of Organizational Life

One of the Hurricanes swim team's traditions was the awards banquet at the end of the season after the league championship. The swimmers all looked forward to the slide show featuring candid shots of the team taken throughout the summer. Coaches Kaitlyn and Kevin also saw the awards banquet as an opportunity to reinforce the values and messages shared throughout the season and a chance to celebrate individual and team excellence. "We made a 'paper plate' award for each swimmer," they told us.

> We handed the award plate out with the final stats for the season on it. It also had a name or title we assigned to each swimmer based on their unique personality and contribution to the team. For example, an eight-year-old boy who was always giggling and making people laugh might get the name "Lucas the Laugh Maker." A swimmer who had made huge strides during the season might be called "Bonnie the Buzzsaw." Sometimes we think they looked forward to those plates more than the ribbons and trophies. It was fun for us to get ready for the event and really reinforced what the summer swim league is all about.

You should put celebrations on your calendar, just as the Hurricanes did with their awards banquet. These scheduled events serve as opportunities to get people together so that you can show them how they are part of the larger vision and have a shared destiny. Celebrations are highly visible ways to affirm shared values, mark meaningful progress, and create community.

You probably already put birthdays, holidays, and anniversaries on your calendar. You also should do it for the significant milestones in the life of your team and organization. Giving them a date, time, and place announces to everyone that these things matter. It also creates a sense of anticipation. Scheduling celebrations doesn't rule out spontaneous events; it just means that certain occasions are of such significance that everyone needs to pay attention to them and remember why they are special.

That's the message Lee LeBoeuf communicated when she started a new tradition to commemorate the accomplishments of her university's senior class before graduation. As class president, Lee led a team to create a celebration for the class that would continue through the years. She conferred with her classmates about experiences that had meant a lot to them as first-year students. One that stood out was The Welcome Tunnel, an event welcoming new students to campus. "I thought it would be really cool to create an event for everyone to celebrate the end of our time together on campus, to kind of bookend the freshman experience," Lee said.

Lee and her colleagues decided to put on an event called "The Final Lap." It would be a symbolic final trip around campus, complete with a party at the end of the race open to everyone. Graduating seniors would jog or walk a lap around the campus as music played. Afterward, they would meet their friends and other students for a celebration with food and dance to mark the end of their collegiate careers.

It was a bigger undertaking than anything the senior class had ever put together for a year-end celebration. It was sometimes tough to keep everyone motivated over the entire year, particularly with their time at the university wrapping up. "I struggled to keep my fellow seniors motivated and working toward the event because their other responsibilities on campus were coming to an end," Lee told us. "My entire team was made up of seniors, so it was difficult to motivate them to work during a time when they wanted to be celebrating all the work they had already put into their undergraduate careers."

Lee broke down each large task—for example, charting the course for The Final Lap—into smaller tasks, such as reaching out to the groundskeeping staff to figure out where they would have electricity to play music and put lights along the course. Completing each task served as a celebration point for the student council members who had worked on that task.

> We'd celebrate each smaller milestone so that we could see how each piece contributed to the entire experience—it wasn't so daunting when we could have small victories along the way. It also made the whole process more fun.

She said that a strong narrative about why the event was important helped motivate Lee's team.

> We had a story to tell about how this was something we'd done as first-year students and how much it would mean to our whole class to be able to re-create that experience in a different context. I could also say to my team, "Look, this is going to be an experience we want to continue in the future; this is going to be the new tradition for graduating seniors, and you got to help start it. When we come back for our ten-year reunion, people will still be doing this run, and they'll have improved it and made it even better." That went a long way to keeping everyone involved and motivated.

Finally, Lee noted that it was important for her student council to know that The Final Lap and the celebration afterward were as much for them as for their fellow graduates. "This was our last chance to have a hoorah as a group, to celebrate all of our hard work and see it embodied for our peers," Lee said. Part of the driving motivation was to have one last time to have fun and celebrate together.

In setting up celebrations, student leaders like Lee decide which organizational values, events of historical significance, or remarkable successes are of such importance that they warrant a special ritual, ceremony, or festivity. Perhaps you want to honor the people who started your organization or created an astounding event. Maybe you want to praise those who reached amazing levels of community service or thank the parents and families of your group members. Whatever you wish to celebrate, formalize it, announce it, and tell people how they become eligible to participate.

The importance of celebrations is borne out by how students feel when their leaders "find ways for people to celebrate accomplishments." Only three out of a hundred students whose leaders *seldom* or *once in a while* celebrate report being highly productive or believe they are making a difference. Similarly, striking results are shown in Figure 10.2 about how finding ways to celebrate strongly impacts students' feelings about the extent to which the leader values their work.

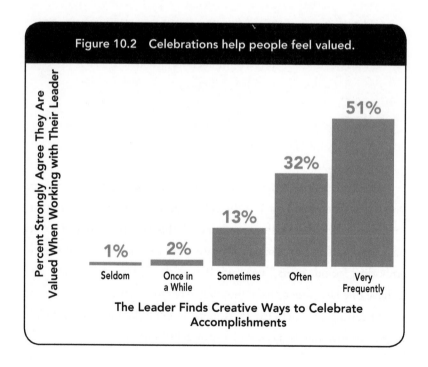

Figure 10.2   Celebrations help people feel valued.

There is no shortage of opportunities to bring people together to celebrate your group's values and victories. In good times or bad, gathering together to acknowledge those who've contributed—and the actions that led to success—signals to everyone that their work and determination are well worth the effort. Their energy, enthusiasm, and well-being—and yours—will be all the better for it.

REFLECT AND ACT: CELEBRATE THE VALUES AND VICTORIES

Celebrating together reinforces the fact that extraordinary performance is the result of many people's efforts. Student leaders create and foster community and sustain team spirit by visibly and publicly acknowledging the team's accomplishments. Student leaders reinforce and sustain people's focus when their celebrations are consistent with core values and recognize small wins.

Social interaction increases the commitment that individuals have to the standards of the group and has a profound effect on people's well-being. When people are asked to go beyond their comfort zones, the support and encouragement of others enhance their resiliency and resistance to stress.

Student leaders demonstrate that recognition and celebration are the norm by getting personally involved. Telling stories about individuals who have made exceptional efforts and achieved outstanding successes provides role models for others to emulate. Stories make people's experiences memorable, often even profound in ways they hadn't envisioned, and serve as a guide for future actions. Making personal connections with people in a culture of celebration also builds and sustains credibility for the cause and the people involved. Leaders make it a point to bring people together to bear testimony about what has been and can be accomplished because of their collective efforts.

Reflect

The second commitment of the leadership practice Encourage the Heart requires leaders to *celebrate the values and victories by creating a spirit of community*. What is the most important idea or lesson about exemplary leadership that you learned from this chapter?

_____

_____

_____

_____

Here are actions you can take to more effectively follow through on your commitment to **Celebrate the Values and Victories**:

- Plan to set aside time at an upcoming group gathering to share evidence of success with everyone.
- Make sure to relate the fundamental principles being honored when you bring people together to celebrate.
- Never pass up any opportunity to publicly relate true stories about how people in your group went above and beyond the call of duty.
- Make sure that everyone understands how they are "part of the whole" and that many others are working to achieve success for the group, even if they don't know those people personally.
- Repeat this phrase—"We are in this together"—at every celebration.
- Don't wait until the whole project is completed to celebrate. Plan a festive celebration for even the smaller milestones that your team reaches or the remarkable efforts people put forth.

- Whatever the celebration, experiment with ways to keep this ritual fresh, meaningful, genuine, and fun.
- Make sure you are personally present and involved with celebrations.

Act

After you have reflected on what you learned, what you can improve, and the preceding suggestions, record your plan here for taking at least one action that will help you become a better leader:

_____

_____

_____

_____

_____

_____

Continue Your Leadership Development

Throughout this book, we have shared stories and research that clearly demonstrate the ability of students to lead others, making extraordinary things happen for their classmates and colleagues, their schools, and their communities. We believe everyone is capable of leadership, and you can do everything we've written about if you want to (remember that the choice is always yours).

The Five Practices of Exemplary Leadership gives you the framework to liberate the leader within. But exploring your leadership potential while you're a student is just the beginning. Let your time in school be the opportunity to learn about yourself, how to work with others, and how to put your heart into doing what you think matters.

That's precisely what Tarek Aly did. He experienced his first leadership opportunity just one week after entering college. His instructor talked about how serving others was a major part of becoming an effective leader, and a hurricane had just hit the Gulf Coast. Tarek and a classmate came up with the idea of creating a carnival to raise funds to support the relief effort. In just about a month, their Emergency Mardi Gras was held, and all told, the students raised nearly $28,000.

This was only the beginning of Tarek's leadership journey. He wanted to do something that could help people in the longer term. The local community was embroiled in a debate about how to feed the people experiencing homelessness in the region. Tarek saw an opportunity to bring students together to address this issue in ways that hadn't even been imagined. With a core group of six students, they targeted an area about an hour away from campus, and every Wednesday, they would get together in Tarek's campus apartment and make a bag of peanut butter and jelly sandwiches. Then they would hop into two cars and drive in search of anyone they found living on the streets. They didn't just want to feed those who were unhoused. "We wanted to do something that could help transform their lives," Tarek said.

It wasn't about the sandwiches; it was about relationships. We wanted to have conversations with the people most others ignored. The peanut butter and jelly sandwiches were just the tool to begin these conversations.

This was the beginning of "Hope in Hand," and within just a few months, there was a caravan of students driving every Wednesday afternoon to hang out with people on the street and talk to them. Week after week, relationships grew as the students would see the same people. The students learned about the experiences and aspirations of unhoused people in a way that would not have been possible if they were working on a soup kitchen line.

Local business owners in the area started coming into the streets on Wednesdays to help out or listen to what the students and street people were saying to one another. What had been a relatively invisible population had become people with names and hope. Within two years, other campus student groups started their programs modeled after Hope in Hand.

Tarek continued to find other opportunities to make a difference as he moved through college. He became one of the founders of his fraternity and worked in a social services agency as a case manager handling some of their most difficult male teen cases. He became the president of the Multicultural Student Association, serving as the campus umbrella group for all ethnic student groups. In that role, he worked to establish a stronger support system for multicultural students on campus.

Tarek's student leadership career is a wonderful example of the ongoing journey at the heart of exemplary leadership. Leadership is not about a box you check or a single event. It's an ongoing experience of commitment and service. Like a deep friendship, it gets defined with each interaction and gets richer with time. Tarek summed it up for us this way:

> The key to leadership is being intentional. If you have pure intentions people will rally behind you and everything else will fall into place. I found out that learning goes side by side with knowing who I was as a person and as a leader. I learned what was important to me and how I could use those things to make a difference in others.

The Five Practices and Ten Commitments of Exemplary Leadership described in depth in this book give you the framework to liberate the leader within. The student leaders we have talked about are from campuses all over the globe and in different stages of their academic lives. Chances are you haven't read about them or heard them mentioned in the press. They're not public figures, celebrities, or megastars. They might sit next to you in a classroom or at another table in the student union, live in the room down the hall, or in an apartment across the street. In short, they are people just like you.

We've focused on everyday exemplary student leaders because leadership is not about position or title. It's not about power or authority. It's not about fame or fortune. It's not about the family you are born into or your cultural heritage. And it's definitely not about being a superhero. Leadership is about relationships and about what you do.

Understanding and utilizing The Five Practices of Exemplary Leadership as an *operating system for leadership* is a place to start. Exploring your leadership potential while you are a student is an essential beginning. But we've learned a few other important lessons from our research that you must remember as you continue your leadership development journey. We close this book with those lessons, the first of which is the most important: "How you behave makes a difference."

YOUR LEADERSHIP MAKES A DIFFERENCE

Right now, whether you hold a position or not in a student organization, classroom project, or community service group, you are impacting the other members of whatever group, project, or team you are involved with. Sometimes that impact is highly visible, and sometimes it happens even when you're not present. Sometimes your actions are bold, and other times they're little things. Regardless, it is how you behave that makes a difference.

Kayla Richard shared her illustrative experience. Kayla tore her ACL in her first year playing on her university's basketball team, and while having to sit out the rest of the season, she believed she still had a role on the team. For example, before each away game, when Kayla couldn't travel because of her injury, she would write a note to each teammate, listing specific individual strengths and offering personalized words of encouragement. "To me," Kayla said, "it was just a way of letting the girls know that I was there with them in spirit, and I believed in them. My teammates loved it! They were really touched and told me that it motivated them to play harder."

Kayla realized, as have so many other students, that even small acts of positive leadership can significantly impact others. Wherever you are in your leadership journey, regardless of whether you now hold an official position or will in the future, and no matter what role you play, you, too, can touch and motivate others. After all, what's really expected of any leader? Is it to improve performance, keep it the same, or make it worse? Admittedly, this is a rhetorical question. All leaders are expected to have a positive impact on results. That's why, in every chapter of this book, we've provided case studies, examples, and empirical data showing how exemplary leadership significantly affects people's well-being, commitment, motivation, school, and project performance, and the success of their organizations. We want you to know that your leadership matters.

How you behave as a leader matters, and it matters a lot. It matters to you. It matters to your classmates. It matters to your family. It matters to your friends. It matters to your neighbors. As shown in Figure E.1, the data makes this point clear: the more students report

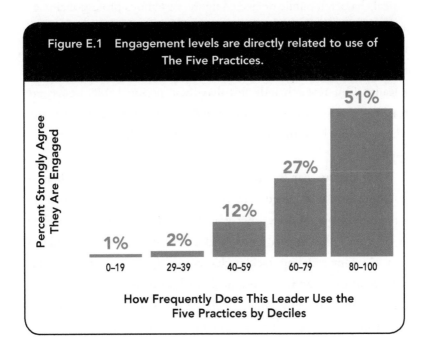

Figure E.1   Engagement levels are directly related to use of The Five Practices.

their leader using The Five Practices, the more strongly they report being engaged.[1] The extent of engagement is nearly negligible for those students in the three lowest quintiles, whose leaders do not often utilize the leadership behaviors associated with exemplary leadership.

You have the potential to make a meaningful difference in the lives of those you lead. It's up to you to determine the difference you want to make, and then you must strengthen your capacity to make it.

YOU ARE THE MOST IMPORTANT LEADER IN THE ROOM

When we ask people to name someone who has been a meaningful role model for them in learning what leadership looks like in action, they mention an individual whom they know rather than some historical character, public or elected figure, or famous professional (e.g., athlete, actor, entertainer, or billionaire), or headline-capturing social media influencer. Most often, they select someone personally close to them (now or in the past) who illustrated what it means to be a leader. Our research indicates that these personal role models are teachers, coaches, parents, relatives, and friends.[2] They're the ones with whom people have the most frequent contact. The same realization applies to you.

This means that to the people you are working with, there is no more important leader in the room than you. What you do sets an example, as does what you don't do. You are being looked at by your colleagues, friends, and classmates for the example of how someone steps up, tackles challenging goals, responds to difficult situations, handles crises, deals with setbacks, or resolves ethical dilemmas. It's not someone else. Like Michael Jackson's song "Man in the Mirror," if you want to make a change, you have to realize that it starts with you. As Samantha Morrow explained in her personal-best leadership experience:

> Not having a position did not stop me from leading. As long as I am actively involved and help ensure that things stay organized, I can be a leader. I can step in and work for those who are unwilling to do their job. Simply motivating other members and helping where no one will is as much of a leadership position as someone who actually holds a title.

No matter your position in a group, you have to take responsibility for the quality of its leadership. You are accountable for the leadership you demonstrate. And because you are the most important leader to those closest to you, your only choice is whether or not to be the best leader you can be. But wait, you ask, "Can anyone (*even me?*) learn to be an exemplary leader?"

LEADERSHIP IS LEARNED

Nearly every time we teach a class, give a speech, or conduct a workshop, someone will ask, "Are leaders born or made?" Whenever we're asked this question, our answer, always offered with a smile, is this: "We've never met a leader who wasn't born. We've also never met an accountant, artist, athlete, engineer, lawyer, physician, professor, teacher, writer, or zoologist who wasn't born. We're all born. That's a given."

You might be thinking, "Well, that's not fair. That's a trick answer. Of course, everyone is born." That's precisely our point. Every one of us is born, and every one of us has the necessary material to become a leader.

The question you and others should ask yourselves is not, "Am I born to be a leader?" Instead, to become a better leader, the more demanding and significant question you should ask is, "Can I become a better leader tomorrow than I am today?" To that question, our answer is a resounding "YES!"

Let's get something straight. Leadership is *not* some mystical quality that only a few people have and everyone else doesn't. Leadership is not preordained. It is not a gene, and it is not a trait. There is no hard evidence to support the assertion that leadership is imprinted in the DNA of only some individuals and that everyone else missed out and is doomed to be clueless.

Remember Katie Szykman and Gi DiMatteo from Chapter 10—they both told us that before starting the queer club and throwing queer prom, they hadn't thought of themselves as leaders. But the practical skills and challenges they had to overcome along the way showed them that leadership is a learned skill. "In college, I had a variety of internships and work experiences. But none of it taught me as much as being co-president of the queer club," Katie said.

> It taught me how to manage a budget, how to manage a team, and how to keep that team moving together in the right direction. Everything I learned from this experience wasn't something I expected to learn in college—but I did, and I'm so grateful I did. I feel like we really became leaders through this experience, and I'm so ready to take that with me into the workforce. I think everyone should explore the opportunities available to them in their university—you really never know where it's going to lead.

We've collected leadership assessment data from millions of people around the world. We can tell you without a doubt that there are leaders in every educational setting, in every profession and function, in every type of organization, in every religion, every country, and from every age, gender, and race. It's a myth that leadership can't be learned—that you either have it or you don't. There is leadership potential everywhere we look.

Leadership is an *observable pattern of practices and behaviors* and *a definable set of skills and abilities*. And any skill can be learned, strengthened, honed, and enhanced, given the motivation and desire, along with practice, feedback, role models, and coaching. When we track students' progress in leadership development programs, the research demonstrates that they improve over time.[3] Similarly, when researchers track the progress of people who participate in leadership development programs in workplace settings, the research demonstrates they get the same results.[4] As is the case with any set of skills, when people engage in activities to strengthen their abilities to use The Five Practices of Exemplary Leadership, they can demonstrate them more frequently.

In challenging times, continuous learning must be a priority for everyone. In school—especially as you transition to the workplace—and throughout your careers—learning leadership must be at the top of the agenda. Why? Very simply, it's this: people who are most actively involved in learning are also the ones who engage most often in The Five Practices of Exemplary Leadership.[5] It has also been reported that those leaders who engage in learning for five or more hours per week, compared to those who spend an hour or less per week, are 74 percent more likely to have *more direction in their careers* and 48 percent more likely to *find purpose in their work*. They are also happier.[6] The more you seek to learn, the better you will become at leadership (or at anything, for that matter). What's clear is that *the best leaders are the best learners*!

Learning Starts by Looking Inside

Engineers have computers; painters have canvas and brushes; musicians have instruments. Leaders have only themselves and their experiences. The instrument of leadership is the self, and mastery of the art of leadership comes from mastery of the self. Leadership development is self-development, and self-development is not about stuffing in a whole bunch of new information or trying the latest technique. It's about leading from what is already in your soul. It's about liberating the leader within you. And it starts with looking inside. You can't lead others until you've first led yourself on a journey of self-discovery. To become the leader you aspire to be, you must take the time to step back and reflect deeply on your past, present, and future.

"As someone who's struggled with self-doubt in the past," Adam Schellenberg told us just before his college graduation:

> I did not believe I had the capacity to be a leader. I believed that leaders were born with many qualities that I simply did not possess. But having the opportunity to think more deeply about my personal values and clarify my aspirations, I now have a path forward and believe I can make a difference.

Like Adam, you need confidence in yourself, and your ability to excel as a leader begins with how well you know yourself. The better you know yourself, the better you can make sense of the often confusing and conflicting messages you receive daily as a student: "do this, do that; support this, support that; decide this, decide that; change this, change that." You need internal guidance to navigate the turmoil in today's highly uncertain environment.

Building your capacity to be an active learner also requires a growth mindset, which is the belief that people's basic qualities can be improved and strengthened through their efforts, in contrast to a fixed mindset, which presumes one's qualities are inherent and carved in stone. With a growth mindset, you believe that you (as well as other people) can learn to be better leaders. Holding a fixed mindset means that you believe that no amount of training or experience will make people better than they already are.[7]

Our research found that those with a growth mindset were more willing than those with a fixed mindset to embrace challenges, persist when facing obstacles, and sustain efforts, even when confronted with resistance. Believing that people can change and grow, growth-minded individuals were willing to foster innovation and focus on learning from setbacks. They showed a greater propensity to support experimentation by others. People with a fixed mindset avoided challenging situations and were unlikely to open themselves to feedback.[8] Mindsets, not just skill sets, make the critical difference in deciding to take on challenging situations.

There is no shortcut to knowing yourself and discovering who you are, what drives you, what's important to you, whom or what you want to serve, and the like. It takes serious self-reflection, and the more you engage in it, the more you discover about yourself. Knowing who you are makes it easier to connect with other people and communicate more effectively about what matters to you. Your leadership becomes authentic—because it is an expression of who you are and not some means to an end.

Three Ways to Learn to Lead

Although leadership can be learned, not everyone wants to learn it, and not all those who learn about leadership master it. Why? Because becoming the very best requires having a deep desire to excel, a strong belief that new skills and abilities can be learned, a willing devotion to deliberate practice, and continuous reflection and experimentation. No matter how good you are, you can always become better.[9]

No matter how many summits you've ascended, you must take a step every day to improve—one reflection at a time, one question at a time, one lesson at a time. Being an exemplary leader requires a lifelong daily commitment to learning. What differentiates an expert performer from merely good ones is hours of practice developing their skills. It doesn't matter whether it's in sports, music, medicine, computer programming, mathematics, leadership, or any other field, you've got to work at becoming the best, and it sure doesn't happen over a weekend or by taking a single class.

The point is that you need to put in the time and effort to sharpen any skill. Leadership is no different. To be a good leader, you'll have to practice. Early in her third year at university, Julie Guillaumin told us:

> What fascinates me is that while there are ladders in corporations for climbing to the top, leadership remains a level playing field. Many people mindlessly trudge through mediocre work and school life because so many "busy" tasks prevent significant reflection and taking initiative. We overlook how school and work can actually be our greatest opportunity for the discovery and growth of our leadership capabilities.

You must have a passion for learning to become the best leader you can be. You must be open to new experiences and an honest examination of how you and others perform, especially when the going gets tough or the future is uncertain. You must be willing to learn quickly from your failures and successes and find ways to try out new behaviors without hesitation. You won't always be right or do things perfectly, but you will get the chance to develop and grow.

In our research, as part of the investigation into personal-best leadership experiences, we asked people, "How did you learn to lead?" There was not one best way to pursue learning leadership; instead, three distinct approaches emerged. The most frequently mentioned learning approach was through direct experiences. Observing others was another helpful learning strategy, and participating in organized education programs was the third.

Experience: Learning through Trial and Error

There's no substitute for learning by doing. Learning from trial and error—that "school of hard knocks" people talk about so often—is not just a saying. More people mentioned experience as the most important way to learn to lead than any other approach. Experience was mentioned almost twice as often as observing other leaders and nearly three times as often as organized education.

It's simply this: dancers dance better by dancing. Runners run faster by running. Writers write better by writing. Leaders lead better by leading. Whether it's facilitating team meetings, leading a special task force, heading a charity fundraising drive, or chairing a school-wide or annual conference, the more chances you have to lead, the more likely it is that you'll develop the skills to lead—and the more likely that you'll learn the vital leadership lessons that only come from the failures and successes of action. We found a strong positive correlation between how many leadership opportunities student leaders reported having and how frequently they engaged in The Five Practices.

Just any experience, however, does not support individual development by itself. Challenge is crucial to learning and career enhancement. Tedious, routine tasks don't help you improve your skills and abilities. You must stretch yourself. You must seek opportunities to test yourself against new and nonroutine tasks. Experience *can* indeed be the best teacher—if it includes the element of personal challenge. Whenever you select experiential activities to boost your performance, choose projects and assignments that involve a stretch.[10] If you are put in a role that doesn't stretch you, figure out how to do it differently so that you *are* stretched.

Additionally, when you practice leading, set specific goals for what you want to learn, focus on a defined skill or technique, and get helpful feedback on how you did. If your goal is to improve how you lead meetings, set a goal, for example, to gather ideas from at least half the participants by asking them direct questions, and then at the end of the meeting, ask people to tell you how they experienced the meeting. What did you do well in engaging others? What could you improve? What would they recommend you do in the future? Without feedback on the goals you set and methods you used, you'll never know how much progress you're making.

Examples: Learning by Observing Others

You can't lead alone, and neither can you learn alone. The top performers in every endeavor, including leaders, all seek out support, advice, and the counsel of others. That has a lot to do with why they are the most successful.

All the people around you are potential sources of learning. Role models are critical to learning anything and essential when learning how to lead. As you design your continuing leadership development, look for role models, coaches, and teachers in your organization or community. Don't hesitate to ask for their help or permission to watch them in action. Ask to sit in on meetings they run or attend presentations they make. Take them out to coffee and interview them on how they handle difficult situations. Ask them for feedback about how they may have seen you operate with your peers. Their feedback is the only way to learn how you are doing. Getting open and honest feedback only happens when there is a foundation of mutual trust.

As you enter your career at work, the relationship that will make the most difference in your performance is your relationship with your immediate manager. Managers not only serve as potential role models, but they can also provide beneficial developmental feedback. The best managers are those who challenge you, trust you, spend time with you, and teach you. If you are fortunate to have one of those managers who is a role model for leadership, take charge of this relationship and make the most of it. If you have one of those managers who'd make a great candidate for the ten worst bosses, observe what *not* to do. Remember, managers can have both a favorable and a damaging impact on others. Adopt the positive and reject the negative.

Peers are also valuable sources of knowledge, skill, and information. Trusted peers can serve as advisers and counselors, giving you feedback on your style and helping you test alternative ways of dealing with problems. If you have a colleague who's strong in an area you need to improve, ask that person to teach you what they know. Ask people to share their best practices and seek opportunities to observe them in action.

Education: Learning through Training and Coursework

Formal training and education can improve your leadership abilities. Even though people devote significantly less time to these, and the opportunities to participate and learn are often not as directly on-the-job or part of everyone's daily routines, they can still be a high-leverage opportunity. Done right, classes, workshops, and seminars enable you to spend a concentrated period with an expert focused on one subject and some specific skills. This focused attention helps you to learn something more quickly, with the benefit of having multiple chances to practice new behaviors and skills and get feedback in a safe environment. As with opportunities to lead, there was a strong positive correlation between the number of "formal" developmental opportunities in leading and learning about leadership student leaders reported having and how frequently they employed The Five Practices.

Increasingly, as many people discovered during the coronavirus pandemic, you can do training on your own through a plethora of learning technologies featuring seminars, workshops, presentations, simulations, how-to sessions, threaded discussions, and the like. Even if your school or organization doesn't sponsor them, take advantage of self-directed learning opportunities that you can complete on your own time and at your own pace. In addition, consider picking up a couple of biographies of contemporary or historical people you admire and read about how they learned to lead and the struggles they dealt with and overcame.

Finally, to get the most out of any educational experience, make sure you take the opportunity to apply what you've learned. Consider these to be "experiments." The probability that you'll apply what you've learned in training decreases each day following the end of an experience. Whenever possible, take the time to describe what you learned with your teacher, mentor, coach, supervisor, fellow students, or colleagues. That's another effective method for taking an essential first step in determining how to apply best what you learned or experienced in the classroom now.

LEADERSHIP AND HUBRIS: NO GUARANTEES

You'll excuse us for not pointing out at the onset of this book that you can execute flawlessly on all five practices and ten commitments, and people may still not follow you completely. You can still get "fired," not end up in first place, not win the contract, lose the contest or election, or whatever. But you probably knew this already. There's absolutely no way that we can say that any of these leadership practices will *always* work all the time with all people. We know for sure that there's a strong probability that they will contribute to your effectiveness, but there's no ironclad money-back guarantee. And if anyone ever stands in front of you and claims that they have *the* three, five, seven, or nine-factor theory that's 100 percent certain to get you results and rewards, grab onto your wallet and run. There's no get-rich-quick, instant weight-loss program for leadership (or for getting rich or losing weight, for that matter).

Here's another caveat. Any leadership practice *can* become destructive. Virtues can become vices. There's a point at which each of The Five Practices, taken to extremes, can lead you astray.

For example, although clarifying values and setting an example are essential to modeling, an obsession with being seen as a role model can lead to being too focused on your own values and your way of doing things. It can cause you to discount others' views and be closed to feedback. It can push you into isolation for fear of losing privacy or being "found out" and cause you to be more concerned with style than substance.

Being forward-looking and communicating a clear and shared vision of the future is what sets leaders apart from other credible people. Yet, a singular focus on one vision of the future can blind you to other possibilities and the realities of the present. It can cause you to miss the exciting possibilities that are just out of your sight or make you hang on just a little too long to an out-of-date technology. Exploiting your powers of inspiration can cause others to surrender their will. Your energy, enthusiasm, and charm may be so magnetic that others stop thinking for themselves and mindlessly agree with your perspective.

Challenging the process is essential to promoting innovation and progressive change. Seizing initiative and taking risks are necessary for learning and continuous improvement. However, take this to extremes and you can create needless turmoil, confusion, and paranoia. Routines are important, and if you seldom pause long enough to give people an opportunity to gain confidence and competence, they'll lose their motivation to try new things. Change for change's sake can be just as demoralizing as complacency.

Collaboration and teamwork are essential to making extraordinary things happen in today's hyperactive world. However, an over-reliance on collaboration and trust may reflect an avoidance of addressing critical issues or cause errors in judgment. It may be a way of *not* taking charge when the situation requires it. Delegating power and responsibility can become a way of dumping too much on others when they're not fully prepared to handle it.

Personal recognition and group celebration create the spirit and momentum that can carry a group forward, even during the toughest challenges. At the same time, if you constantly worry about who should be recognized and when you should celebrate, you can become a gregarious minstrel. You can lose sight of the mission and any sense of urgency because you're having so much fun, so consumed by all the perks and pleasures that you forget the purpose of it all.

Far more insidious than these potential problems, however, is the dangerous lure of hubris. It's fun to be a leader, gratifying to have influence, and exhilarating to have scores of people cheering your every word. In many all-too-subtle ways, power and importance make it easy to be seduced. All evil leaders have been infected with the disease of hubris, becoming bloated with an exaggerated sense of self and pursuing their own sinister ends. How do you avoid this?

Humility is the antidote for hubris. You can avoid excessive pride only when you recognize that you're human and need the help of others. Exemplary student leaders know that they "can't do it alone," and they act accordingly. They lack the pride and pretense displayed by many leaders who succeed in the short term but leave behind a weak organization that fails to remain viable after their departure. They remain interested in the ideas of others, learning about matters for which they don't already have the answers. They are resilient and demonstrate a willingness to experiment. They appreciate the lessons learned from experience, including the disappointments. With self-effacing humor, deep listening to those around them, and generous and sincere credit to others, humble leaders achieve higher and higher levels of performance.

It takes a lot of courage to admit that you aren't always right, that you can't always anticipate every possibility, that you can't envision every future, that you can't solve every problem, that you can't control every variable, that you aren't always congenial, that you make mistakes, and that you are, in a word, human. It takes courage to admit all these things to others, but it may take even more courage to admit them to yourself. If you can find the humility to do that, you invite others into a courageous conversation. When you let down your guard and open yourself up to others, you invite them to join you in the creation of something that you alone could not create. When you become more modest and unpretentious, others have the chance themselves to become visible and noticed.

Nothing in our research hints that leaders of any age should be perfect. Leaders aren't saints. They're human beings, full of flaws and failings like everyone else. They make mistakes. Perhaps the very best advice we can offer to all aspiring leaders is to remain humble and unassuming—always to remain open to learning more about yourself and the world around you.

LEADERSHIP IS IN THE MOMENT

Sometimes leadership is imagined as something quite bold and majestic—about grand visions, world-changing initiatives, and transforming the lives of millions, saving the planet if not the universe. These are noble possibilities, but authentic leadership generally occurs one moment at a time. Every interaction and situation you find yourself in presents an opportunity to provide leadership.

In reflecting on his journey to becoming a better leader, Sergey Nikiforov, as a graduate student, once asked us, "Where do I start becoming a better leader?" Before we could answer, he offered on his own this simple yet profound realization:

> This question has been nagging me for some time. Naively, I assumed that to become a better leader meant to perform formidable tasks: moving mountains, saving lives, and changing the world for the better. As you have pointed out, these noble, grandiose tasks are often insurmountable for a single person.
>
> Then it occurred to me—I was thinking selfishly. What I envisioned was instant gratification and recognition of my skills and talent. Although the issues at work matched well with the book's materials, the way I dealt with them was far from ideal. In most cases, I used the wrong tools and methods.
>
> I found that every day I had an opportunity to make a small difference. I could have coached someone better, I could have listened better, I could have been more positive toward people, I could have said "thank you" more often, I could have . . . the list just went on. At first, I was a bit overwhelmed by the discovery of how many opportunities I had in a single day to act as a better leader. But as I have gotten to put these ideas into practice, I have been pleasantly surprised by how much improvement I have been able to make by being more conscientious and intentional about acting as a leader.

Sergey nailed it. Each day provides countless opportunities to make a difference. The chance might come in a private conversation with a friend or in a meeting with colleagues. It might come over the family dinner table. It might come when you're presenting at a student leadership symposium or when you're listening to a friend talk about a current conflict with a peer. There are many moments each day when you can choose to lead and many moments each day when you can choose to make a difference. Each moment serves up the prospect of contributing to a lasting legacy.

Legacies aren't the result of wishful thinking. They're the result of determined doing. The legacy you leave is the life you lead. You lead your life daily. You leave your legacy daily. The people you see, the decisions you make, the actions you take—they are what tell your story. It's the sum of everything you do that matters, and the most critical leadership actions are the ones you take today.

Now, and not at some point in the future, is the time to pause and ask yourself, "What kind of a leader do I want to be?"

Let's jump-start that conversation with yourself by imagining that it is ten years from today, and you are being recognized at a ceremony in your local region as being one of the "35 Outstanding Leaders under 35." Many people will come to the stage to talk about your leadership and how you have made a positive difference in their lives. Use the L.I.F.E paradigm in Figure E.2 to jot down what you hope people will say about you that day.

After you've written down your responses to these questions, ask yourself: Right now, even while I am in school, how am I doing at teaching these *lessons*, living up to these *ideals*, creating these *feelings*, and providing the *evidence* that I am contributing as a leader? Don't stop there! Ask yourself: What can I do to do even better?

Find a trusted friend, colleague, coach, or mentor to share your reflections with. Ask them for feedback. We know from research that going with your aspirations can strengthen your commitment to take steps in the direction you want to go.

Becoming an exemplary leader fundamentally changes who you are. It changes your relationship with yourself. You're no longer just an individual contributor. You're someone who takes people on journeys to places they've never been.

Figure E.2   The L.I.F.E. paradigm.

Lessons: What vital *lessons* do you hope others will say you pass on? (For example, I hope they will say: I am teaching people how to face adversity with grace and determination, and I inspire them about the importance of giving back to those who've given to them.)

Ideals: What *ideals*—values, principles, and ethical standards—do you hope people will say you stand for? (For example, I hope they will say: I stand up for freedom and justice and believe in always telling the truth, even when it isn't always what people want to hear.)

Feelings: What *feelings* do you hope people will say they have or had when being with you? (For example, I hope they will say: They always felt, when working with me, capable of doing the impossible. I make them felt that they matter and that what I had to say was worthwhile listening to.)

Evidence: What is the *evidence* that you have made a difference; what lasting expressions or contributions—tangible and intangible—will people say that you provided to them? (For example, I hope they will say: Together, we turned around this project/division/organization when others had lost hope, and that my dedication to others is evident not only in the workplace but also in what I've contributed to the community.)

Becoming an exemplary leader changes how you present yourself day in and day out. You are expected to be a role model for your and the organization's values.

- It changes how you see the future. You are expected to be able to imagine exciting future possibilities and communicate them to others.
- It changes how you respond to challenges. You are expected to be comfortable with uncertainty, champion experimentation, and learn from experiences.
- It changes how you relate to others. You are expected to build relationships, foster collaboration, strengthen others, and forge trust.
- It changes how you show others that you appreciate them. You are expected to recognize contributions and celebrate team successes genuinely.

You never know whose life you might touch. You never know what change you might initiate and what impact you might have. You never know when that critical moment might come. What you do know is that *you can make a difference*. You can leave this *world*—be it a classroom, group paper or project, your residence, community, internship, workplace, or family—better than you found it because you were there.

REFLECT AND ACT: CONTINUE YOUR LEADERSHIP DEVELOPMENT

To become the best leader you can be, now and in the future, you must recognize that you matter. Leadership is a relationship, and the decisions you make and the actions you take have an impact on others. It's up to you to determine the kind of difference that you want to make.

Leadership is learned. It's an observable set of skills and abilities that along with can be developed and strengthened with motivation, practice, feedback, and coaching. You also have to believe you can be a better leader. A growth mindset is a prerequisite to learning to lead.

There are three general approaches to learning to lead—you can learn and grow through experience, observe and consult others, and participate in training and coursework. Each has its benefits, and the more time you devote to learning, the more skilled you'll become.

The Five Practices and Ten Commitments do not guarantee success, although they do increase the probabilities. The antidote to hubris on the part of leaders is humility.

Your future leadership self is not predetermined by who you are today. You can grow and change as time passes. An initial step in becoming your best leadership self is to reflect on the lessons, ideals, feelings, and evidence that describe how you want others to experience you in the future.

Finally, becoming the best means making exemplary leadership a daily habit. There are countless opportunities to lead. Take advantage of each to demonstrate that you are committed to leaving a legacy of significance.

Reflect

Your leadership development journey has reached a milestone. Congratulations on completing this stage of becoming an exemplary leader. Take a few moments to reflect and answer these questions:

1. What are the three most important ideas or lessons about continuing your leadership development that you learned from this chapter?

   _____

   _____

   _____

2. Considering the preceding suggestions and the lessons you've recorded from the other chapters in this book, if you were going to give a presentation to someone who's not yet read this book, what are the three most important lessons you'd share?

_____

_____

_____

Here are actions to follow through on your commitment to **Continue Your Leadership Development** journey most effectively.

- Create a personal board of directors—a group of four to seven people whom you respect and trust to whom you can turn when you need counsel on tough questions, guidance on your career and transitions in the workplace, advice on personal and professional development, and the like.

- Fill in the blank to finish this sentence: "When I think about what it takes to become an exemplary leader, I am curious about _____."

- Repeat this daily affirmation every morning: "Who I am, what I do, and how I do it make a difference."

- At the end of each day, ask yourself: "What did I learn in the last 24 hours that will help me become a better leader?" Keep a journal of your responses and periodically review what you record. Give yourself a high-five for all the things you've learned!

- Set a near-term stretch learning goal for yourself. It could be about improving your public-speaking abilities, learning to resolve conflicts, or having difficult conversations with your peers. Keep pushing yourself to learn outside of your comfort zone.

Act

What is one small thing you can do in the next few weeks or month to apply one of these lessons to continue your leadership development journey? For example: What project would give you a chance to learn from the experience? Whose leadership could you observe? Who could coach you on one of the practices? What course or training could you enroll in to improve in an area of importance to you?

_____

_____

_____

_____

_____

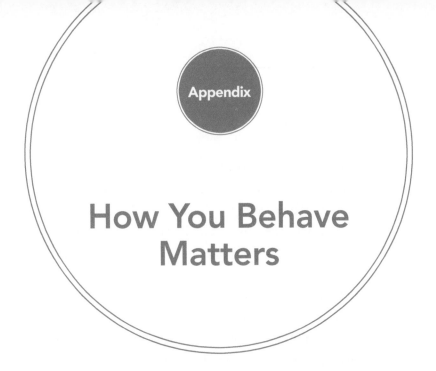

Appendix

How You Behave Matters

The Prologue provided a brief overview of The Five Practices and Ten Commitments of Exemplary Leadership, which can serve as an operating system for becoming the best leader you can be. To improve, however, you first need to create a baseline from which to establish and chart your progress. To serve that purpose, we created the *Student Leadership Practices Inventory*®.

The *Student Leadership Practices Inventory* (S-LPI)® measures how frequently students engage in the behaviors that lead to the best leadership outcomes. It allows you to understand your behaviors, own your development, and identify where to improve.

You can access the S-LPI at this URL: www.studentlpi.com/ebook.

The inventory takes about ten minutes to complete. Use this appendix to review and make sense of the data you generate. Responses are entirely confidential, and no one other than you can access the results. There are opportunities at the end of each chapter to further reflect on your data in connection with exploring each of The Five Practices and Ten Commitments in depth.

Let's begin with reviewing four questions students commonly ask about the Student LPI:

1. "What are the 'right' answers?"

    There are no universal "right" answers when it comes to leadership. The inventory is intended to be descriptive and developmental. The more candid you are in responding to each statement, the more accurate and useful the results will be to you.

2. "What is a 'good' or 'bad' result?"

    Just as there are no "right" answers, there are no "good" or "bad" results. No matter your current response, it is what it is. Again, consider your current results as a baseline. Then, the question to ask yourself is, "What can I do about my behavior and actions to become an even better leader?" Your responses to this question will help reveal how you see yourself behaving now and what you can do more often and more skillfully as you progress in your leadership development.

3. "Can I change my leadership behavior?"

    It is certainly possible—even for experienced leaders—to learn new skills. You will increase your chances of changing your behavior if you receive feedback on your present skill level, observe a positive model of that skill, set some improvement goals for yourself, practice the skill, ask for updated feedback on your performance, and then set new goals. The practices assessed using the Student LPI fall into the category of learnable skills. However, you also need the will and the way to improve these skills and change current behaviors. You first need a strong and genuine inner desire to make a difference. But enthusiasm alone is insufficient. You also need methods for learning and improving in each area you desire to grow.

4. "How reliable and valid is the Student LPI?"

The question of reliability can be answered in two ways. First, the Student LPI has shown sound psychometric properties. The scale for each leadership practice is internally reliable, meaning that the statements within each practice are highly correlated. Second, results of multivariate analyses indicate that the statements within each leadership practice are more highly correlated (or associated) with one another than they are between the five leadership practices.

Concerning validity—or, "what difference do the scores make?"—the Student LPI has good face validity and predictive validity. This means, first, that the results make sense to people. Second, scores on the Student LPI significantly differentiate high-performing leaders from their less successful counterparts. We present some of this data later in this appendix as we have throughout the book.

Use the information from your Student LPI to better understand how you currently behave as a leader. Reflect on which leadership practices and behaviors you feel comfortable engaging in and those where you feel uncomfortable. Determine those leadership practices and behaviors you can improve and take steps to develop your leadership skills and confidence in leading other people and groups.

MAKING SENSE OF YOUR STUDENT LPI FEEDBACK

To better understand your current use of The Five Practices, transcribe your responses from the Student LPI Feedback Report to the following spaces.

MODEL THE WAY

1. ___ 6. ___ 11. ___ 16. ___ 21. ___ 26. ___ **TOTAL:** ___

INSPIRE A SHARED VISION

2. ___ 7. ___ 12. ___ 17. ___ 22. ___ 27.___ **TOTAL:** ___

CHALLENGE THE PROCESS

3. ___ 8. ___ 13. ___ 18. ___ 23. ___ 28. ___ **TOTAL:** ___

ENABLE OTHERS TO ACT

4. ___ 9. ___ 14. ___ 19. ___ 24. ___ 29. ___ **TOTAL:** ___

ENCOURAGE THE HEART

5. ___ 10. ___ 15. ___ 20. ___ 25. ___ 30. ___ **TOTAL:** ___

Using the preceding responses, several ways exist to make sense of your Student LPI Feedback. Start by getting a "big picture" perspective by plotting your five leadership practice results (total) in Figure A.1. In Figure A.1, designate your scores for each leadership practice (Model, Inspire, Challenge, Enable, and Encourage) by marking each of these points with a capital *S* through the number in each column that corresponds to the number for your Student LPI score on each dimension. Connect the five resulting "*S*-scores" with a solid line.

Next, rank order (from most to least frequent) the leadership practices. That is, place the number "1" by the leadership practice with the highest total self-rating, a "2" by the next-highest total self-rating, and so on. This ranking represents the leadership practice that feels most comfortable (or natural) to you, second-most comfortable, and so on until you label the leadership practice with which you feel least comfortable.

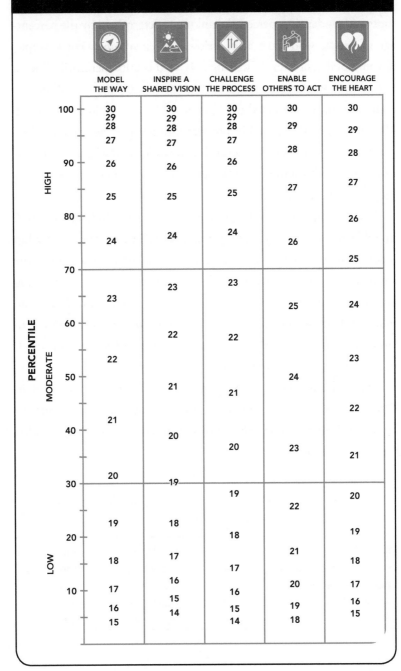

Figure A.1 Chart for graphing your S-LPI scores.
© James M. Kouzes & Barry Z. Posner. All rights reserved.

How do your scores compare with other students who have completed the Student LPI? The column to the far left in Figure A.1 represents the Student LPI-Self percentile rankings for several hundred thousand students. A percentile ranking is determined by the percentage of people who score at or below a given number. For example, if your total score for "Challenge" is at the 60th percentile line in Figure A.1, you assessed yourself higher than 60 percent of all students who have completed the Student LPI; you would be in the top 40 percent in this leadership practice. Studies indicate that a "high" score is one at or above the seventh percentile, a "low" score is one at or below the thirtieth percentile, and a score that falls between those ranges is considered "moderate."

Now, using the preceding criteria, circle Low, Moderate, or High in Table A.1 for each leadership practice. Where do your leadership practices tend to fall compared to other student leaders around the country? Remember that while this information may be interesting and somewhat informative, the "competition" is not with others—all those students worldwide who have completed the S-LPI—but with yourself. What's most valuable to you is what you need to do yourself to become an even better leader.

Take another look at the graph of scores that you created in Figure A.1. Here are some questions you should consider in making sense of this information. Record your responses in the space provided for each question:

Table A.1   Comparison of your scores with other student leaders.

Model the Way	Low	Moderate	High
Inspire a Shared Vision	Low	Moderate	High
Challenge the Process	Low	Moderate	High
Enable Others to Act	Low	Moderate	High
Encourage the Heart	Low	Moderate	High

- Where is this data consistent or inconsistent with your self-perceptions (before completing the Student LPI)?

  _____

  _____

  _____

- How far apart are the total scores for your most and least frequently engaged-in leadership practices? Are they three points or less apart? Three to six points? More?

  _____

  _____

  _____

- In which leadership practices do you feel most comfortable?

  _____

  _____

  _____

- In which leadership practices do you feel least comfortable?

  _____

  _____

  _____

- Are there leadership practices you don't engage in because you don't (or didn't) consider them all that important or critical to getting the job done? If yes, what are they?

  _____

  _____

  _____

- How does your use of these various leadership practices seem to be consistent or inconsistent with their use by other student leaders?

  _____

  _____

  _____

- What else does your feedback say to you?

  _____

  _____

  _____

To gain a deeper understanding and insight into your leadership practices, review each of the thirty behavioral statements on the Student LPI. One or two of the six behaviors that comprise each leadership practice may be higher or lower than the rest. Make some notes to yourself in response to these questions:

- Within each leadership practice, on which specific statement is there considerable variation? What do these differences suggest?

  _____

  _____

  _____

- What does it tell you if there are agreements across each of the statements for a leadership practice?

  _____

  _____

  _____

Record your five or six least frequent leadership behaviors and respond to these questions: Do these behaviors cluster in one leadership practice, or are they scattered across several practices? How do you feel about these specific behaviors? What would be required for you to engage in any one of them more than you do currently?

_____

_____

_____

_____

_____

As you read through the chapters in the book and learn about The Five Practices and Ten Commitments of Exemplary Leadership, take a few more moments to review your S-LPI Feedback and the notes you made to yourself above. Summarize your thinking as you begin your leadership development journey in this book and the course or workshop in which you are enrolled.

STRENGTHS: Which leadership practices and behaviors are you most comfortable with? Why do you think this is the case? Can you do even more with these strengths than you are currently doing?

_____

_____

_____

AREAS OF IMPROVEMENT: Which leadership practices or behaviors do you need to improve? What can you do to use a practice more frequently? What will it take to feel more comfortable when you use a particular leadership behavior?

_____

_____

_____

_____

In the final analysis, leadership is a choice. No one can make you a better leader. That's your choice. Likewise, we can teach leadership, but only you can choose to learn to become an even better leader.

THE FIVE PRACTICES MAKE A DIFFERENCE

Exemplary student leaders' behavior makes a profoundly positive difference in the commitment, motivation, and work performance of the students they work with. In generating a high level of commitment and performance, student leaders who most frequently use The Five Practices of Exemplary Leadership are considerably more effective than those who less often or seldom use them.

In other words, how student leaders behave explains how hard their colleagues work and how engaged these individuals feel in the work, projects, and programs they are doing. Our research tells us that the more you use The Five Practices of Exemplary Leadership, the more likely it is that you'll positively influence others, their efforts, and their commitment to their group, team, campus, or cause. That's what all the data adds up to. If you want to have a significant impact on people, organizations, and communities, you need to invest in learning the behaviors that enable you to become the very best leader you can be.

The Student LPI data consistently shows that the more frequently the colleagues and constituents of student leaders observed their student leaders engaging in The Five Practices, the more they reported being satisfied with that person's leadership. The use of The Five Practices was nearly 27 percent higher by those being strongly satisfied versus those reporting the least satisfaction levels. Similar relationships were found between student leaders' frequency of The Five Practices and how their colleagues and constituents felt appreciated and valued, agreed that their efforts were making a difference, and felt highly productive. Moreover, student leaders were viewed by others as more effective as a direct function of using The Five Practices. There was a dramatic relationship between how students assessed the leadership skill level of their leaders and how frequently these leaders were seen engaging in The Five Practices. The research also revealed something else that's extremely important to appreciate: individual characteristics, such as gender, age, ethnicity, and year in school, are not the reason why student leaders were reported as effective or not.

These findings are well aligned with the perspectives of student leaders themselves. For example, a strong direct relationship is consistently found between how student leaders evaluated their leadership skills and their use of The Five Practices compared with their peers. Those who reported their leadership skills as "not well developed" used The Five Practices 6 percent less than those indicating their leadership skills were only "somewhat underdeveloped." The frequency increased by 7 percent for those student leaders who claimed their leadership skills were "somewhat developed" over those reporting "somewhat underdeveloped" and by nearly 14 percent for those reporting "not well developed." Those student leaders who viewed their leadership skills as "well developed" compared with their peers reported using The Five Practices 8 percent more than those indicating their skills were "somewhat developed" and 15 percent more than those whose skills were "somewhat underdeveloped," and 23 percent more often than those who viewed their leadership skills as "not well developed" in comparison with their peers.

To sum it up, what matters is how you behave.

YOU MAKE A DIFFERENCE

Engaging in The Five Practices of Exemplary Leadership makes a significant difference—no matter who you are or what you are leading. How you behave as a leader matters, and it matters a lot. It makes a difference. You make a difference. We believe it is the responsibility, even the moral obligation, of all students to look into their hearts, determine what they believe in, and make the world a better place by acting on that belief.

Notes

Prologue: When Leaders Are at Their Personal Best

1. Unless otherwise noted, all stories and quotations are from student leaders around the world who shared with us, in their own words, their personal-best leadership experiences and the lessons they have learned about leadership. Most have now graduated and moved on, and the organizations in which their personal-best leadership experiences occurred may no longer exist by the time you read this, but the details on their roles, organizations, and experiences were accurate at the time of this writing.

2. When we use the term *team* or *group*, we mean any collective organization a student participates in, whether as a member or in a leadership position. For example, an athletic team, a club, a choir, a common-interest group, any specialized activity or project, an academic program, or even a class project group or group of housemates. We also use the word *leaders* to refer to students we have studied, not just students in formal leadership positions, but students who have taken the challenge and worked with others to make extraordinary things happen in the teams and groups to which they belong. For example, in many classroom situations, no one is officially designated as "the" leader of the group.

3. Visit www.studentleadershipchallenge.com for continuing updates on personal-best leadership stories from young leaders around the world. For detailed information on our research methodology, the theory and evidence behind The Five Practices of Exemplary Leadership, Personal-Best Leadership Experience questionnaire, the psychometric properties of the *Student Leadership Practices Inventory* (S-LPI), and abstracts of studies that have used The Five Practices framework and S-LPI, take a look at the research section of our website: www.studentleadershipchallenge.com.

4. J. M. Kouzes and B. Z. Posner, *The Truth about Leadership: The No-Fads, Heart-of-the-Matter Facts You Need to Know* (San Francisco: Jossey-Bass, 2010). Also, see B. Z. Posner, "Understanding the Learning Tactics of College Students and Their Relationship to Leadership," *Leadership & Organization Development Journal* 30, no 4 (2009): 386–395.

5. We use the terms *cooperate* and *collaborate* synonymously. Their dictionary definitions are very similar. In the *Merriam-Webster Unabridged* online dictionary, the first definition of *cooperate* is, "To act or work with another or others to a common end: operate jointly" (http://unabridged.merriam-webster.com/unabridged/cooperate). The first definition of *collaborate* is, "To work jointly with others or together, especially in an intellectual endeavor" (http://unabridged.merriam-webster.com/unabridged/collaborate).

6. The research described here and throughout this book draws from the normative database of online responses to the *Student Leadership Practices Inventory* (S-LPI), which includes nearly one million respondents. The sample used for this edition are respondents from 2017–2022, including 91,561 self-reports and 365,747 observer reports. For information about the psychometric properties of the S-LPI, see: B. Z. Posner, "Effectively Measuring Student Leadership," *Administrative Sciences* 2, no. 4 (2012): 221–234; and B. Z. Posner, "A Leadership Development Instrument for Students: Updated," *Journal of College Student Development* 45, no. 4 (2004): 443–456.

    Fifty-nine percent of the SELF *respondents* were women. The vast majority of respondents were from the United States (76%). For U.S. respondents, by race or ethnic background, the majority were Caucasian (58%), followed by Asian/Pacific Islander (23%), Black (8%), Hispanic/Latinx (8%), Mixed (3%), and Native American (0.5%). Sixty-two percent were college undergraduates, 23 percent were in high school, and 15 percent were in graduate school. The majority were 18–23 years of age (58%).

    Fifty-nine percent of the OBSERVER *respondents* were women. Most respondents were from the United States (61%). For U.S. respondents, by race or ethnic background, the majority were Caucasian (50%), followed by Asian/Pacific Islander (37%), Hispanic/Latinx (6%), Black (6%), Mixed (1%), and Native American (0.3%). Thirty-nine percent were college undergraduates, 19 percent were in high school, and 42 percent were in graduate school. About one-third were 18–23 years of age.

    The S-LPI contains thirty behavior-based statements constructed from the personal-best leadership experiences of students and will be familiar to you if you complete it as part of reading this book. Each statement is measured on a five-point Likert scale in terms of the frequency with which the individual completing the instrument or being reported about engages in the particular behavior, with the following response categories: (1) seldom, (2) once in a while, (3) sometimes, (4) often, and (5) very frequently. Six statements make up the scale of each of The Five Practices: Model the Way, Inspire a Shared Vision, Challenge the Process, Enable Others to Act, and Encourage the Heart.

The analysis of the impact of the leader's behavior uses data *only* from observers. In addition to indicating how frequently they observed the leader engaging in various leadership behaviors, these respondents also provided information about how they felt working with this leader. For example:

- When working with this leader, I'm highly productive in what I do.
- I'm proud to tell others that I am working with this leader.
- I feel like this leader values my work.
- When working with this leader, I feel like I am making a difference around here.
- Overall, I am satisfied with the leadership exhibited by this person.

Responses to these statements are on a five-point scale: (1) strongly disagree, (2) disagree, (3) neither disagree nor agree, (4) agree, and (5) strongly agree.

Combining the responses to the first four questions above produced an "engagement" scale, with scores ranging between 4 and 20, and the internal reliability coefficient for this scale was quite strong (Cronbach's alpha = .911). In addition, observers were asked if "the leadership skills of the person I just reported about compared to their peers" are (1) not well developed, (2) somewhat underdeveloped, (3) similar to their peer group, (4) somewhat developed, and (5) well developed. A similar question was asked of the leaders themselves.

All of the analyses presented in this book meet the criteria of being *statistically significant* ($p < .001$). Most compare the responses of those who *strongly agree* with a statement, often looking at the differences between the respondents along the five continuum points.

Chapter 1: Commitment #1: Clarify Values

1. C. Daniels, "Developing Organizational Values in Others," in D. Crandall (ed.), *Leadership Lessons from West Point* (San Francisco: Jossey-Bass, 2007), 62–87.
2. R. A. Stevenson, *Clarifying Behavioral Expectations Associated with Espoused Organizational Values*, Ph.D. dissertation, Fielding Institute, 1995.

Chapter 2: Commitment #2: Set the Example

1. F. A. Blanchard, T. Lilly, and L. A. Vaughn, "Reducing the Expression of Racial Prejudice," *Psychological Science* 2, no. 2 (1991): 101–105.
2. B. D. Rosso, K. H. Dekas, and A. Wrzeniewski, "On the Meaning of Work: A Theoretical Integration and Review," *Research in Organizational Behavior* 30 (2010): 91–127.

Chapter 3: Commitment #3: Envision the Future

1. D. Gilbert, *Stumbling on Happiness* (New York: Knopf, 2006), 5–6.

2. For an in-depth discussion of what people look for in their leaders, see J. M. Kouzes and B. Z. Posner, *Credibility: How Leaders Gain It and Lose It, Why People Demand It*, 2nd ed. (San Francisco: Jossey-Bass, 2011). See also J. M. Kouzes and B. Z. Posner, *The Leadership Challenge: How to Make Extraordinary Things Happen in Organizations*, 6th ed. (Hoboken, NJ: Wiley, 2017). What's also true is that the importance placed on "forward-looking" increases with both years of work experience and level in the organization.

3. J. P. Schuster, *The Power of Your Past: The Art of Recalling, Recasting, and Reclaiming* (San Francisco: Berrett-Koehler, 2011); J. T. Seaman Jr. and G. D. Smith, "Your Company's History as a Leadership Tool," *Harvard Business Review*, December 2012, 44–52. For an example of learning from the past, see E. Florian, "The Best Advice I Ever Got," *Fortune*, February 6, 2012, 14.

4. See E. L. Deci with R. Fiaste, *Why We Do What We Do: Understanding Self-Motivation* (New York: Penguin, 1995). For another excellent treatment of this subject, see K. W. Thomas, *Intrinsic Motivation at Work: Building Energy and Commitment* (San Francisco: Berrett-Koehler, 2000); and for an extensive academic treatment, see C. Sansone and J. M. Harackiewicz (eds.), *Intrinsic and Extrinsic Motivation: The Search for Optimal Motivation and Performance* (New York: Academic Press, 2000).

5. D. Pink, *Drive: The Surprising Truth about What Motivates Us* (New York: Penguin Group, 2009); and L. Freifeld, "Why Cash Doesn't Motivate," *Training* 48, no. 4 (July/August 2011): 17–22.

6 Deci with Fiaste, *Why We Do What We Do*, 25.

7. J. M. Kouzes and B. Z. Posner, "To Lead, Create a Shared Vision," *Harvard Business Review*, January 2009.

8. B. L. Kaye and S. Jordon-Evans, *Love 'Em or Lose 'Em: Getting Good People to Stay*, 5th ed. (San Francisco: Berrett-Koehler, 2014).

Chapter 4: Commitment #4: Enlist Others

1. "'I Have a Dream' Leads Top 100 Speeches of the Century," press release from the University of Wisconsin, December 15, 1999, http://news.wisc.edu/i-have-a-dream-leads-top-100-speeches-of-the-century/. The full list is available online at http://news.wisc.edu/archive/misc/speeches/ and http://www.americanrhetoric.com/top100speechesall.html. See also S. E. Lucas and M. J. Medhurst, *Words of a Century: The Top 100 American Speeches, 1900–1999* (New York: Oxford University Press, 2008). Other leaders often seen on international lists of great speakers from recent history are Winston Churchill, Charles de Gaulle, Mahatma Gandhi, Vaclav Havel, Robert Kennedy, Nelson Mandela, Jawaharlal Nehru, Barack Obama, Ronald Reagan, Eleanor Roosevelt, Gloria Steinem, Mother Teresa, Margaret Thatcher, and Lech Walesa.

2. The audio version of the "I Have a Dream" speech that we have found to be most instructive is the version running 6 minutes and 11 seconds that contains the most famous passages. It is in the collection Greatest Speeches of All Time (Vol. 1) available from Amazon.com: www.amazon.com/Greatest-Speeches-All-Time-Various-Artists/dp/1885959435/ref=tmm_abk_swatch_0?_encoding=UTF8&qid=1499268211&sr=8-1-spell. A printed version of this portion of the speech is in C. S. King (ed.), "The Words of Martin Luther King, Jr." (New York: Newmarket Press, 1983), 95–98. A video can be viewed on YouTube at www.youtube.com/watch?v=smEqnnklfYs.

3. D. Goleman, *Social Intelligence: The New Science of Human Relationships* (New York: Bantam, 2006).

4. H. S. Friedman, L. M. Prince, R. E. Riggio, and M. R. DiMatteo, "Understanding and Assessing Nonverbal Expressiveness: The Affective Communication Test," *Journal of Personality and Social Psychology* 39, no. 2 (1980): 333–351; D. Goleman, R. Boyatzis, and A. McKee, *Primal Leadership: Realizing the Power of Emotional Intelligence* (Boston: Harvard Business School Press, 2002); J. Conger, *Winning 'Em Over: A New Model for Management in the Age of Persuasion* (New York: Simon & Schuster, 1998); and M. Greer, "The Science of Savoir Faire," *APA Monitor* 36, no. 1 (2005): 28.

5. J. L. McGaugh, *Memory and Emotion* (New York: Columbia University Press, 2003), 90. See also R. Maxwell and R. Dickman, *The Elements of Persuasion: Use Storytelling to Pitch Better Ideas, Sell Faster, & Win More Business* (New York: HarperCollins, 2007), especially "Sticky Stories: Memory, Emotions and Markets," 122–150.

6. McGaugh, *Memory and Emotion*, 92.

7. McGaugh, *Memory and Emotion*, 92.

8. D. A. Small, G. Loewenstein, and P. Slovic, "Sympathy and Callousness: The Impact of Deliberative Thought on Donations to Identifiable and Statistical Victims," *Organizational Behavior and Human Decision Processes* 102 (2007): 143–153.

Chapter 5: Commitment #5: Search for Opportunities

1. T. S. Bateman and J. M. Crant, "Proactive Behavior: Meaning, Impact, Recommendations," *Business Horizons* 42, no. 3 (May–June 1999): 63–70; J. M. Crant, "Proactive Behavior in Organizations," *Journal of Management* 26, no. 3 (2000): 435–463; J. A. Thompson, "Proactive Personality and Job Performance: A Social Capital Perspective," *Journal of Applied Psychology* 90, no. 5 (2005): 1011–1017; S. E. Seibert and M. L. Braimer, "What Do Proactive People Do? A Longitudinal Model Linking Proactive Personality and Career Success," *Personnel Psychology* 54 (2001): 845–875; and D. J. Brown, R. T. Cober, K. Kane, P. E. Levy, and J. Shalhoop, "Proactive Personality and the Successful Job Search: A Field Investigation of College Graduates," *Journal of Applied Psychology* 91, no. 3 (2006): 717–726.

NOTES

2. E. L. Deci with R. Fiaste, *Why We Do What We Do: Understanding Self-Motivation* (New York: Penguin, 1995). See also D. Pink, *Drive: The Surprising Truth about What Motivates You* (New York: Riverhead Press, 2011); and K. W. Thomas, *Intrinsic Motivation at Work: What Really Drives Employee Engagement* (San Francisco: Berrett-Koehler, 2009).

3. See, for example, J. Ettlie, *Managing Innovation*, 2nd ed. (Abingdon, UK: Taylor & Francis, 2006); S. Johnson, *Where Good Ideas Come From: The Natural History of Innovation* (New York: Riverhead Press, 2010); E. Ries, *The Lean Startup: How Constant Innovation Creates Radically Successful Businesses* (New York: Penguin Group, 2011); T. Davila, M. J. Epstein, and R. Shelton, *Making Innovation Work: How to Manage It, Measure It, and Profit from It*, updated ed. (Upper Saddle River, NJ: FT Press, 2012); and I. Asimov, "How Do People Get New Ideas?" *MIT Technology Review*, October 20, 2014, www.technologyreview.com/s/531911/isaac-asimov-asks-how-do-people-get-new-ideas/.

4. G. Berns, *Iconoclast: A Neuroscientist Reveals How to Think Differently* (Cambridge, MA: Harvard Business School Press, 2008); and B. Andreatta, *Wired to Resist: The Brain Science of Why Change Fails and a New Model for Driving Success* (Santa Barbara, CA: 7th Mind Printing, 2017).

5. A. W. Brooks, F. Gino, and M. E. Schweitzer, "Smart People Ask for (My) Advice: Seeking Advice Boosts Perceptions of Competence," *Management Science* 61, no. 6 (June 2015): 1421–1435.

6. Z. Achi and J. G. Berger, "Delighting in the Possible," *McKinsey Quarterly*, March 2016, 5.

Chapter 6: Commitment #6: Experiment and Take Risks

1. For a history of the research, see S. R. Salvatore, "The Story of Hardiness: Twenty Years of Theorizing, Research, and Practice," *Consulting Psychology Journal: Practices and Research* 54, no. 3 (2002): 175–185. See also S. R. Maddi and S. C. Kobasa, *The Hardy Executive: Health under Stress* (Chicago: Dorsey Press, 1984); S. R. Maddi and D. M. Khoshaba, "Hardiness and Mental Health," *Journal of Personality Assessment* 67 (1994): 265–274; and S. R. Maddi and D. M. Khoshaba, *Resilience at Work: How to Succeed No Matter What Life Throws at You* (New York: AMACOM, 2005).

2. R. A. Bruce and R. F. Sinclair, "Exploring the Psychological Hardiness of Entrepreneurs," *Frontiers of Entrepreneurship Research* 29, no. 6 (2009): 5; P. T. Bartone, R. R. Roland, J. J. Picaño, and T. J. Williams, "Psychological Hardiness Predicts Success in US Army Special Forces Candidates," *International Journal of Selection and Assessment* 16, no. 1 (2008): 78–81; and P. T. Bartone, "Resilience under Military Operational Stress: Can Leaders Influence Hardiness?" *Military Psychology* 18 (2006): S141–S148.

3. K. E. Weick, "Small Wins: Redefining the Scale of Social Problems," *American Psychologist* 39, no. 1 (1984): 43. For a related treatment of this topic, see P. Sims, *Little Bets: How Breakthrough Ideas Emerge from Small Discoveries* (New York: Free Press, 2011), 141–152.

4. D. Bayles and T. Orland, *Art and Fear: Observations on the Perils (and Rewards) of Artmaking* (Eugene, OR: Image Continuum Press, 2001).

5. R. W. Eichinger, M. M. Lombardo, and D. Ulrich, *100 Things You Need to Know: Best Practices for Managers & HR* (Minneapolis, MN: Lominger, 2004), 492.

6. L. M. Brown and B. Z. Posner, "Exploring the Relationship between Learning and Leadership," *Leadership & Organization Development Journal*, May 2001, 274–280. See also J. M. Kouzes and B. Z. Posner, *The Truth about Leadership: The No-Fads, Heart-of-the-Matter Facts You Need to Know* (San Francisco: Jossey-Bass, 2010), 119–135.

7. C. Dweck, *Mindset: The New Psychology of Success* (New York: Random House, 2006), 6–7. See also C. Dweck, "Carol Dweck Revisits the 'Growth Mindset,'" *Education Week*, September 22, 2016, www.edweek.org/ew/articles/2015/09/23/carol-dweck-revisits-the-growth-mindset.html. See also T. K. Kouzes and B. Z. Posner, "Influence of Mindset on Leadership Behavior," *Leadership & Organization Development Journal* 40, no. 8 (2019): 829–844.

8. J. Barash, M. Capozzi, and L. Mendonca, "How Companies Approach Innovation: A McKinsey Global Survey," *McKinsey Quarterly*, October 2007.

9. A. Bandura and R. E. Wood, "Effects of Perceived Controllability and Performance Standards on Self-Regulation of Complex Decision Making," *Journal of Personality and Social Psychology* 56 (1989): 805–814. See also Dweck, *Mindset*, for a discussion of numerous research studies in these and other domains.

10. A. Carmeli, D. Brueller, and J. E. Dutton, "Learning Behaviours in the Workplace: The Role of High-Quality Interpersonal Relationships and Psychological Safety," *Systems Research and Behavioral Science Systems Research* 26 (2009): 81–98.

11. A. L. Duckworth, *Grit: The Power of Passion and Perseverance* (New York: Simon & Schuster, 2016).

12. M. E. P. Seligman, "Building Resilience," *Harvard Business Review*, April 2011, 101–106. For a more complete treatment of this subject, see M.E.P. Seligman, *Flourish: A Visionary New Understanding of Happiness and Well-Being* (New York: Free Press, 2011).

13. It may be difficult to overcome a habitual pattern of avoidance, but it is possible to learn to cope assertively with stressful events. For example, see Maddi and Kobasa, *The Hardy Executive*; D. M. Khoshaba and S. R. Maddi, "Early Experiences in Hardiness Development," *Consulting Psychology Journal* 51 (1999): 106–116; S. R. Maddi, S. Kahn, and K. L. Maddi, "The Effectiveness of Hardiness Training," *Consulting Psychology Journal* 50 (1998): 78–86; Maddi and

Khoshaba, *Resilience at Work*; K. Reivish and A. Shatte, *The Resilience Factor: 7 Keys to Finding Your Inner Strength and Overcoming Life's Hurdles* (New York: Broadway Books, 2003); and J. D. Margolis and P. G. Stoltz, "How to Bounce Back from Adversity," *Harvard Business Review* 88, no. 1 (January–February, 2010): 86–92.

Chapter 7: Commitment #7: Foster Collaboration

1. P. S. Shockley-Zalabak, S. Morreale, and M. Hackman, *Building the High-Trust Organization: Strategies for Supporting Five Key Dimensions of Trust* (San Francisco: Jossey-Bass, 2010).

2. P. Lee, N. Gillespie, L. Mann, and A. Wearing, "Leadership and Trust: Their Effect on Knowledge Sharing and Team Performance," *Management Learning* 41, no. 4 (2010): 473–491.

3. R. Axelrod, *The Evolution of Cooperation*, rev. ed. (New York: Basic Books, 2006). See also W. Poundstone, *Prisoner's Dilemma: John Von Neumann, Game Theory, and the Puzzle of the Bomb* (New York: Anchor, 1993). These findings were replicated in an extensive probability analysis, which used high-powered computing to run hundreds of "games" and found that cooperativeness, rather than selfishness, won in the end. For more information, see C. Adami and A. Hintze, "Evolutionary Instability of Zero-Determinant Strategies Demonstrates That Winning Is Not Everything," *Nature Communications* 4, no. 2193 (2013), available online at http://dx.doi.org/10.1038/ncomms3193.

4. Axelrod, *Evolution of Cooperation*, 20, 190.

5. H. Ibarra and M. T. Hansen, "Are You a Collaborative Leader?" *Harvard Business Review*, July–August 2011, 69–74; "Secrets of Greatness: Teamwork!" *Fortune*, June 12, 2006, 64–152; A. M. Brandenburger and B. J. Nalebuff, *Co-Opetition: A Revolution Mindset That Combines Competition and Cooperation: The Game Theory Strategy That's Changing the Game of Business* (New York: Currency, 1997); P. Hallinger and R. H. Heck, "Leadership for Learning: Does Collaborative Leadership Make a Difference in School Improvement?" *Educational Management Administration & Leadership* 38, no. 6 (2010): 654–678; W. C. Kim and R. Mauborgne, *Blue Ocean Strategy: How to Create Uncontested Market Space and Make the Competition Irrelevant*, expanded ed. (Boston: Harvard Business School Publishing, 2015); and D. Tjosvold and M. M. Tjosvold, *Building the Team Organization: How to Open Minds, Resolve Conflict, and Ensure Cooperation* (New York: Palgrave Macmillan, 2015).

6. M. Moriesen and T. B. Neeley, "Reflected Knowledge and Trust in Global Collaboration," *Management Science* 58, no. 12 (2012): 2207–2224. See also D. Cohen and L. Prusak, *In Good Company: How Social Capital Makes Organizations Work* (Boston: Harvard Business School Press, 2001), 20.

7. D. Brooks, *The Social Animal: Hidden Sources of Love, Character, and Achievement* (New York: Random House, 2011).

Chapter 8: Commitment #8: Strengthen Others

1. L. Wiseman, Multipliers: *How the Best Leaders Make Everyone Smarter* (New York: HarperCollins, 2010).

2. A. Bandura, *Self-Efficacy: The Exercise of Control* (New York: Freeman, 1997); M. J. McCormick, J. Tanguma, and A. S. Lopez-Forment, "Extending Self-Efficacy Theory to Leadership: A Review and Empirical Test," *Journal of Leadership Education* 1, no. 2 (2002): 34–49; D. L. Feltz, S. F. Short, and P. J. Sullivan, *Self-Efficacy in Sport* (Champaign, IL: Human Kinetics, 2007); F. C. Lunenburg, "Self-Efficacy in the Workplace: Implications for Motivation and Performance," *International Journal of Management, Business, and Administration* 14, no. 1 (2011): 1–6; and J. E. Maddux, "Self-Efficacy: The Power of Believing You Can," in S. J. Lopez and C. R. Snyder (eds.), *The Oxford Handbook of Positive Psychology*, 2nd ed. (New York: Oxford University Press, 2011), 335–344.

3. A. Wrzeniewski and J. Dutton, "Crafting a Job: Revising Employees as Active Crafters of Their Work," *Academy of Management Review* 26, no. 2 (2001): 179–201; and M. S. Christian, A. S. Garza, and J. E. Slaughter, "Work Engagement: A Quantitative Review and Test of Its Relations with Task and Conceptual Performance," *Personnel Psychology*, 64 (2011): 89–136.

4. Evolutionary psychology demonstrates that in ecosystems, collaboration is what assists species to survive rather than become extinct; the group ends up eradicating bad or inefficient behavior. See R. Wright, *The Moral Animal: Why We Are the Way We Are: The New Science of Evolutionary Psychology* (New York: Vintage, 1995). For another interesting look at the origins of social cooperation, see: A. Fields, *Altruistically Inclined? The Behavioral Sciences, Evolutionary Theory*, and the Origins of Reciprocity (Ann Arbor: University of Michigan Press, 2004).

5. Psychologists often refer to this as *self-efficacy*. See, for example, Bandura, *Self-Efficacy*; and E. Chester, *On Fire at Work: How Great Companies Ignite Passion in Their People without Burning Them* Out (Shippensburg, PA: Sound Wisdom, 2015).

6. P. Sweeny, V. Thomson, and H. Blanton, "Trust and Influence in Combat: An Interdependence Model," *Journal of Applied Social Psychology* 39, no. 1 (2009): 235–264.

Chapter 9: Commitment #9: Recognize Contributions

1. Hundreds of research studies have since been conducted to test this notion, and they all clearly demonstrate that people tend to act in ways that are consistent with the expectations they perceive. See, for example, D. Eden, *Pygmalion in Management: Productivity as a Self-Fulfilling Prophecy* (Lexington, MA: Lexington Books, 1990); D. Eden, "Leadership and Expectations: Pygmalion Effects and Other Self-Fulfilling Prophecies in Organizations," *Leadership Quarterly* 3,

no. 4 (1992): 271–305; S. Maddon, J. Willard, M. Guyll, and K. C. Scherr, "Self-Fulfilling Prophecies: Mechanisms, Power, and Links to Social Problems," *Social and Personality Psychology Compass* 5/8 (2011): 578–590; and A. Smith, L. Jussim, J. Eccles, M. Van Noy, S. Madon, and P. Palumbo, "Self-Fulfilling Prophecies, Perceptual Biases, and Accuracy at the Individual and Group Levels," *Journal of Experimental Social Psychology* 34, no. 6 (1998): 530–561.

2. K. S. Cameron, *Positive Leadership: Strategies for Extraordinary Performance* (San Francisco: Berrett-Koehler, 2008). Fostering virtuousness, according to Cameron, is about facilitating the best of the human condition. He argues that an inclination exists in all human systems toward goodness for its own intrinsic value.

3. J. E. Dutton, R. E. Quinn, and K. S. Cameron, *Positive Organizational Scholarship: Foundations of a New Discipline* (San Francisco: Berrett-Koehler, 2003); K. S. Cameron, *Positive Leadership: Strategies for Extraordinary Performance;* D. Whitney and A. Trosten-Bloom, *The Power of Appreciative Inquiry: A Practical Guide to Positive Change*, 2nd ed. (San Francisco: Berrett-Koehler, 2010); and M. E. P. Seligman, *Flourish: A Visionary New Understanding of Happiness and Well-Being* (New York: Free Press, 2011).

4. J. E. Sawyer, W. R. Latham, R. D. Pritchard, and W. R. Bennett Jr., "Analysis of Work Group Productivity in an Applied Setting: Application of a Time Series Panel Design," *Personnel Psychology* 52 (1999): 927–967; and A. Gostick and C. Elton, *Managing with Carrots: Using Recognition to Attract and Retain the Best People* (Layton, UT: Gibbs Smith, 2001).

5. K. A. Ericsson, M. J. Prietula, and E. T. Cokely, "The Making of an Expert," *Harvard Business Review* 85, no. 7/8 (2007): 114–121, 193.

6. For more on this topic, see Truth 9 in J. M. Kouzes and B. Z. Posner, *The Truth about Leadership: The No-Fads, Heart-of-the-Matter Facts You Need to Know* (San Francisco: Jossey-Bass, 2010).

7. J. A. Ross, "Does Friendship Improve Job Performance?" *Harvard Business Review* 54, no. 2 (March–April 1977): 8–9. See also K. A. Jehn and P. P. Shah, "Interpersonal Relationships and Task Performance: An Examination of Mediating Processes in Friendship and Acquaintance Groups," *Journal of Personality and Social Psychology* 72, no. 4 (1997): 775–790

8. E. Harvey, *180 Ways to Walk the Recognition Talk* (Dallas, TX: Walk the Talk, 2000); J. W. Umias, *The Power of Acknowledgment* (New York: International Institute for Learning, 2006); L. Yerkes, *Fun Works: Creative Places Where People Love to Work*, 2nd ed. (San Francisco: Berrett-Koehler, 2007); B. Nelson, *1501 Ways to Reward Employees* (New York: Workman, 2012); and B. Kaye and S. Jordan-Evans, *Love 'Em or Lose 'Em: Getting Good People to Stay*, 5th ed. (San Francisco: Berrett-Koehler, 2014).

9. B. Fredrickson, *Positivity: Top-Notch Research Reveals the 3-to-1 Ratio That Will Change Your Life* (New York: Random House, 2009).

Chapter 10: Commitment #10: Celebrate the Values and Victories

1. D. Brooks, *The Social Animal: The Hidden Sources of Love, Character, and Achievement* (New York: Random House, 2011); and E. Aronson, *The Social Animal*, 11th ed. (New York: Worth Publishers, 2012).

2. S. Achor, *The Happiness Advantage: The Seven Principles of Positive Psychology That Fuel Success and Performance at Work* (New York: Crown Books, 2010), 176.

3. J. W. Shenk, "What Makes Us Happy?" *Atlantic*, June 2009. Available from www.theatlantic.com/magazine/print/2009/06/what-makes-us-happy/7439/.

4. R. D. Cotton, Y. Shen, and R. Livne-Tarandach, "On Becoming Extraordinary: The Content and Structure of the Developmental Networks of Major League Baseball Hall of Famers," *Academy of Management Journal* 54, no. 1 (2011): 15–46.

5. T. Rath, *Vital Friends: The People You Can't Afford to Live Without* (New York: Gallup Press, 2006), 52; and T. Rath and J. Harter, *Wellbeing: The Five Essential Elements* (New York: Gallup Press, 2010), 40–43.

6. R. E. Baumeister and M. R. Leary, "The Need to Belong: Desire for Interpersonal Attachment as a Fundamental Human Motivation," *Psychological Bulletin* 117 (1995): 497–529; H. W. Perkins, "Religious Commitment, Yuppie Values, and Well-Being in a Post-Collegiate Life," *Review of Religious Research* 32 (1991): 244–251; D. G. Myers, "The Funds, Friends, and Faith of Happy People," *American Psychologist* 55, no. 1 (2000): 56–67; and S. Crabtree, "Getting Personal in the Workplace: Are Negative Relationships Squelching Productivity in Your Company?" *Gallup Management Journal*, June 10, 2004. Available from www.govleaders.org/gallup_article_getting_personal.htm.

7. Myers, "The Funds, Friends, and Faith of Happy People"; M. Csikszentmihalyi, "If We Are So Rich, Why Aren't We Happy?" *American Psychologist* 54 (1999): 821–827; D. G. Myers and E. Diener, "The Pursuit of Happiness," *Scientific American* 274 (1996): 54–56; and D. Gilbert, *Stumbling on Happiness* (New York: Knopf, 2006).

8. D. Westen, *The Political Brain: The Role of Emotion in Deciding the Fate of the Nation* (New York: Public Affairs, 2008), 28.

9. G. Klein, *The Power of Intuition: How to Use Your Gut Feelings to Make Better Decisions at Work* (New York: Crown Business, 2004). After studying professionals in life-and-death situations, Klein concludes, "the method we found most powerful for eliciting knowledge is to use stories."

Epilogue: Continue Your Leadership Development

1. To assess "engagement," students were asked: (a) "How satisfied are you with the leadership exhibited by this student leader?," (b) "When working with this leader, I am highly productive in what I do," (c) "I am proud to tell others that I am working with this leader," and (d) "How developed are the leadership skills of this leader?," along with indicating how frequently that leader engaged in The Five Practices. The internal reliability of this scale was very strong (Cronbach alpha = 0.88).

2. B. Z. Posner, "When Learning How to Lead, An Exploratory Look at the Role Models," *Leadership & Organization Development Journal* 42, no. 5 (2021): 802–818.

3. B. Z. Posner, "A Longitudinal Study Examining Changes in Students' Leadership Behavior," *Journal of College Student Development* 50, no. 5 (2009): 551–563; and B. Z. Posner, R. G. Crawford, and R. Denniston-Stewart, "A Longitudinal Study of Canadian Student Leadership Practices," *Journal of Leadership Education* 14, no. 2 (2015): 161–181. See also, B. Z. Posner, "Effectively Measuring Student Leadership," *Administrative Sciences* 2, no. 4 (2012): 221–234; and, B. Z. Posner, "The Impact of Gender, Ethnicity, School Year and Experience on Student Leadership: Does It Really Matter?" *Management and Organizational Studies* 1, no. 1 (2014): 21–31.

4. J. M. Kouzes and B. Z. Posner, "Learning to Lead," in L. Ukens (ed.) *What Smart Trainers Know* (San Francisco: Jossey-Bass, 2001), 339–351; B. Z. Posner, op. cit.; R. J. Jones, S. A. Woods, and Yves R. R. Guillaume, "The Effectiveness of Workplace Coaching: A Meta-Analysis of Learning and Performance Outcomes from Coaching," *Journal of Occupational and Organizational Psychology* 89, no. 2 (June 2016): 249–277.

5. L. M. Brown and B. Z. Posner, "Exploring the Relationship between Learning and Leadership," *Leadership & Organization Development Journal* 22, no. 6 (2001): 274–280; B. Z. Posner, "Understanding the Learning Tactics of College Students and Their Relationship to Leadership," *Leadership & Organization Development Journal* 30, no. 4 (2009), 386–395; and S. Konuk and B. Z. Posner, "The Effectiveness of a Student Leadership Program in Turkey," *Journal of Leadership Education* 20, no. 1 (2021), 10.12806/V20/I1/R6. https://journalofleadershiped.org/jole_articles/the-effectiveness-of-a-student-leadership-program-in-turkey/.

6. J. Bersin, "New Research Shows 'Heavy Learners' More Confident, Successful, and Happy at Work," 9 November 2018, www.linkedin.com/pulse/want-happy-work-spend-time-learning-josh-bersin/.

7. C. S. Dweck, *Mindset: The New Psychology of Success* (New York: Random House, 2006), 6–7. Also see C. Dweck, "Carol Dweck Revisits the Growth Mindset," *Education Week*, 22 September 2016, www.edweek.org/ew/articles/2015/09/23/carol-dweck-revisits-the-growth-mindset.html.

8. T. K. Kouzes and B. Z. Posner, "Influence of Mindset on Leadership Behavior," *Leadership & Organization Development Journal* 40 no. 8 (2019): 829–844.

9. For a detailed discussion of the essentials of learning, see: J. M. Kouzes and B. Z. Posner, *Learning Leadership: The Five Fundamentals of Becoming an Exemplary Leader* (San Francisco, CA: The Leadership Challenge: A Wiley Brand, 2026).

10. For more on the relationship between challenge and peak performance, see: M. Csikszentmihalyi, *Flow: The Psychology of Optimal Experience* (New York: Harper & Row, 1990).

Acknowledgments

One of the truths about leading is that you can't do it alone. This is equally true about writing. One of the great joys of writing a book is the opportunity to work with scores of talented, dedicated, and inspiring people. We are profoundly grateful to them and cherish the opportunity to thank all who have joined us on this journey.

Foremost, a shout-out of appreciation to the thousands of students we've worked with over the years. You inspire us and bring us hope. You give us immense confidence that the future is held in capable hands and generous hearts. A special round of applause and appreciation for all those students whose stories, experiences, lessons, and wisdom make up the centerpiece of this fourth edition of *The Student Leadership Challenge*. Thank you for what you've accomplished and for who you are. And many thanks to scores of other students who have shared their experiences with us, even if we couldn't put everyone's stories into this book. We know that people will become better leaders from reading about the lessons of their experiences.

We had a behind-the-scenes partner in this endeavor, Kezia Endsley, whom we had the privilege of working with on *The Leadership Challenge, 7th edition*. As our developmental editor, with craftsmanship and guidance, she helped bring clarity and focus to our writing.

ACKNOWLEDGMENTS

Our colleagues at John Wiley & Sons have been our constant companions on our journey of developing emerging leaders since before the first edition's publication. Amy Fandrei, executive editor, was the champion of this fourth edition. Her focus on crafting high-quality resources in the education field has enabled us to produce a book that builds on the solid foundation of the past while creating a unique and distinctive volume that includes the most up-to-date research and integrates new resources into its pages. Halley Sutton played a unique role in researching and developing new stories based on student leaders' personal best leadership experiences.

We are blessed to be working with such a passionate team of Wiley professionals for their value-added contributions to our leadership books and educational materials. Thanks to Tricia Weinhold, our senior brand manager at Wiley, for her ongoing support in expanding the global reach and practical application of *The Leadership Challenge*.

As always, we cannot say enough how appreciative we are of our immediate loved ones. We have witnessed—and experienced—their extraordinary feats of leadership; they have taught us more than we can ever imagine. To our respective spouses, Tae Kyung Kouzes and Jackie Schmidt-Posner, we publicly express our deepest gratitude for their love, encouragement, sacrifices, and graciousness. Big hugs to Nicholas and Kimberly Lopez, Amanda Posner, and Darryl Collins for continuing to inspire our quest to develop new generations of leaders.

We wrote this book, as we have each of our books, to liberate the leader within each person and increase the quality and quantity of leaders for the world. That's our mission and our passion. Every individual makes a difference. The real challenge is to make sure that we're leaving the places we are now and will be in the future better because we were there. Let's be sure to live life forward.

About the Authors

Jim Kouzes and **Barry Posner** have been working together for over forty years, studying leaders, researching leadership, conducting leadership development seminars, and providing leadership in various capacities, with and without titles. They are co-authors of the award-winning, best-selling book *The Leadership Challenge*, which has sold over three million copies worldwide and is available in more than twenty-two languages. It has won numerous awards, including the Critics' Choice Award from the nation's book review editors and book-of-the-year awards from the American Council of Healthcare Executives and Fast Company. *The Leadership Challenge* is listed in *The Top 100 Business Books of All Time* as one of the Top 10 books on leadership.

The Student Leadership Challenge: Five Practices for Becoming an Exemplary Leader has become a standard leadership development book and resource for young people and students from middle to high school, undergraduate to graduate levels. More than 500 colleges and universities use *The Student Leadership Challenge* and the *Student Leadership Practices Inventory* in their classes, seminars, programs, and workshops.

Jim and Barry have co-authored more than a dozen other award-winning leadership books, including *Everyday People, Extraordinary Leadership*; *Leadership in Higher Education*; *Stop Selling & Start Leading*; *Learning Leadership: The Five Fundamentals for Becoming an*

Exemplary Leader; Turning Adversity into Opportunity; Finding the Courage to Lead; Great Leadership Creates Great Workplaces; Credibility: How Leaders Gain and Lose It, Why People Demand It; The Truth About Leadership: The No-Fads, Heart-of-the-Matter Facts You Need to Know; Encouraging the Heart: A Leader's Guide to Recognizing and Rewarding Others; A Leader's Legacy; Extraordinary Leadership in Australia and New Zealand; and *Making Extraordinary Things Happen in Asia.*

Jim and Barry developed the widely used and highly acclaimed *LPI®: Leadership Practices Inventory* and the *Student Leadership Practices Inventory (S-LPI).* These 360-degree questionnaires provide insights into how frequently leaders use empirically identified behaviors as essential to bringing out the best in people and teams. Worldwide, nearly one million students have completed the Student LPI, and over five million people have taken the LPI.

Over a thousand research studies around the globe have been based on The Five Practices of Exemplary Leadership® framework. More information about these books, inventories, and studies is available at www.leadershipchallenge.com.

Among the honors and awards that Jim and Barry have received are the Association for Talent and Development's (ATD) highest award for their Distinguished Contribution to Workplace Learning and Performance, named Management/Leadership Educators of the Year by the International Management Council, ranked by *Leadership Excellence* magazine in the top 20 on their list of the Top 100 Thought Leaders, named by Coaching for Leadership in the Top 50 Leadership Coaches in the nation, considered by *HR Magazine* as one of the Most Influential International Thinkers, and, listed among the Top 75 Management Experts in the *World by Inc.* magazine.

Jim and Barry are frequent keynote speakers, and each has conducted leadership development programs for hundreds of organizations, including 3M, Apple, Applied Materials, ARCO, AT&T, Australia Institute of Management, Australia Post, Bank of America, Bose, Charles Schwab, Cisco Systems, Clorox, Community Leadership Association, Conference Board of Canada, Consumers Energy,

Deloitte Touche, Dow Chemical, Egon Zehnder International, Federal Express, Genentech, Google, Gymboree, Hewlett-Packard, IBM, Jobs DR-Singapore, Johnson & Johnson, Kaiser Foundation Health Plans and Hospitals, Intel, Itaú Unibanco, Lawrence Livermore National Labs, L.L.Bean, Lucile Packard Children's Hospital, Merck, Motorola, NetApp, Northrop Grumman, Novartis, Oakwood Housing, Oracle, Petronas, Roche Bioscience, Siemens, Topgolf/Callaway Brands, Toyota, USAA, U.S. Postal Service, United Way, Verizon, VISA, the Walt Disney Company, and Westpac. In addition, they have presented seminars and lectures at well over 100 college and university campuses.

Jim Kouzes is a fellow at the Doerr Institute for New Leaders at Rice University and has been the Dean's Executive Fellow of Leadership at the Leavey School of Business, Santa Clara University. He lectures on leadership worldwide to corporations, governments, and nonprofits. He is a highly regarded leadership scholar and an experienced executive. *The Wall Street Journal* hailed him as one of the twelve best executive educators in the United States. Jim has received the Thought Leadership Award from the Instructional Systems Association, the most prestigious award given by the trade association of training and development industry providers, and the Golden Gavel, the highest honor awarded by Toastmasters International.

Jim served as president, CEO, and chairman of the Tom Peters Company for eleven years, and led the Executive Development Center at Santa Clara University for seven years. He was the founder and executive director for eight years of the Joint Center for Human Services Development at San Jose State University and was on the staff of the School of Social Work, University of Texas. His career in training and development began in 1969 when he conducted seminars for Community Action Agency staff and volunteers in the war on poverty. Following graduation from Michigan State University (BA with honors in political science), he served as a Peace Corps volunteer (1967–1969). You can reach Jim directly at jim@kouzes.com.

Barry Posner chairs the Management and Entrepreneurship Department at the Leavey School of Business, Santa Clara University, where he previously served for six years as associate dean for graduate education, six years as associate dean for executive education, and twelve years as Dean of the School. He holds the Michael J. Accolti, S.J. Professorship, teaching leadership courses with both undergraduate and graduate students. He has been a distinguished visiting professor around the globe: Hong Kong University of Science and Technology, Sabanci University (Istanbul), University of Western Australia, University of Auckland (New Zealand), and Seattle University. At Santa Clara, Barry has received the President's Distinguished Faculty Award, the Leavey School's Extraordinary Faculty Award, and several other outstanding teaching and academic honors. An internationally renowned scholar and educator, he is the author or co-author of more than 100 research and practitioner-focused articles. He serves on the editorial review board for the *Leadership & Organizational Development Journal*, *Journal of Business Ethics*, *Administrative Sciences*, and *Frontiers in Psychology*.

Barry received his baccalaureate degree with honors in political science from the University of California, Santa Barbara; his master's degree in public administration from The Ohio State University; and his doctoral degree in organizational behavior and administrative theory from the University of Massachusetts, Amherst. Having consulted worldwide with many public and private sector organizations, he also works strategically with several community-based and professional organizations. He has served previously on the board of the American Institute of Architects (AIA), Big Brothers/Big Sisters of Santa Clara County, Center for Excellence in Nonprofits, Junior Achievement of Silicon Valley and Monterey Bay, Public Allies, San Jose Repertory Theatre, SVCreates, Sigma Phi Epsilon Fraternity, Uplift Family Services, and several start-up companies. Barry can be reached at bposner@scu.edu.

Index